IBIZA '99

IBIZA '99

Ready For Another Round?

LUKE ATWOOD

FOREWORD

The people and places here are no more. At the decree of Ibiza lawmakers, and expanding on their curfews of 2020, strict rules now discourage the very tourists and operators you are about to meet (or be reunited with, if you read the first instalment).

You should treat this book as an unrepeatable account of an unparalleled heyday—a time of carefree self-indulgence and mischief, the likes of which neither holiday-makers nor local residents will see again. Today, bars and restaurants must serve no more than six drinks per customer. Shops selling booze must close at 9:30pm. Party boats remain in dry dock.

"It is neither the kind of tourism we want nor what residents deserve," said Balearic President Francina Armengol, subsequently identified by police outside The Hat in Palma after neighbours made complaints about noise and the bar being open when the rules said it should be shut.

As a successful rep with the area's most successful operator, my friend Luke was responsible for organising the sorts of experience Ibiza lawmakers clearly still enjoy.

Maybe he was the friendly face of Ibiza in charge of you and your friends. Maybe your story is one of the tales in this book. Will a long forgotten penny finally drop?

One thing is for sure. Where Luke's life in the nineties was a series of real world escapades, many of today's adolescents live for meaningless reactions on social media. Even those who make it out to the island's dwindling number of superclubs become a sea of bright white screens recording dark and fuzzy footage for Instagram. What book will they write, a decade or two from now, and could you stay awake reading it?

P.W.

10/7/22

INTRODUCTION

On return to the UK from my first season in Ibiza, I could see clearly how much I'd changed. When I was out and about, if I saw someone I was attracted to, I went over to them immediately. It didn't matter if we were on a train or in the gym. It didn't matter if they were on their own or in a group. If anything, I preferred the group approach because it allowed you to play one off against the other and you could muddy the waters a little, particularly if things weren't quite going to plan. Any hint of shyness or hesitation had evaporated as quickly as the sunny weather.

By the time I got back to University, I was a complete weapon. Not always in a good way either. That was the toll that working as a holiday rep had taken. For good or for bad. Meeting Jess helped to keep me under wraps (and most probably stopped me from dropping out of University), but when the chance came to return to the shores of San Antonio, swapping summer work for summer fun, there was no chance I was giving that up.

Spending a second season out there with Nigel, my

partner in crime, was amazing. That's not to say it all went smoothly. Sometimes there were tears, other times there was penicillin! But as Grandma used to say, you can't make an omelette without breaking some eggs...

PREFACE

When I published Ibiza '98 last year, it was with a great deal of trepidation. As I'd mentioned previously, I was extremely nervous about it. I'd wanted to tell the world for more than twenty years, but as time moved on, the landscape to speak openly and freely about experiences has changed dramatically. The night before publishing, I felt the need again to dampen things down a little, nervous my stories would cause offence. Nervous I would be vilified and chastised for daring to put in writing what had previously remained in memory. Despite my fears, I went ahead and published it anyway.

The response and positive feedback I've received since has been amazing. Thankfully, the majority of readers have taken the book in the good nature that it was intended and I received numerous requests to write a sequel. I loved writing the first book and, given I did in fact return to Ibiza in 1999, it seemed to be a no-brainer to write the follow up.

It was a different era. People behaved differently then. I know every generation says that about their "glory days" but, given what happened out there actually occurred before smartphones or social media, things really were different. No public shaming, no image conscious selfies, no desperation to #liveyourbestlife. You get my point. It really was a case of what goes on tour, stays on tour!

You're going to get a predominantly male point of view from this book, because, guess what… I have a little soldier. That's not to say that it was one sided. The female reps were absolutely as raucous as the males. I saw many guests get used and abused by the female reps, but that's their story to tell, not mine.

Again, please enjoy the book. Whether you're somewhere on a beach, a plane, or sat on a cramped bus or train, I hope it raises a smile! If you were on a lads or a girls holiday in the 90s, I hope it unlocks as much nostalgia for you as it did me.

CHAPTER 1
STUDENT LIFE

I'll always fondly remember my second year at University. Not because of a particular house we moved into, not because of a tutor or course I liked, and not because of a relationship. It was because of the size of my beanbag.

Returning to 'normal' life after working as a holiday rep in Ibiza for the 6 months prior was a double-edged sword. I was a very different person to the one that had said goodbye to his course mates just before the summer. I was wilder, more fun to be around, larger than life. Socially, I had supreme confidence bordering on arrogance. I would approach girls at University in the same manner I'd been approaching girls in the West End of San Antonio. Direct, confident and unflinching. Thing is, my uni town wasn't exactly the white island and, with no rep tag hanging around my neck to break the ice, it meant that the outcomes weren't always great.

As with all extreme things in life, I became polarising. On the one hand, I was picking up far more talent than I'd done previously, but on the other, I was probably upsetting more people than I'd managed to offend in the whole of my life prior. I can only deduce that some girls thought I was the life and soul of the party—the crazy one, the wild child, the one needing taming. I guess others simply thought I was a complete tosser with an ego the size of Nelson's column (and a dick the size of Nelson's toothpick). I obviously aimed for the first variant, but sometimes the second caught up with me. It didn't deter me though. It was a number's game with an infinite number of entry tickets.

The thing is, I'd actually managed to squirrel away a fair bit of cash when I was working abroad. I'd had a good rapport with the hoteliers and pretty much ate for free everywhere. I never paid for a drink while there, and a lot of the guests would always leave me stuff they didn't want to take back with them. Everything from pasta and cereal, to shower gels and medicine. In fact, bar a few items of clothing that needed to be replaced and things like trainers, I didn't really spend a cent. We received a UK wage that went straight into my bank account here at home, and I would pay my resort wages directly into my Spanish bank account that I had been smart enough to open when I first got there. Believe it or not, by the time I got back to university, I'd managed to save about £6,000.

As a student this was a king's ransom. I wish I could tell you that I acted responsibly with it, but really it just meant I could party harder and more frequently, thereby dragging out my reversion to a normal student life. Most of us were working the summer to pay down debts and to accumulate funds for the year ahead; it usually meant that the first term was the most active, as people were less concerned with financial caution. This suited me fine as I wanted to start the year off with a bang.

We were always in the Student Union bar chasing girls and pints in equal measure. Mike and I were big fans of all day drinking, and would often settle in around lunchtime on a Saturday. The day always got pretty messy because mid-afternoon the rugby teams would descend, post-match, and that's when things kicked off.

Rugby was really popular where we studied, and there was a decent following in the university. It meant that not only were you likely to witness an adolescent downing a pint through his team mate's sock, it also meant that there were likely to be a fair few female groups in tow as well.

Rugby socials were magnets for girls. We were quite friendly with the rugby lot and had several links to the teams through various individuals on our courses. As time went on, we would often get invites to join them on the piss, despite the closest thing I'd come to catching anything oval shaped was a girl I'd snagged in Ibiza who had a funny shaped head. Mike had played rugby at school, so he was able to converse with them. Me? I was just there for enter-tainment. They often liked the drinking games I would come up with, or my ability to roar into a crowd of girls at the drop of a hat. The thing is, the Rugby boys' behaviour was probably the closest thing I could get to Ibiza, and so I was keen to foster it.

Normal life felt boring. Nights out in the pub became stale. By all accounts, I wasn't the only one feeling it. I'd kept in touch with Nigel, my partner in grime. He, too, was back in University and missing Ibiza just as much as I was. If people thought I was misbehaving they should have seen him. By all accounts, he'd been thrown off the end of Brighton Pier by some local bouncers. The story goes that he'd gotten totally wasted, thrown up on himself on the dance floor of the club on the pier, and was taken into the bathroom to clean himself up. Rather than wipe himself down, he proceeded to take his clothes off there and then in the Gents. Naked as the day he was born, he decided he was going to have a walk around the dance floor to see if there was any action. You can imagine the reaction of his fellow clubbers. In his own words, he said he got about 25% of the way across the dance floor before he was lifted into the air above the bemused crowd. Nigel told me that the main bouncer calmly walked through the club with him above his head and proceeded to jettison him into the cold black sea below. They refused to let him back in the club to collect his things and chose to laugh at him instead. At the doorway he tried to rationalise why he should be allowed back in, and explained he had suffered a quick error in judgement. Needless to say, the bouncers refused, leaving Nigel to stand outside in the cold, showing nothing but contempt for the door staff and a healthy amount of shrinkage due to the southern winds whipping across Brighton beach. Remember, this was a time pre mobiles, so it was only when one of his mates was due to leave, did they notice this poor shivering naked dude outside the main entrance, was the alarm raised, and someone managed to track down his clothes.

While Nigel and I didn't get to see each other back in the UK at that time, we would speak on email. Well, when I say speak, what I mean is we mainly forwarded to each other porn pics and adult jokes. I mean, why else was email invented? It wasn't until we broke up for Christmas that we actually managed to get on the phone. Both of us were staying with our parents, and both of us were facing the main issue most male students were faced with when back in with Mum and Dad: where to shag?

It was nice to hear his voice. We hadn't actually spoken since Ibiza, and while a lot had happened since then in terms of uni life and trying to readjust to civilian rules of engagement, we skipped over all of that and immediately began to reminisce about Ibiza.

Nigel kicked it off. "I don't like the UK. The weather is shit, the clubs are crap, and talking to girls is too much hard work." I chuckled at this. It was all I could do not to give an amen in response. I let him continue. "I can't fucking wait to get back out to Ibiza. Have you received a letter yet?"

"Nope. Not a dicky bird," I replied. The deflation penetrated my every word.

Funny thing is, I hadn't actually thought about going back out before the call. I mean, we'd only just got back. I'd spent the past three months putting into practice everything I'd learnt from the first season—with a fair amount of success I might add. In my mind, going back out for the second season was something I was going to contend with as and when around Easter. I was a little bit torn. On the one hand, who wouldn't want to go back out there large and in charge to pick up where we left off, but on the other, I needed to think about the future. I needed to decide what I wanted to do and make inroads to get myself in a position to be hired. Everyone went to university nowadays; it wasn't like my parents' generation, where those few who went were thought of as gifted and handsomely remunerated immediately because of it when they were hired. Everyone had a degree.

I was convinced, and still am, that most people go to university not to become eligible for employment but to basically get pissed for three years and to meet, fuck, starve and maybe even study along the way. Some would even try and drag it out. Either those not bright enough to pass their exams would repeat the year, or if you were really trying to keep the dream alive, you'd do a gap year abroad where you would basically drink, meet, starve, fuck and maybe study only this time in a different language. If you wanted to get ahead when the job offers were floating around, you needed to have something extra on your CV. If you were looking to get into one of the high payers—finance, law, insurance—that meant doing internships. That meant courting and allowing yourself to be courted at various high brow events or sessions where some bellend with two middle names and a double-barrelled surname would basically give you a speech about how we were the future, and how they'd once stood where we were now. They'd go on to say that choosing Rectum, Bandit & Swindler set them on their way and was the best choice they'd ever made. As if Cuthbert Cuntingdon-Huntley was going to stand up there and say anything else. "I'm glad I chose Rectum as the starting point of my career because they worked me to the absolute bone for no money and no perks. I believe prisoners of war have more fun and more opportunities for growth than the junior ranks. In fact, if it wasn't for the fact that I'm a penny short of a pound, I probably would have stepped off the terrace of the executive restaurant on the 21st floor. I thank you!"

Some students had already pondered their career paths and had spent their first and second summer break working as interns in various law firms, banks, brokerages and asset managers. Others had worked on the whole life experience bit, volunteering, helping, couch surfing. Whenever there were these high-profile career fairs, you would have to wear a big name badge which would stretch across your chest like a banner. You would herd through the sports hall like sheep being driven to the shearing pen. Meet and greet. Meet and greet. Meet and greet. It was like a scratched record stopping off at the various company stands. There would be some you'd be interested in and others you had no interest in, but you chose to engage purely because the female representative looked decent and happened to glance across a 180 degree arc which you happened to be standing in. Game time.

The room was full of brown nosing and self-promotion. The air was littered with such openers and responses like, Tiffany what did you do during the break? Oh, I travelled down through South America reaching Argentina. Patrick, what did you do? I volunteered in Botswana. Philip, what did you do? I spent time teaching English in Myanmar to disadvantaged children. Maximillian, what did you do in the holidays? I spent four months in a hedge fund and then the last month in Antigua learning to dive. I couldn't feel more out of place.

They would get to students like myself and Nigel. Nigel what did you do in the break? Oh, I worked in Ibiza where I effectively shortened my lifespan by several years by drinking, dancing and going bareback through enough girls to form a netball league. As the representative recoiled in shock, instinct kicked in. You'd see the cogs turn behind bewildered eyes. Their brains would be urging them, quick, say something funny. Change the subject, lightly chuckle, but move on quickly and politely. "Oh Nigel, you have been a busy bee. Did you have an epiphany while away?" "Not sure, don't remember that name. I smashed a few Tinas and a Hyacinth though!"

Needless to say, neither Nigel nor myself had actually arranged any internships. My first summer was spent working in a supermarket as a supervisor and helping some of Dad's clients out with some mundane IT tasks. The second summer brought me to Ibiza—which brings me back to where this all started off. I hadn't thought about returning yet, so wasn't nervous about an invitation or lack of.

Nigel was concerned. "Mate, what if they don't invite us back? What are we going to do then?"

I was somewhat surprised how worked up he was. "Relax, how would they not invite us back? Everyone loved you out there, you are hilarious and great on the mic. They'd be mad not to have you back."

"Yeah, but my sales were dog shit, not a patch on yours."

"OK, so maybe you need some work on the figures side of things, but my sales were only good because we were great as a team. You had them pissing themselves as they got to the table, where I then closed them. Seriously, stop panicking."

He seemed to lighten up at the point, or at least he stopped whining about it. Neither of us could control what the company did next, but I was still pretty sure of my position. We both had our strengths and weaknesses, but I was confident we would be invited back.

The subject changed to uni life. We were exchanging war stories. It sounded like Nigel was going through the exact same motions that I had been going through, despite being hundreds of miles away in a different university. When pushed on his hit rate he owned up to getting laid more often, but also upsetting more girls than ever before. It was a reflection of my own experience. Difference being, I actually didn't want to irritate anyone and it generally bothered me when I was taken the wrong way. I am not sure if that was insecurity on my part or I just didn't want to upset anyone. Probably a bit of both. Nigel on the other hand did not give a shit. His conscience had a time span measured in seconds. We must have spoken for about an hour before hanging up and wouldn't actually speak on the phone again for another few months, although the email porn kept coming.

The rest of the holiday was spent largely with family. We had a nice Christmas break. I'd managed to keep in contact with some of the guests from my hotel, mainly by email, but we managed to arrange a few meet-ups around the country. It was good fun. I was still managing to get laid although you can't plant the flag twice.

Time flew, and it wasn't long before I found myself sitting on a national express coach again, freezing my tits off heading back to uni. I was looking forward to seeing Mike and our other housemates. It had only been a month or so, and while it was nice to be back with school friends and acquaintances from my area, I'd been missing the independence of student life. I was looking forward to not having to sneak girls out of the house, trying to avoid my parents as I went.

CHAPTER 2
JESS

There was another reason I was looking forward to getting back to university. I'd been exchanging emails with a girl that had stayed in my hotel during the summer. She was an angel. She was studying law. She had blonde hair, blue eyes you'd get lost in, and a smile that would light up the room. I remember meeting her early on in my repping campaign. Truth be told, I could feel myself falling for her right off the bat and I was gutted when she left. She even shed a slight tear as she hugged me before getting on the coach. We'd been writing to each other since I got back. I assumed she'd had a boyfriend, as it was all kept very casual and cool, different to how we left things in resort.

Initially this put me out, as I did like her, but at the same time I wasn't in a rush to get hitched up as I was enjoying my post Ibiza rampage. Over the Christmas break though, I'd detected a change. Things had become more flirtatious. The banter had increased and she'd begun to flirt and abuse me in her emails. She was fiercely intelligent, so it wasn't just the obvious banter you'd get in the pub where someone's digging for a compliment or playing coy so that you would make the first move. This girl was actually testing me and I was getting hooked. I figured she'd had a change of heart with her fella at home, or she too had enjoyed our exchanges and reconsidered her own position. Either way I didn't want to upset the trajectory, say anything awkward or rush in, so I kept quiet and played it cool.

It wasn't until a few weeks into February that she suggested we meet up somewhere. Bingo. Music to my ears. We picked a neutral place to meet, halfway between our universities—we couldn't have been studying any further apart if we'd tried—and set a date. I didn't want to presume anything, so I let her control the details. Last thing I wanted to do was start talking about hotels and sharing rooms if she only had a day trip in her mind. Thankfully, we were on the same page and she said it would be silly to go all that way for a day trip and too expensive if we got separate rooms. Naturally I agreed. We made the necessary bookings and set the date for the middle of February. We would be missing Valentine's Day, so we would both be free of any cupid awkwardness. Well, by that, I meant I'd be spared the pain of it.

The next few weeks seemed to fly past. Mike and I did our best to party hard and to attend every single Valentine's club night that was going on. Thankfully at university, every club in the town seemed to have its student night. You'd go here on Monday, there on Tuesday, a different place on Wednesday, and so on. It helped to ensure that each one had a relatively busy night and they weren't all competing and diluting themselves down. This meant that there were potentially six different Valentine's Parties we could attend.

Mike and I had a ball. The trick was not to overcook it on Monday or Tuesday as, by the time Wednesday arrived, you'd be hungover, tired, or worse; skint. Mike and I had been brewing our own alcohol in the house. I'd made 40 pints of lager, and he'd done bitter. My lager was passable, or at least you could drink it without retching. His bitter was basically filth in a glass. Thankfully, we had a backup plan. He'd also been making crème de menthe. This was somewhat more successful. It tasted better than his faecal beer but resembled a liquid kryptonite. All I know is that it tasted minty and got you tipsy. Between us, this set up meant we could get smashed on beer and spirits at home for free. We'd then hit the club horny and warmed up, both smelling like a pair of polo mints. All the clubs put on free buses for us every 15-30 minutes, including returns at 2am. We basically didn't even have to spend a penny until we got to the bar inside the venue. This was great. Pound a pint and 1.50 for a shot, meant you were having a night out for £10-15. Rinse and repeat.

Valentine's passed with mixed fortunes. I'd managed to snatch a couple and even Mike pulled one out the bag, so to speak. Unfortunately for me, while my first one was nice, the last one was somewhat of a rotter. Although there were no regrets, the abuse that I received from the boys had been somewhat costly in terms of my pride. Despite me being happy with the week's performance, it took a good few days for Mike to stop smirking every time he looked at me. I think it was this small piece of shame that contributed to my mental state at the time, and some impact on what happened in the weeks following.

It was the weekend. I was about to take a four hour National Express coach trip to meet my angel. I'd made the mistake of taking some homework with me to do while sitting there, but all thoughts of study soon evaporated once I got to the station. I was in a good mood, a little apprehensive perhaps, but in a good way. What would she be like? Is she how I remembered her? Will she still like me? Am I getting laid? What if she's nothing like I remember? Everything was racing through my mind.

I put my bag on the coach and wondered if I'd be able to sleep. For those of you who have never been on a National Express coach, if you're slightly taller than a hobbit you've got no chance of being able to put your heels on the floor, let alone grabbing forty winks. As I sat there, compressed in my seat, my mind started to wander. Clearly a pre-smash sleep wasn't going to happen. In terms of study, I was pushed to even fit a Twix on the tray that had unfolded in front of me, let alone a folder or a book, so that was out the window. Might as well have a drink then.

There was a refreshment trolley out on the platform. I casually walked over to it, only to end up bent over while the station worker effectively fisted me. "Four quid for a can of Fosters!?" He could tell my amusement was waning. He shrugged his shoulders. Begrudgingly, I handed him my hard saved cash as we traded. Saying I was unimpressed was somewhat of an understatement. I started to do the maths as I slumped back into my high chair. I'd effectively handed over 40-50% of a night out on just one can of beer. It was daylight robbery. He should have been wearing a mask. The feelings of being a victim began to ebb away as we pulled out of the station. Pretty soon we were on the M1 and I was on my way.

By the time I got to the city, my vertebrae had fused. As I painfully straightened myself out, all thoughts of tearing into my blonde bombshell had dissipated. Or so I had thought. As I stepped off the coach, I was met with the broadest of smiles and a big pair of blue smiling eyes.

"What time do you call this?" she teased. I just threw my arms around her and gave her a hug. She was every bit as pretty as I had remembered, and she was wearing spray on denim and a tight-fitting top. Her coach had pulled in half an hour before mine, so the timing was perfect. We got a taxi to the hotel and dropped our stuff off.

I'd like to tell you it felt weird at first, or rattle on about the tension in the air, but to be honest, it was just nice. We headed straight into the centre to look for somewhere to have lunch. We had a great day, lots of laughs and a few drinks. We had planned to go out to a bar and a club but, by the time we got around to having to get ready, neither of us could be bothered. We grabbed a couple of drinks to go in the hotel bar, got back to the room, and crashed out. Both of us were tired from the journey, and the early start booze. In fact, when it was time for bed, we ended up having a quick fondle before falling asleep.

The rest of the weekend passed really quickly. We were having a great time just hanging out, and we got on really well. By the time I was back in the coach station I'd been well and truly bitten. Her coach left 20 minutes before mine, and I'd be lying if I didn't feel sad seeing her leave. We had already arranged to meet up again, so I took that as a good sign.

Once her coach had disappeared out of the station, I turned my mind towards my own journey. I could see the guard standing next to the refreshment cart. He was already locking eyes on me but there was no way I was going to get violated again. I skipped out of the station to the nearest supermarket where I grabbed a couple of cans of Stella. It's not that Stella Artois was the weapon of choice —I mean, I've never owned a string vest or a tank top—but it was on special. I didn't even check the expiry date (why ruin a nice end to a nice day?). Ten minutes later I was shoehorning myself into the seat on the coach like a fucking contortionist. Thankfully no one sat next to me for the journey back.

I didn't want to appear too keen when I got back to university. Of course, I opened up to Mike that I had a lovely time with her and that I hoped to see her again. He simply caned me mercilessly, called me a soppy twat and left for lectures. Jess and I exchanged emails with each other over the next week until we'd booked up another weekend away. Well, it was a weekend away for me. She'd invited me to go and stay with her and meet her friends. We'd arranged it for the following weekend. I even decided to skip Friday's lectures just so I could travel across and sneak in an extra night of adult cuddles.

A few weeks afterwards I invited her to mine, and she effectively did the same. When she arrived, I introduced her to my housemates. We opened a bottle of wine and everyone was getting on like a house on fire. When I was alone, Mike pulled me to one side and remarked that she was absolutely fit as fuck and he could clearly see what all the fuss was about now. He patted me on the back, quipped "Good lad," and went back into the living room to rejoin the group. Although it was only a simple gesture, it helped to reinforce and validate what I'd already known. I'd got myself a good one and that it was time to put away my spurs. For now (at least) I was off the market.

Over the next couple of months, we were pretty much doing a weekend on followed by a weekend off. Sometimes we'd skip a weekend if either of us were particularly busy with studies, or we were seeing our own families elsewhere in the UK. I got to know the National Express coach service intimately. I even think I managed to lose an inch of height in the process. It was as if my body decided to rein in the growth and actually shed some skeletal mass just so I could fit in the fucking seat. When we weren't together, I was still out partying with Mike and the others, but it just wasn't the same. Any thought of going out on the pull and hunting for the smash seemed to evaporate. Sure, I'd go out and talk to girls, but deep down I wasn't interested in any of them.

If anything, this just made some of the girls even more determined to chase me. I've always marvelled at this. You get a single guy going out on the town looking for action and most of the girls will steer clear. You put the same guy out there with some degree of commitment—wife, girl-friend, significant other—and those same uninterested girls suddenly do an about turn. I guess it's all about the forbidden fruit. Much the same way as you wanting to nail your best mate's sister...

CHAPTER 3
THE INVITATION

Jess and I had already been seeing each other for the best part of three months when I got an email from Nigel. In true Nigel fashion, the title of the email was as subtle as ever.

"OH, MY FUCKING GOD, IT ARRIVED..."

I knew instantly what he was referring to. I double clicked his email and began to read. You could immediately tell his mind was made up. He'd received a formal letter from the company inviting him to be a Senior Overseas Representative in Ibiza for the upcoming summer. He'd accepted immediately. There was no way he was going to turn this down.

I called home that evening to ask Mum if any mail had arrived for me. There was indeed a letter addressed to me. I asked her to open it and read it out to me. It was from the company and, like Nigel, I had been invited back as a Senior Rep in Ibiza. Mum didn't even ask if I wanted to return or not and instead just said, "what about Jess?" That was indeed the million-dollar question.

Prior to this email from Nigel, our communications had somewhat slowed over the previous few weeks. I think there was a general email porn drought going through the UK's universities, and I'd been preoccupied with Jess so the usual exchange of debauchery after a weekend on the pull had waned somewhat. I replied to his email that I too had received the letter, and was pleased I'd been invited back. This triggered an avalanche of emailing that went back and forth furiously.

I had already told him I'd "met a nice bird" and that we'd been seeing each other, but Nigel didn't give it a second thought. As far as he was concerned, the band were back together. I would continually receive emails with lurid titles such as, "WE'RE GOING TO GET SO MUCH ASS", "DOOR OR WINDOW? FK IT, LET'S SMASH THEM BOTH" and a personal favourite of mine, "WE'RE GOING TO GET SO MUCH KNOB ROT WE'LL APPEAR AS EXTRAS IN THE DAY OF THE DEAD!" Seriously, my screen looked more suspect than a Nigerian Internet Café's inbox. Each email would be an infectious attempt to hype me up. There was a constant outpouring of nostalgia and reminiscence.

The emails didn't just read like a victory speech; there was a practical aspect to it too. Nigel had immediately given them his acceptance. He'd told them when he would be able to fly out and in return had received a second letter with more details. They gave a list of the things that he needed to bring out to resort. He was asking me what I thought about this and that. I answered as best as I could.

The thing is, I hadn't sent back my acceptance yet. Things were going relatively well with Jess, and despite a couple of drunken rows here and there, we were solid. I hadn't told her I'd been invited back, and I certainly didn't tell Nigel that I was in two minds. As far as he was concerned, I was the other half of his spit roast.

I mentioned it to Mike. As soon as the words had left my mouth, he grimaced. He knew immediately the painful choice that was facing me. He knew the lifestyle. He knew the temptation. He also knew it was good money and a damn sight better than stacking shelves at Tesco's or having to brown nose some prick in a pair of loafers and an expensive suit in London. He helped me focus on the choice in hand. I was going back out to Ibiza, the question was, would it be with a girlfriend in tow, or would I be single. "Besides, it's still a couple of months away. Plenty of time to split up before then!"

I laughed when I heard this. Thing was, he was right. Last thing I wanted to do was knock back the invite, only to then find out that Jess was having some waiter from Pizza Hut hanging out the back of her and was now feeling 'confused.'

Nigel's filth laden emails began to clutter my inbox again. He was making me laugh and seemed to become even bolder with every email he sent. You'd think he wasn't using official university email. I mean not only was I receiving actual images of naked girls in varying yoga like poses, but the titles were getting worse. "NOTHING BUT SLAGS", "FIRST TO GET A BLOWJOB ON THE COACH AT THE AIRPORT WINS", "NEW RULES FOR KNOCKADOOR SMASH!" The thing is, it was beginning to get to me. I was beginning to amp myself up. I don't think he even knew he was doing it, but he was slowly but surely putting that spring back in my step.

I decided to man up and talk to Jess. She was due to come over at the weekend, so I figured I'd talk to her rather than do it over email. Things between us had already settled into a routine. As soon as we would see each other, we'd get back to either place, sit down, have a cup of tea or a drink, say hi to each other's flatmates, then go up to the room under the pretence of dropping off our bags. We'd smash the granny out of each other, before going out for a bite to eat.

As soon as she arrived, though, it was different. I needed her onside and open-minded. Something somewhere in my neanderthal bonce was telling me that approaching the subject post coitus was a mistake. The moment she turned up, I chucked the bags in my room and took her out for a drink instead. Mike knew what was going on and wished me luck on the way out.

I think she was a little confused. The cuddles were good between us, and both of us were horny, so for us not to go immediately horizontal meant something was up. As she sat in the pub sipping her drink, she asked me what the matter was. I told her I'd been invited back to Ibiza. You could tell she was saddened to hear it. She just sank into her chair. Having seen what the reps were like in Ibiza, and how the girls were throwing themselves at them, she feared the worst.

"What are you going to do?" she asked quietly. It was like she needed to hear the answer, but it was a question she didn't want to ask.

I told her that I wanted to go back to San Antonio for the summer, but quickly followed up that I wanted her to come out there with me.

"Really?"

You could see a huge wave of relief roll over her.

"Definitely. It'll be great."

I began to sell it to her. "You'll be able to stay with me for free out there, we won't pay for clubs, food or drink. It will be like one long amazing holiday." Her eyes lit up, and she began to get excited. I was feeling relieved, but I still needed to put out a couple of important disclaimers. "Thing is, if we're going to do this, I need you to be onboard with a few things." The movie playing out in her head of her lounging by the pool for 4 months and working on her tan was momentarily placed on hold.

"Go on," she said.

"Well, as you know, I don't have any days off, and I will need to work every single day, and until late. You remember how I was always rushing or tired when you were out there? Well, I don't want you being upset with me if I'm at work and you're suddenly bored or missing me."

"Okay, won't be a problem, I'll be on the beach or by the pool." I could tell she had pressed play on the movie again.

"I'm serious, I can't be getting shit for working late all the time, because that's the job. What's more, you know my job is going to involve heavy flirting, drinking, and enter- taining. Girls will chase, and I will have to tease and flirt back. Sometimes this might be in front of you. Are you sure you're cool with that? I mean, I'm not going to lie and say I'm single, in fact you'll probably be coming to the clubs with us, but I just want to put that out there!"

She kept still for a moment, pondering on what I'd just said. We trusted each other, and she knew I was flirty anyway, but harmless enough. "I'm cool with that. It won't be a problem; besides, the guys will be flirting with me!"

She had a point. I guess it was a sign of the size of my ego that I didn't even consider how guys would be hitting on her. Jess was a good-looking girl and turned heads wherever we went. Whenever I would go to the toilet in a restaurant, when I returned the waiters were always chat- ting her up. I was cool with that. It was par for the course. I laughed, but reiterated my point again. As long as we were clear, there shouldn't be any issues.

Now that everything was out in the open, I felt a huge weight lift off from my shoulders, followed by an excitement that I was going back to the white island. We finished our drinks and practically sprinted back to the house. We burst through the door and made a beeline for my room, much to the amusement of my housemates.

After Jess left on the Sunday, I made a call back home to Mum, asking her to reply to the letter, accepting their offer. I'd already checked when my last exam was and decided to literally fly out a couple of evenings later. I didn't even think about spending more time in the UK celebrating the end of exams. I wanted to be drinking and dancing out there as soon as possible. I didn't tell Nigel that I had only just accepted. I figured he was going to kill me for bringing a bird out with me anyway, but that could wait. Main thing is I was going back and we'd all have a wicked time. Jess included.

It was a good five or six weeks before I actually came clean to Nigel that I was essentially coupled up and that I was going to be out there with her as well. Nigel reacted better than I thought he would. He understood I'd somehow got attached. He even remembered Jess and totally understood. That being said, he also offered me many emails of encouragement. Subject lines like, "Are you SURE you want to go out there with a bird?" or, "Why are you bringing your own hamburger to McDonalds" cluttered my inbox. I'd be lying if I said there wasn't a small part of me that was thinking the exact same thing. I mean, I was potentially throwing away a huge slice of adult action to be with this girl. I just hoped she would appreciate it when we were out there.

As the weeks went by, when I wasn't studying for the impending exams, I was in charity shops trying to pick up props for the summer. Jess and I had even put a pause on the weekenders because she too had exams, and though we were enjoying each other's company, the travelling was pretty exhausting. We both realised that we needed to pass the exams first and foremost. After the exams we would be able to party like animals.

CHAPTER 4
PRE-SEASON

Unfortunately, given the exam timetable and the studies that year, I was unable to attend the annual training in Majorca. The company was cool with it, I mean, they knew I wasn't lying. Who would pass up a jolly in Majorca? They still had confidence in me and my selling was already proven. Nigel, however, got more shit for not being able to make it. He had exams at the same time as well. The seniors were putting some pressure on him to attend the sales part, as that was his weak point, but it didn't amount to much. They ultimately accepted he couldn't go and, well, that was that.

Nigel and I had colluded already and decided to fly out together on the same date. We figured they would give us a few days to settle in and adjust, as well as observe the existing reps there like we did last time. If we were going to have a few days out there to relax before, we might as well spend them together. I'd arranged for Jess to fly out a week or so later to give me time to get into the swing of things and sort out accommodation, etc.

Before we got to resort, we each received a phone call

from the company. It was during our easter break. I was at my parent's home when the phone rang. Mum handed me the phone.

"Hello dickweed, how are you?"

I started to smile. It was a voice I hadn't heard for a while. It was Damien, my manager from the first season.

"Long and Strong. How are you?"

He laughed. "Very good matey, very good. We missed you at training. Apparently, you and your boyfriend had exams to sit or some shite! I won't keep you long. I wanted to ask you something." Before I had a chance to question what, he continued. "How do you fancy being in my team again this year? Think you could suffer me for another year?"

I was flattered. "Yeah, definitely. Dream team!" As soon as the words left my mouth I felt like a tool.

"You soft cock!" Damien pounced on the opportunity to cane me. Thankfully, I was quick on my feet. I decided to try my luck.

"Mate, you know how I was your number one sales last year, and how I kept you all paid?" Damien could sense something was coming.

"What do you want now?" he interjected.

"Well, the thing is…"

Damien interrupted, "Just spit it out you knob!"

I just came out with it. "I've got a serious bird now, and she's going to be coming out with me too. It won't interfere with my work, but do you think you could try and sort something on the accommodation front?"

I waited for his response. Uncharacteristically for Damien, he was silent for a moment. "Why the fuck are you bringing a Doris to Ibiza? You and that boyfriend of yours were cleaning up with the girls last season, why would you want to bring baggage with you this year?"

"I can't help it, we're serious."

Damien laughed. "Okay Casanova, leave it with me. I'll see what I can do, but don't you DARE tell any other reps about this. I don't want anyone else hearing of this at all. Others will be three to a room, and if they find out you're on your own with your girl, my life will be made a misery. As you know, shit rolls downhill, so if they're fucking me, I'm fucking you! One more thing. Regardless of what the official targets are for the area, your sales targets are going to be a magnitude higher. Are we clear?"

I agreed immediately. It was the perfect outcome. I'd talked things up to Jess before about us having free accommodation, but truth be told, I'd been winging it. I didn't know what the score was going to be when we got there, but it looked like my prayers had just been answered. This would save us both some cash, and with Damien knowing that she was there and likely to be hanging about, I wouldn't have to keep anything hidden, which was always the right move with him.

I felt a weight lift. He was giving me a few more details. As we were finishing the conversation, I asked him, what was happening with Nigel? I wanted to know if he was going to be under his wing and in our group again.

"I was waiting for you to ask about that sales numpty boyfriend of yours," he teased. "What is it between you two? That fucker asked me the same thing about you!"

I immediately twigged. If he'd spoken to him already, then it would only have been to ask him if he wanted to be in his area as well. Why else would Damien have called him? "Is the band back together?" I joked.

"Well, it would be, if one dick head didn't bring his missus." I recoiled. It was harsh but fair. "You two fuckers better not cause me any grief out there. No punching drug dealers!"

I laughed. "We'll be good as gold, I promise."

"Sure, sure. Anyways, I'll leave you to it. Good luck with the studies and I'll be waiting for you in San An'!"

I thanked him for the wishes, and muttered, "dream team" once more. He called me a prick, laughed and promptly hung up. I was happy. Jess was sorted, Nigel would be with me once more. I immediately began to get excited about the prospects ahead.

Shortly afterwards, I was back in university gearing up for my second year exams. These were more important than the first year ones. You see, the first year in university was treated like a warm up in terms of study. You had everyone coming together from all over the UK and the wider world, from all sorts of backgrounds, with all sorts of levels of education. Most of the first year was spent consolidating and building on the basics, so that everyone could push forwards in the second and third year, at the same pace, from the same starting position.

The first year was also the time to work out who you were in the absence of parental supervision. People would experiment with drink and drugs. Some would experiment sexually. Some would find religion. Some would find weird and wonderful groups to belong to. The second year was where things were kicked up a notch though. Head down, books out. Well, that was the theory anyway. The whole house had basically gone into overdrive. When we weren't writing pages and pages of coursework, we were cramming for tests. We were also being forced to pay ridiculous sums of money for books that would be heavy enough to qualify for the free weights area of Fitness First. The party dial had been turned right down, and besides, by the final term we were all running low on readies.

I still remember Mike's words from the previous year regarding getting fit. I needed to get in shape for Ibiza.

Even if I wasn't looking to shag, I needed to still look the part. Jess and I were basically on a self-imposed break from visiting each other, so when I wasn't at my desk I was in the gym.

I can hardly remember that final term. I'd already amassed most of the props and items needed to take out to Ibiza. One of my housemates was handy with a needle and thread, and so if anything needed to be altered or sewed, she helped me. By the time I'd finished my exams I was desperate to unwind.

Even Nigel's porn train of emails had slowed to a snail's pace. He too was clearly feeling the squeeze given his own workload. I knew when his last exam had finished because I received an email with the following subject title in my inbox: "WE SRE GOIING T OPLOUGH S OMANY BIRDS OUT THERE, SHULD BE ILEGAL!!!!" Clearly, he'd had a drink. I'd finished the day before, so I was already nursing a thick head. I quickly opened it to see what it contained, but it was gibberish.

He'd basically told me he'd finished, declared his undying friendship to me, and then told me a story about buying condoms in bulk, or words to that effect. It was difficult to decipher, because a) I was hungover and b) he'd clearly been on the piss when he wrote it. I didn't have time to check in with him, as I was being picked up by my parents, so I logged out and finished packing. I wouldn't have long to wait before seeing him as we were both due to meet at Gatwick in a couple of days anyway to fly out.

CHAPTER 5
THE FLIGHT OUT

Nigel and I met in the South Terminal at Gatwick. We didn't have mobile phones then so planned to arrive two hours before the flight (like normal) and we both saw each other as we were approaching the check-in queue. There were man hugs all round as soon as we got close. Nigel was there with his mum, but I had the full contingent. Mum, Dad and my sister had all turned out to see me off. We all exchanged pleasantries, but sensing that Nigel and I had a lot to catch up on, everyone else left pretty quickly.

We were gassing like a couple of old girls in a care home. We were both excited to be going out there but our reasons were slightly different. I was looking forward to the whole experience of partying for free, getting on the piss, and earning good money, all while being in one of the best places on earth. Nigel was looking forward to going balls deep. Real deep.

On the plane we were already four or five beers in and deep in conversation. He kept trying to discuss new rules for shagging and things he wanted to accomplish. Normally I would have liked nothing more than to discuss the ins and outs of what constitutes additional points in a threesome, but the fact that we were sat either side of the aisle on a plane at 30,000 feet made me feel uncomfortable. We literally had an audience of families surrounding us. Nigel made no attempt to moderate himself, and continued on as if we were sat at a bar on a stag do.

"Do you think if you're in bed with two girls and they're related, you should get extra points?" and "What's more valuable in the grand scheme of things, a blowy in the pool toilets, or getting a hand job on the coach?" and "Who did you most want to fuck from last year who's coming back out this year?" The list went on.

He was clearly psyching himself up, but was also totally oblivious to the stares and tuts flanking us from all sides. I was on the outside of the aisle, so I only had a young guy next to me by the window, but he was sitting next to a family. He was next to the father and son, the other aisle, then mum and daughter last. He was so loud, even the mum could hear the topic of conversation and she was on the other side of the plane. At one point I thought she was going to strangle him.

My attempts to wind him in failed miserably. It wasn't until he started telling me about a girl he and his mates had piled through at university, did the old man get involved. He was a big lump and on the wife's orders, he leant in to Nigel and in a deep northern accent, asked Nigel to pack it in. He was quite polite about it, just saying it was inappropriate as he was with his family. Nigel immediately apologised, owning up to too many beers in the airport, and said he would keep the noise down. He leant forward, mouthing the words sorry to the wife who was casting a watchful eye over proceedings. She didn't react. Next he turned to me, rolled his eyes, and moved on to discuss anal. There was going to be no stopping him in San Antonio.

CHAPTER 6

TOUCHDOWN

Despite my embarrassment and the newfound concern that Nigel was rapidly becoming a sex pest, I was beginning to feel a bit put-out. I really wanted to share in the banter and attack the challenges of San Antonio with the same degree of energy and enthusiasm, but it was different. I was different. I had a serious girlfriend, and while I was going to be drinking, dancing, messing about and flirting as much as possible, the thought of not getting laid at the end of it, or not partaking in the bedroom games as we'd done the season before, was bothering me.

Maybe it was a mistake to come back out with Jess in tow. Damien might have been right. Maybe I'd been foolish, thinking I could enjoy it the same way as before. Only time would tell. Listening to Nigel discuss his plans for going on the pull and working out new rules for knockadoor smash, which we both had played so fondly the year previously, had me feeling conflicted. It was as if there was a loose thread in my head, and the more I heard and the more I saw, the more it would be lightly tugged on, bit by bit.

By the time we touched down in Eivissa, we were tired but weary. While the rest of the herd stood up out of their seats immediately, desperate to get to the queue at passport control, Nigel and I stayed seated. I pretended to read an article from the in-flight magazine, trying to avoid eye contact with any of the parents in a 15 metre radius who might have listened to how Nigel got his balls sucked during fresher's week, or how he was planning to fuck one of the girls from last year who was returning as a senior.

The wait was agonising. Nigel as ever was oblivious to it. Once through passport control, we grabbed our suitcases and made our way towards the coaches. My suitcase was large enough to fit a fully grown body in, as I wasn't just bringing out stuff for me, but Jess had also managed to sneak in a couple of items, much to my annoyance.

As the double doors opened and we exited customs, we turned right. I don't think we made two steps before we were greeted by a flurry of wolf whistles and abuse.

"Oi Oi, you pair of English wankers!"

I knew that voice. It was Edinburgh. The rep from Scotland, who in our first season's training had been unceremoniously forced to toss the senior rep's salad. I hadn't even thought about him since we left resort the year before. He was on airport duty and was picking up the guests, which in our case, included us.

Standing next to him were another couple of reps that were unknown to us. Edinburgh introduced everyone and immediately launched into some war stories from the season before. Despite being tired, we chose to hang around there at the airport rather than wait on the coach with the other guests. Desperate to get an update, we asked Edinburgh how the resort was. How was everyone? We were filled with questions. All he could do was smile.

He gave his clipboard to one of the juniors, rested a

hand on both our shoulders and pointedly told us that this season was already shaping up to be better than last season. "How so?" I asked. He went on to tell us that, because we were seniors now, it meant that any shitty jobs we didn't want to do, we could just delegate to the juniors, leaving us with more time to focus on what was important. Namely, sneaking in naps and drilling anything in a bikini.

He took us to one side, out of earshot of the juniors, as he continued. "You remember how we were all a little nervous last year, what with this being our first time and all? It took us a while to find our feet, right? Speaking in front of crowds, talking to strangers, bantering with birds?" Nigel and I both knew exactly what he was talking about. "Well, this time it's completely different. You know what to expect, you know how to do it, and you know that everyone will love you regardless! You'll be able to fire into the lasses immediately, and you (gesturing at me) can sell the hind legs off a donkey, so you're already proven. There's no stress."

Nigel was beside himself. You'd think he'd walked through the gates of Eden. All he heard was napping, banging and no stress. He broke out into a huge grin. I too was smiling, but I felt another pull on the thread. Nigel couldn't wait to tell Edinburgh about Jess. "This dickhead has only gone and got a bird, and he's bringing her out next week."

It was as if the airport fell silent. I glared at Nigel, before switching my attention to Edinburgh. He pulled a puzzled face similar to the look a child has when it sharts for the first time. "Get to fuck. Tell me he's joking! Tell me he's pulling my todger." It was like listening to an irritated Sean Connery. Edinburgh was the last person I'd want to tell first, and Nigel had well and truly dropped me in it. It didn't stop there. "Why have ye done that? You don't bring an apple to an orchard."

I stood there motionless. If he had tugged lightly on that thread of doubt in my mind earlier, both he and Nigel were fucking bungee jumping on it right now. I was trying to quickly think what to say to try and rescue any sense of street cred I had left and not look like a sap.

Right on cue, Nigel stepped out of the silence. "Oh, but he loves her." Edinburgh roared with laughter, with Nigel quickly following.

I had to say something. I was being trashed here and within a few hours everyone would know. "Fuck off the pair of you!" was the best I could come up with. I needed a follow up. "You prick!" Nigel laughed even more, so I gave him a dead arm.

Edinburgh changed tack at this point. "Well, I hope she's worth it mate, because you're giving away a lot of fanny for this one bird. It's okay though, just means more for us, right?" gesturing to Nigel. I just smiled. I was tired from the flight and frankly this was a sensitive subject.

We returned to the juniors who were still ticking names off. We continued to catch up with Edinburgh, receiving updates on the rest of the team, until everyone was on the correct coach and we were cleared to leave the airport.

Nigel and I were dropped off alongside the guests at our respective units, where keys were given to us, along with a message about what time we were meeting. Thankfully, it would be just after lunchtime, so we had time to sort ourselves out and not have to sit through welcome meetings first thing.

Nigel and I were both given rooms in different hotels. We'd known ahead of time which hotels we were going to be responsible for. I was given a couple of medium sized apartment blocks with a room in the smaller of the two.

Frankly, it more resembled self-catering apartments than the usual quality of hostel the company was leasing. This suited me. It was off the beaten path, away from the other rep accommodation blocks.

The place was also big. It was a single room apartment with a seating area, a couple of sofas, a big bed and a kitchen you could actually make something in. Not that I intended to cook as I would be eating mainly in the hotel restaurant, but it meant it would be something Jess could use during the day. It didn't have any laundry facilities, but a nice sized balcony overlooking the sea.

Now, this apartment block didn't have a communal area or bar, but the other I was in charge of did. The guests of this block would be using the pool, bar and restaurant of the other hotel I was responsible for. I didn't think this would be an issue as it was literally 75m up the road on the left and a proper cheap and cheerful zoo of a thing. It would be packed full to the rafters of horny drunk adolescents doing their best to drink away brain cells, bang the life out of each other and hopefully not get arrested in the process. The fact that I was living just away from the madhouse, meant I could keep some degree of separation.

Nigel had been given a room actually located in his hotel. This was a double-edged sword. It meant that he could sneak back for a nap whenever he wanted, and he would be able to save time by not having to commute anywhere. If he forgot clothing, or simply needed to do something, he could literally just pop up to the room. It also meant if he needed somewhere to run through a guest, he could sort out a hasty rendezvous there and then. You could easily overturn any objection about not having time or not wanting the friend to find out, or whatever. They were in the same building.

He used this trick with great success. If one of the girls

was feeling horny, or wanted to knock him off on the quiet without anyone else knowing, they would announce they were "just popping out to grab an ice cream from the mini market next door," and would find themselves chowing down on his cornetto literally two minutes later. As everyone was on holiday, no one was keeping track of time. She could grab a couple of magnums and be back in the room within 20 minutes and her mates would be none the wiser.

The other edge of this blade was that you couldn't escape. You were literally on call 24/7. Any issue in the hotel, knock at the door. Anyone drunk and looking to party on, knock at the door. Anyone needing to know where to buy condoms or tampons, knock at the door. Anyone forgetting what time their coach was taking them to the airport, knock at the door. He had virtually no chance of sneaking a girl into the hotel undetected, as he'd have to walk through the main reception with her and, if he was having a good week, he stood a high chance of getting caught out. Girl A would come looking for round two when he was already hanging out the back of Girl B. You can imagine the potential for fireworks. The continual pain and drama that he endured living there during our second season caused me no end of joy.

CHAPTER 7
MEET THE TEAM

Nigel and I had already agreed to meet for a quick lunch before meeting up with the rest of the team. We were both relaxed and happy to be there. We shared a San Miguel and a paella. I say paella, but it was basically yellow rice, some oil, a couple of peas, and the remnants of what once may have resembled a prawn. I joked that the prawn looked like Nigel's cock. All head and no body. We both chuckled into our beers.

Despite the culinary shortcomings, it was the same meal we'd finished just prior to leaving the year before, so it seemed fitting to pick up as we left off. I was glad I'd put my exams behind me and was happy to see the sea. It was a view I'd forgotten about at university. Nigel was happy that the waitress had tits. In fact, I think he remarked on those of the cashier, the manager, other diners and even the ticket tout who was standing a stone's throw away on the corner trying to sell club tickets to passers-by. I could tell he was just about ready for launch!

We were both wondering how long we'd get to settle into the rep life again. Last year it was a complete cycle, i.e., two weeks. Neither of us thought we would be so lucky this time round, although it didn't stop us dreaming about a fortnight off. We weren't new to the game. We knew how much hard work this was going to be, so a week or two to chill and get with the program wasn't such a tough ask. Or so we thought.

Nigel and I walked into the office after lunch. There were five reps sitting there filling out their welcome meeting paperwork, and we immediately recognised two of them from last year. One of the reps was Laura. She had met us initially the season before and helped to show us the ropes when we first reached the island, but neither Nigel nor myself had seen her since. We immediately gave her a big hug. She was one of the good ones and we were glad she was in the team again.

Another of the reps we recognised but couldn't place. She was pretty, slim, with short dark hair in a bob. We both knew her, though neither of us remembered her name — not that memory loss meant much out here. Neither of us could explicitly recall shagging her (I verified this with Nigel shortly afterwards), but neither of us could definitively say we hadn't, either.

We both stood there motionless as our cogs slowly turned and eventually she broke the trance. "It's me, Emma. I was staying at the Tropicana last year? Come on Nige, don't you remember?"

The pieces immediately slotted into place. I was off the hook as she wasn't in my hotel specifically, and how was I supposed to know everyone who'd stayed in his hotel? But sure, I did remember her. She was cool. Nigel instantly hammed up remembering her. His performance was so bad you'd think he was making his debut on Pornhub. Either way, we both hugged her, then made our way to the other three who we hadn't met before.

We didn't even get a chance to shake hands with the juniors before a familiar voice rang out. "Oh my god, who let these tarts in?"

It was Damien. I gave him a big man hug, and, much to my surprise, found he reciprocated. Nigel went to do the same but Damien instantly recoiled, explaining that cuddles were for closers—a reference to Alec Baldwin's Glengarry Glen Ross. Nigel protested, and still flung his arms around him. It was comical to watch. Damien eventually relented and gave him a hug back while the juniors watched with interest. Damien ushered us to a seat and introduced us to the rest of the team.

We were meeting the new members and I was curious to work out how the pecking order would fall. Though both Nigel and I were seniors we were still newcomers to the team, and I wondered how the inexperienced reps would take us. Laura was sound, and I was less worried about Emma, as she knew us already and had seen us in action, but to the other three we were complete strangers. Damien introduced us one by one.

We had Jack, who was a lad from Kent. He was relatively short, but slim and reminded me of a football player. He seemed friendly enough with nothing bolshy about him. In fact, he seemed very genuine. Just a really nice guy.

Next up was Tony. He was a big lump from London, south of the river. He was mixed race, but no one could tell you where he was actually from. To look at you'd think he had Indian roots, but then when he spoke there was almost a Caribbean twang to his voice. I liked him, he made me laugh and had a very infectious laugh himself. He seemed relaxed, but Damien started caning him almost immediately, so I figured maybe he was a little too relaxed and wondered if he might steal the crown from Nigel for being Damien's bitchin' bag for the season.

Last but not least was Frank. Now, right from the start I thought Frank was a complete and utter bell end. He was from Glasgow with a very strong accent. He was even more fiery than Damien and Edinburgh put together. He seemed to resent us being there as it pushed him down the pecking order. In the weeks to come he would do anything to prove himself by being overly competitive, argumentative, not particularly funny, and lecherous. Basically, he thought his shit didn't stink. I couldn't see why any bird would fancy a go on him, and to get laid he must basically irritate girls into eventual submission. He probably thought the same about me.

Once pleasantries were out the way, we sat down for a general update. Damien lobbed us our packs of promotional gear and general repping stuff. This included new t-shirts, shorts, trainers, and even some funky foam hand things for signalling and waving at guests in the airport. No chance I was taking them with me as I'd look a proper twat. I glanced across at Nigel who had already made his gesturing polyurethane glove show the middle finger and was grinning back at me. Point proven.

Damien went through a quick sales meeting with everyone. Nigel and I listened intently, but knew it wasn't really applying to us so we didn't pay much attention. Once he dismissed the others to go back to their respective hotels, he switched to us. Finally, the bit we'd been waiting for. He reconfirmed the hotels that we would be responsible for, which reps were currently covering them, and then proceeded to go through details on each unit. How many were in each hotel, what max capacity was, who the hotelier was, what other properties (if any) they had on our books, and just general info we would need to know. While this would be useful, it was also boring. All we wanted to know was when our start date would be. Neither Nigel nor myself wanted to ask though, so we just sat there trying not to nod off as we went further into the statistics.

Eventually, Damien got to the crucial question. "I suppose you helmets want to know when you're starting?" We both nodded and he let out a broad smile. "I bet you thought you were going to be given a week or so to settle in?"

Our hearts sank. I could feel Nigel was about to say something, but Damien continued. "Well, in a minute I'm going to introduce you to the hoteliers, and then you can get acquainted with them for the rest of the day. You won't need to partake in any rep entertainment in the evening until you've gone through rehearsals with the team, but essentially, tomorrow you'll be manning your units. I'm leaving the girls on the hotels with you for a couple of days to ensure everything is smooth, but then you're on your own."

Bollocks. No holiday. No settling in period. No sunbathing. I kind of suspected as much. It was fantasy to think that we were going to be given time off to relax on the company's dime, and I blamed Nigel for getting my hopes up. Without either of us saying a word, Damien told Nigel he'd take me to see my units now, but he was to meet him outside his one in an hour. Nigel agreed and left us to it.

Damien and I were alone now. "So when's your bird getting out here?"

I told him Jess was flying out in a week's time, and that I needed a week to settle into it. He agreed it was a good idea to have some alone time. He told me that he had made a deal with the office. Jess would be able to stay with me rent free for the whole period, as long as I made whatever target was given to me. He said if at any time things went wrong between us, or her being here was impacting me or the team, then that would be an issue that he would have to act decisively on. He wouldn't or couldn't allow anything to fester for weeks on end. I understood.

Damien then went on to add that if I performed for him like I did last year, he'd make sure that not only would there be no issues with Jess staying with me, but there'd be perks coming my way too. I assumed by this he meant early nights, late starts, low on the priority list for airport duties, and so on. He asked me if we had a deal?

I nodded keenly and shook his hand. I thanked him for sorting it out and that I wouldn't let him down on the figures front. I did say that I couldn't guarantee my sobriety but he just laughed and told me he didn't expect anything less. Shortly after that we packed up and he took me on the back of his moped to go and see my new masters at the hotel.

The first unit we visited was where I was already staying. Damien introduced me formally to the owner and his wife. Neither of them could speak English very well and our Spanish was comical. Short of ordering a cheese baguette or saying "I love melons" we were pretty much out of vocabulary within seconds. It didn't matter, they were very friendly, and seemed genuinely pleased to meet me. They already knew to give me the upgraded room, and Damien had told them that my 'wife' was due to join me the following week. I guess it was just less awkward all round having to explain who Jess would be and why she was staying over, but I was a tad concerned that he felt the need to confirm it.

I just hoped that the security in the hotel wasn't going to be difficult about randoms and strays coming back in the evening. Not for me, but for the guests. Last thing I wanted to have to deal with would be the endless confrontations with security because he'd stopped someone bringing a girl or guy back etc. Thankfully, the security guard was relaxed and knew the score and, as the season went on, we got on well and I'd often bring him back a bottle of schnapps from the bodega whenever we went, just to help grease the wheels.

We made our excuses and headed up the road to the other unit. This was the fun house with the pool and the bar I was going to be responsible for. As soon as we walked in, we were greeted warmly by some guests. I was somewhat surprised by this, as Damien didn't have any 'hotels or guests', so to speak, and I hadn't begun repping here yet. Apparently, Laura had already put the word out that she was going to be letting the unit go under my wing and that I was a great guy, and that they should look after me for my first couple of days.

It was a nice touch actually. I said hello to everyone while Damien went off to find Pepe the hotelier to make the introduction. He must have been gone no more than five minutes before returning with Pepe to see me necking a San Miguel. They stopped in their tracks. I'd been challenged by one of the lads who could down a beer quickest. Naturally I wasn't going to bend and stretch at that. I said I'd do it, only if every person in the bar joined in.

Two minutes later, 21 bottles of San Miguel had been bought and paid for. The bar man backed me up. On hearing this, Pepe let out a deep Spanish laugh, put his arm roughly around me and told me we were going to get on just fine. The message was simple: get the guests to spend money and not do too much damage to the property and essentially everything for me was on the house.

I could tell Damien was conflicted. He was irritated that I was already getting on the piss in front of the hotelier, which didn't look great or reflect well on him, but was also impressed that I'd managed to get everyone in the bar to buy drinks and make a good impression on Pepe. I guess the latter sentiment won, because he also managed to squeeze out a little more for me. He told Pepe that my other half was due to join me in a week's time, and asked if she could have a tab too, saying the company would cover it in the event I was unable to. Pepe dismissed the idea with a wave of his hand. "I will not hear of it. She will be welcome any time, you look after me, I look after you both." He extended his hand to both of us. We both shook it. This was a perfect start. We bid him farewell and began to make tracks.

On the way out, one of the lads who I'd been drinking with earlier asked me why we were going and why we weren't having another drink. "Dry your eyes princess, you'll see me soon enough. Get some rest, because I'll be seeing you here in the bar tonight. Bring your best drinkers and leave your excuses in the room." There, shots fired. He quipped that I was on, and returned to his pals chuckling.

Damien looked at me, shaking his head. "Just don't fuck this up. You've got a good gig on here!"

I nodded, thanked him for helping out there re Jess, and left him to it. He shot off to meet Nigel at his unit. I made a swift exit and dragged my new assortment of rep clothes and accessories with me. I had a couple of hours to kill so proceeded to unpack and sort myself out.

CHAPTER 8
MEET THE GUESTS

I was relaxing on the balcony when there was a knock on the door. It was Laura. She was asking if I wanted to come with her on her rounds and be introduced to the guests personally.

As I opened the door, she walked in, and clearly couldn't believe what she was seeing. "Wow, is this your place? They've looked after you here! It's twice the size of mine and I have to share!"

She caught me unawares. I didn't know what to say. I didn't want to tell the truth about Jess coming over, as it would look like unfair treatment, and I remember what Damien said about keeping my mouth shut.

I immediately lied. "It's temporary, unfortunately. I think they're trying to sort out the flats so I can share with Nigel, but someone else wanted to move or something. I'm here for a couple of weeks to get sorted, then the owners want it back for their own use. No idea, it's all drama."

I wasn't sure if she bought it or not, and I felt bad telling porkies to her, but the last thing I wanted to do was to mess this up. "Well, lucky you for now. Do you want to come and meet the guests? I'm going to be handing out tickets. I can introduce you."

This was a great idea and another nice touch from Laura. Nigel and I had both arrived on the changeover flights last night and, while we hadn't been doing much in the way of repping today, the others had been on full sales mode and had been conducting welcome meetings throughout the whole time. They'd collected payment and already handed in their paperwork to the office. The only thing to do now was to hand out the various bundles of tickets that had been purchased and to tell the guests what time we were meeting in the bar.

Thankfully for me, Laura was working in another unit just up the road from me, but it too didn't have a pool or much of a bar, so they were using Pepe's facilities alongside my lot. This was nice because she was thoughtful and decent and we got on well, so we'd be able to back up and cover for each other throughout the rest of the season. It made me chuckle deep inside knowing that Nigel didn't have a second this season and he might actually have to get off his arse and do some work! She told me to get a rep top on and meet her downstairs in a few minutes.

Door by door we went. Laura would knock, we'd be invited in, she would introduce me as their new rep and I'd make small talk while she was rummaging around in her satchel digging out the correct club tickets and venue slips that the guests had bought. All the guests were friendly and I was relieved that no one was funny with me.

Sometimes guests could get prickly on hearing they would be dropped by their rep and would feel rejection. Others would be territorial, like I'd stolen them from her. Fortunately, Laura had a good spiel and implied that, as we were approaching peak season, we had more guests and more bodies were needed. I was very experienced and while she wasn't going to be the primary contact now, she would be the secondary, as I would be for her guests. It was 100% accurate but I really liked the way she delivered it. For the guests that had just arrived when we did, they didn't really care as they had no time to form an impression —good or bad— on either of us, but for those that were already a week into it, they more often than not gave her a big hug and would shake my hand. This was a good sign, and really helped to put any pregame butterflies to rest. I remember what Edinburgh had told me in the airport about being senior now and knowing how it works, but I was still feeling a little unsettled. I knew after a couple of days in, I would be fine, but I'd still only been on the island for less than 24 hours. We quickly went through the apartments before wandering up to the hotel.

On arrival at the hotel, Laura was met with enthusiasm all round. All the guests liked her and wanted to spend time with her. The guys were very protective of her and she of course flirted and played right up to it. They were trying to buy us drinks, but she politely managed to swerve them and we went up to the first floor. She continued with the handover and within about 45minutes we only had a couple of rooms to go. Much like the experience in the apartments, everyone was very friendly and enthusiastic towards me. I could tell that Laura was at pains to hand everyone over, but even she herself had said how difficult it was managing all the hotels on her own. She said she knew it was only temporary from the start, and that Damien had made it very clear that he wanted me in these two units, so she was totally cool about it. I couldn't believe how smooth sailing this was and nothing like the deep end I'd been unceremoniously dropped into during my first season.

Just before we knocked on one of the last doors, Laura told me to prepare myself. When I inquired as to why and what the guests were like, she replied that they were a couple of girls who had come out for a good time but hadn't really gelled with the rest of the hotel. They didn't really want to do any of the trips and every time Laura had tried to interact with them, they had been a bit pissy. Laura described them as 'up themselves.' She tried to tell me in advance that, as they hadn't bought anything or tried to interact with the hotel as a whole, she had effectively given up on them and that I shouldn't be bothered if they're not friendly. I totally understood where she was coming from. We weren't everyone's cup of tea. That said, I was still somewhat apprehensive.

Laura knocked twice. We could hear the music lower from inside and muffled voices. Laura knocked again. I heard the clunk of the key turning in the lock. After what Laura had just said, it felt like a horror film. I was waiting for a cenobite to be on the other side of the door, the Lament Configuration having just been opened by some rusty old key. The door was slowly opened.

I couldn't have been any more wrong. The girl standing in front of me was gorgeous. Short pixie hair, a beautiful face, dark eyes. I think I was shell shocked for a moment. She had the most gorgeous kissable lips, and I'm not talking about the modern-day version where you take a perfectly normal looking girl, add some filler and out pops a five feet ten inch human duck, complete with a stupid puzzled look. I'm talking early career Angelina Jolie. Not what I was expecting.

She too seemed to lock eyes on me, both of us a little puzzled to be gawping at a stranger. It wasn't until Laura said "hi" and asked her how she was doing that we broke off eye contact. She seemed flustered and asked Laura to repeat the question. Laura just smiled and asked again how they were doing. The girl invited us both in. I stood there like a bit of a wally, but Laura led the way.

The friend came in from the balcony and said hello. They both seemed to be friendly enough and not how Laura had described them initially. I just stood there smiling while Laura proceeded to tell them that I would be covering them from now on. She skipped the part about her being a secondary contact or making any other kind of niceties about them still seeing each other. She just asked the first one if they were ok to be 'under' me. Pixie looked across, having avoided eye contact up until this point. I continued to smile, and to my surprise, she smiled back but then immediately started to blush. I couldn't believe it. This girl was dynamite and it was looking like I'd got her rattled. Laura picked up on it too.

Saving the girl from any more embarrassment (must have been a chick thing) she quickly moved attention to the friend who was still standing by the balcony. "We're going to be meeting in the bar at 8 if you fancy a drink. All the new arrivals will be there. You never know, you might see some decent ones." With that she turned to leave.

Just as we got to the door, I couldn't resist one more eye fuck. "It was really nice to meet the pair of you. Hopefully we'll get to know each other a bit more over the next few days." I smiled again directly at pixie, who was just about holding it together, before closing the door behind me.

I won't lie, I felt my apples swell. Any thoughts I had about Jess had evaporated during that brief moment. "Well, they seemed alright," I said to Laura.

"Mate, she was big time into you," came the response. "That's the friendliest I've seen the pair of them in a week."

"I didn't notice," I replied meekly.

"Shut up you didn't notice! You were teasing her."

Laura was no fool, there was no point trying to play coy with her. I broke out into a broad grin.

"Still got it," I joked. Laura laughed as she knocked on the next room.

The last couple of doors revealed less memorable inter-actions, but everyone was super friendly, and I was relieved. If this was anything to go by, early indications were that I had a good group of friendly guests and the hotels already had momentum due to Laura's efforts. It meant that I was going to be able to hit the ground running.

I tried to put Pixie out of my mind. Sure, she was fit, and her blush in front of Laura had my ego stroked more than a Bond villain's cat, but I had to remind myself about Jess and that I wasn't about that this time round. I still needed to have some fun though, so I decided early on I was going to be all about the tease. I mean, we needed some ground rules here. I figured, no numbers, no kissing, no holding hands etc, just banter was above board. That put me on the side of being faithful, but didn't totally choke me of fun.

CHAPTER 9
THE FIRST NIGHT

Once we'd finished with the guests, Laura headed off to her place to get ready. We had an hour before we needed to be back in the bar. I was starving, and given it was our first night I thought it wise to get some grub in me before hitting the booze.

I was on my way out towards the apartment when I saw Pepe. "Hola, how are you, my friend?" he said in his deep voice.

"Very good thanks Pepe, you, ok?" I replied. He asked me where I was going, I told him to grab a bite to eat and to get changed for the evening's events. He asked me what I was going to eat. I was a bit taken back by this, and so just shrugged my shoulders, answering something quick and easy. Pepe said he would fix it, and without giving me a chance to say anything, he shouted towards the back of the bar. I didn't hear what he asked for, all I heard was "Si Pepe" come back. He showed me to the bar, poured me a beer and we made small talk. I was both welcomed and flattered, this was like a dream come true. If Carlsberg did first days at work!

Within a few minutes, two plates turned up, one was a seafood salad, with prawns the size of sausages, and the other was a plate of chips with some chorizo at the side. "I know how the English like their chips," he teased.

I smiled, and paused just long enough to appear polite before ripping through the plates. Thankfully, the rest of the bar was empty. The last thing I needed was to come across the guys from before, challenging me to drink and getting me sideways before I'd even had a chance to line my stomach. I already figured I'd need to build up my tolerances again, but as you can't really control the amount you drink, I decided to just eat more instead, hoping it would help soak it up.

Both plates were clear within a few minutes. I tried to pay, but was immediately shot down by the barman. "Pepe's orders señor!" I put my wallet away. Shook his hand and left.

I got back to the apartment. I took a quick shower and laid down for half an hour. I was stuffed. I felt like a prawn enthused walrus. Thankfully I was told to wear a black t-shirt this evening, so I figured I could hide my meal. It wasn't that I was lardy, it was literally I just smashed two meals in five minutes and both felt and looked pregnant. Laying there wasn't helping, so I tried to walk around the apartment to ease the bloat.

In the end there was only one thing for it. An emergency turn-out. One strong black coffee later and within minutes I was purged. That sorted me out. Within ten minutes I was walking back to the bar to start the night's entertainment.

By the time I got to the bar, the place was busy. The new arrivals were buzzing and keen to get their party on, and as soon as I got there I started to socialise. This was what I had missed back in the UK. The ability to go up and talk to anyone you wanted for no reason or purpose, and to be met openly without barriers.

Everyone was mixing and getting on like a house on fire. The main lad from before suddenly appeared with his lot and another group of lads they'd bonded with. Unfortunately for me, they had no interest in mingling or chatting up the opposite sex, they just wanted to drink and drink hard. "Here's the lightweight, how are we feeling?" he quipped, in front of his mates.

I just smiled. "I hope you lined your stomach, Tinkerbell."

I was anticipating Laura arriving to save me or to try and distract them, but alas she was not. I walked him over to the side of the bar. Like chickens, his mates just silently followed. A few guys who were there made a clearing for us. "Choose your weapon?" I told them. After a quick discussion within the group, tequila was picked. "You want a bottle or shots?"

"Up to you."

"You lot are paying, you choose." They looked at each other before they went for the bottle.

I asked the barman for a new bottle of tequila, and he put it on their room. They immediately started pouring. A few others had started to notice and I could sense the noise in the room had begun to lower. I looked at another group of lads who were watching from across the bar. You could see they were weighing it up. "You in?" I asked, much to their surprise.

"Yeah, we're in," claimed the leader proudly, thinking he was going to get a free shot of tequila.

"Good lads, get yourself a bottle too then, we'll wait for you." At that point the barman was already preparing their glasses. The guys couldn't really back down, given how public it was. They accepted their bottle and the barman put it on their tab.

The shots were lined up. We must have had ten lads on my side of the bar, and a further six or seven on their side. "Last group to stop wins," I said. "Has everyone else got a drink?"

A few said they hadn't, so I managed to usher them to the bar where the barman quickly poured them. The general noise in the bar had faded to almost a silence.

"Let's raise a toast, if I may. We have new arrivals today, myself included. For those of you who have already been out here, it will be our first chance to get to know you." I raised my shot of tequila above my head. "First night," and proceeded to down my shot.

The rest followed. At which point, Laura walked through the door. I don't think she could quite believe it. The whole bar was necking shots and it was only 8:05pm. I just smiled and turned to the lads who were busy pouring out another round. "Keep an eye on the lot on that side. Make sure they're not cheating," I hollered in the direction of the lads on the other side.

Thankfully, they took it in good spirits and we all went again. And again, and again. Luckily, we only had 25ml shot glasses, which is 30 shots out of a bottle of tequila. Within no time the bottle was empty, and the guys were reaching for another from the barman. I respectfully asked if we could switch to vodka, as I believed that tequila would impair my ability to get a boner. The boys laughed and the barman handed them a bottle of Smirnoff. Fortunately, at this point, Laura pulled me out of there as we needed to sort out logistics for later.

We stood outside the hotel's main reception discussing what the timing was and where we would be taking them. I knew the drill, but still needed to know what bars and what times. I let Laura take the lead. I was happy to follow. She remarked that Pepe had already told her that I was a good guy and that I was going to get on well there. On hearing this, I asked her for a favour. "Does Pepe know what time we normally leave here? Is he normally about?"

"Every time. He's clued up and he knows when we leave, and he can see what's been ordered. Why do you ask?"

"Would you mind if I took them out late today? Maybe 10-15 minutes?"

"What about Damien?"

"I'll handle that. We'll say it's my fault and I took us to the wrong bar or something. He'll be okay. You won't get blamed. I want to really get into Pepe's good books, as I am sure over the next couple of months shit will hit the fan and it will buy me some political capital."

Laura was uneasy about this, but understood where I was coming from. "Okay, just don't get me in trouble." We then spoke a bit more about the rest of the evening's itinerary before heading back into the bar.

By the time we walked back in, the place was heaving. The two groups of lads had managed to forget about me and were busy doing shots together. They'd even roped in some stragglers into the arrangement and they too were downing vodka. I kept to the opposite side of the bar with plenty of people between us, hoping they wouldn't see me. My tequilas had just kicked in and I was feeling the mood too. Any nerves or apprehension had seeped away. I was in full flow when something caught my attention in the corner of my eye.

It was Pixie. She and her mate had come down to the bar and they both looked gorgeous. You could feel the eyebrow of every lad raise as they graced through the room to the bar. I continued my conversation, forcing myself to play it cool.

In fact, it was a further 15-20 minutes before I even glanced in her direction. Her back was towards me, standing at the bar, but I managed to catch a glimpse of her in the mirror behind her. She'd been looking at me. I just smiled. She smiled back, showing more composure than earlier. I continued to talk to the group I was with. Eventually I approached the bar under the premise of getting a beer, but I paused next to the pair of them. I asked them how they were doing. I told them they both looked very nice and thanked them for joining us. I asked if they were coming onwards with us to the next bar.

Pixie looked at her mate who appeared to be calling the shots. Neither of them said anything for a moment. I used this awkward silence to play my hand. "Well, if you don't want to go it's fine, I understand. It would have been nice to have a drink with you both. I'm sure you've got a huge night planned anyway, as you're both dressed to kill. If you change your mind you know where we are. I need to get the group ready to move now, so I need to cut, but if I don't catch you this evening, hopefully we'll chat more tomorrow?"

I threw Pixie a massive smile and looked her deep in the eyes. I think this irritated her mate as she could have been a huge horse in a pink tutu and I still wouldn't have looked at her. I felt Pixie begin to crack, so I made my excuses and rejoined the crowd.

Another 20-30 minutes passed before Laura gave me the nod. It was officially time to leave. Any minute spent longer in the hotel bar was on my ass.

I walked over to the barman, took him to one side and said what's the quickest cocktail you can make in a few minutes? He said he could do a really quick Moscow mule.

Basically, vodka and ginger beer with a twist of lime. I asked him if he had enough ginger beer and limes to do a lot? He replied he could do as many as I needed. Challenge accepted.

At that point I went over to the lads who were already two bottles of tequila, a bottle of vodka and some beers down and asked them if they wanted a Moscow mule. I said I was having one and that they were great. They were all keen. So, we ordered 17 of them. They weren't particularly expensive, and the number sounds big, but it's just because usually you don't have two groups ordering together or drinking the same drink.

On hearing this, others started to inquire. Before you knew it, we had a further ten on order, and as the first ones started to be handed out (mine included), I started giving them to others to try. This only caused more of a backlog, as others wanted them too.

This was exactly what I was hoping for. In the space of the next 15 minutes, we proceeded to take the bar out of all their ginger ale, another bottle of vodka, and most of their limes. Pepe took me to one side. He just said, "Thank you."

"That's for the prawns!" I replied, smiling. We both laughed, and he returned to the back of the bar.

By the time we got out we were already 15 minutes late, and trying to move everyone was like herding cats. We got to the first venue on the strip 25 minutes late. Damien was on the door and far from impressed. I walked straight up to him and apologised. I told him Laura had tried to move off earlier, and that I had stupidly ordered a large number of cocktails for the guests and it took longer than I thought. I said it wouldn't happen again and I was still a bit rusty. He looked me straight in the eye and asked me if I did it for Pepe.

"Yes, I threw him an extra 15 minutes. I've taken him

out of all his ginger, most of his limes, two bottles of tequila, maybe two if not three bottles of vodka, and more beer than a rugby team can drink. Our lot are ready to launch."

"Fair play. Don't do it again though, spread the love!" He beckoned everyone in. He didn't say anything to Laura, but just gave her a look as if to say, keep an eye on me. She scuttled past him and went inside with the others.

Once inside the venue, selfishly, any thought I had for entertaining the guests went out the window. I wanted to find Nigel as we had heaps to talk about. I found him hiding at the back with a beer in his hand. "Oi, oi, sailor, how are you doing?" I bellowed as I walked up to him.

"Not as great as you, by the looks of it, " he replied.

"What's wrong? Everything ok?" I was surprised by how downtrodden he seemed.

"The guests hate me. The hotelier thinks I'm a dickhead. My room looks like something from Beirut, and it's covered in insects."

I couldn't help it. I pissed myself laughing. "I got to hear this one. Go on…"

Nigel proceeded to explain what had happened. Damien, having left me, found Nigel and introduced him to his hotelier. This guy, by the sounds of it, was a staunch Catholic, no-sex-before-marriage type, who seemed to question Nigel's moral standpoint before he'd even had a chance to do anything wrong. Nigel said the hotelier didn't speak any English and already he had a feeling he'd pissed him off. Apparently, the only English that this guy did speak was "No Girls!"

I couldn't believe my ears, this was karma. Next, there'd been a mix up in the hotel because there was an overflow. This was when the hotel for one reason or another had been overbooked, meaning that some of the guests who were due to be staying there were suddenly being told that the hotel was no longer available and they were being moved to another one with availability. In this instance, rather than staying in the West End, in the thick of it, they were now being moved to San Antonio Bay. Now while the bay in itself was nice enough, quaint, with a few bars and some big hotels dotted around, it was nothing like staying in the West End. Understandably, a number of guests were pissed off but were nonetheless moved onwards in the early hours.

Well, this afternoon they came back trying to get into the hotel they had originally booked. As Nigel was the rep at the time—and even though this initially happened before he arrived—he had to try and deal with it. Nigel could be described as a chocolate teapot at the best of times, let alone in a high-pressure situation. He just melted.

Apparently, there was a huge confrontation and security needed to be involved, something which made him look bad in front of his existing guests, many of whom sympathised with the group that were ousted to begin with. To top it all his room backed onto the rear of the hotel near the kitchen. Directly beneath his window was a small area where they stored the waste products like small vats of oil and fat after cooking etc., and they stank. He couldn't open a window and the place was overrun by ants. Nigel, having stolen a couple of hours' kip earlier (rather than meet his guests) woke up to find them crawling all over his pillow and face.

I couldn't take any more. There was nothing he could say that would not make me piss myself any harder. I literally had to pinch the end of it to stop any wee leaking. This was hilarious.

Coupled with the fact that I had basically a dream start to my second season, it was too much to take. Nigel could see how funny I found it, and even he began to laugh. "I suppose you've had a dream start to the day, right?"

I just smiled and nodded.

Nigel proceeded to invert a San Miguel above his face and turned it upright only when every last drop of silly juice had hit his throat. He was like an angry pelican. "Still, at least I can fuck something."

Ouch. Spiteful bastard. He felled me with that one sentence. He also made me realise that I'd completely forgotten to phone Jess. I was supposed to call her once I was set up in the accommodation and hotel and to let her know how it all was. She was going to be pissed. Nothing I could do now though. I'd call her in the morning. Hopefully she'd understand that I was just busy as opposed to knee deep in guests.

As expected, she was pissed. As soon as she picked up the phone, I could tell she had a mood on. I apologised immediately. I was very cognisant of the fact that she met me as a rep and knew precisely the sort of things that reps got up to. For all she knew, I could have been putting Pixie through her paces and already lining up an afternoon cuddle with the mate. Nothing could have been further from the truth. While I would have liked nothing more than to roar through Pixie, my evening took a different turn of events.

I did in fact get to spend a bit of time talking to her and her friend. They wandered into the bar fashionably late and hung out by the bar most of the time. We had a decent chat for about 20 minutes. They were pretty cool. Her mate softened up a bit and we actually had a pleasant conversation with a bit of banter. God knows why, but I even tried to bring Nigel into the fold with her. Despite his efforts to burst my bubble, I felt like he needed a lay to lift his spirits. Her mate wasn't interested at all though, and Pixie could just about keep a straight face without blushing while looking at me, so it wasn't long before Nigel lost interest and sloped off into the crowd to find his soulmate for the night.

To tell you the truth, it was a strange feeling. As much as I fancied Pixie, and I was pretty certain she would have liked a slice, I didn't want to get to a point where I had to decline or make things awkward. I still wanted Jess and was excited about having her out there with me. Thing is, the more I slowed things down, or the less I pushed forward, the more she did. It was something that I was beginning to notice a lot. All this did was stroke my ego further.

I began to think maybe this season wasn't going to be so traumatic after all, despite tying myself up to Jess. Our little group conversation the night before had been inadvertently cut short by one of my lot projectile vomiting on the dance floor. Predictably, it had been the one with the mouth that had challenged me earlier on at lunch time. The rest of his mates weren't exactly up to scratch either. One had stripped off in the bathroom to his underpants and was being walked out by security, and a third had fallen asleep on a speaker in the corner.

While theoretically, Laura or I could have dealt with it, I chose to get involved immediately, given it was me that helped to put them in that state. I grabbed the other two or three lads who could still speak and got them to help me drag the others out. We walked them back to the hotel, stopping only once for a quick chunder before managing to put them in their rooms. As I walked back out past security, Pepe was there. He found the whole thing funny. It wasn't anything he hadn't seen a hundred times before, but with me managing it all, something tickled him.

In his deep Marlboro accent, he said, "Same again tomorrow night?"

I just smiled. "You look after me, I look after you!"

He beckoned me over to the bar, poured a couple of shots out, and we both took one. "Salut!"

He polished his off in one fell swoop. Not wanting to be outdone, I followed suit. "Cheers Pepe," and slammed it down. Then it hit me.

Oh, my fucking God. Sweet Jesus. What the hell was that? Complete shite. It was a taste I hadn't experienced for over a year and bad memories instantly began to flood my synapses. It was Hierbas, a traditional liquor I'd been introduced to last season. It was as if a camel had taken a shit directly on my taste buds. I spluttered and pulled the face of a three year old eating a lemon.

Pepe threw out a hearty laugh, patted me on the back and retired to the rear of the bar. By the time I got back to the last venue of the night, everyone had already pretty much dissipated. I was fortunate enough to catch the end of Damien's sales meeting where Nigel was conspicuously absent. When pushed on where I was, Laura had spoken up for me, so he was cool, and if anything, probably impressed that I bothered to return at all. It was clear that Nigel, on the other hand, was going to get fisted in the morning.

I tried explaining what had happened to Jess, but it went in one ear and out the other. I felt bad. I could see where she was coming from. Of course, she was excited to be coming out to Ibiza and she wanted to know all about the accommodation and what the hotels were like. I don't think it was a trust thing with her, more disappointment. I apologised again, and asked if she wanted to hear about the apartment?

Her tone softened, and we went through it. She was pleased to hear that it looked like she was going to be eating and drinking for free in the hotel, too. I told her she shouldn't take the piss, but if I can keep Pepe and the barman on side, it should be pretty cheap to live out here.

She already had it in her mind that she was going to try and find some work to keep her occupied. I figured I'd be able to probably help her find some cash work once I got settled in. We cut the conversation short, and agreed we'd speak in a few days. I was keen not to put a specific time on the next call, in case I missed it, so left things casual.

On hanging up, I decided to go and find Nigel. I was keen to hear what had happened to him on his first night out, so popped into his hotel for a cup of tea. I said "hi" to his hotelier who just grunted and pointed to the back of the restaurant.

There was Nigel. He was slumped in a chair nursing a hangover. I asked how he was doing, and the minute I saw him look up, I could tell he was hurting. "What happened to you?"

"Mate, I got ruined last night and blacked out. One minute I was snogging a bird in the club, and the next I woke up on the reception couch with no keys, no cash, and a lump on my head." He pointed to this rather swollen looking bulge protruding from his right temple.

"Did someone smack you or you just fell down pissed? Who found you?"

"No idea, it just hurts. One of the guests woke me up this morning. Am hoping the security or hotelier didn't see me. They already think I'm a cock."

I began to smirk. "Have you spoken to Damien yet?"

"No, why?" he replied.

"Because you were missing at the sales meeting last night. We all assumed you were with a bird or were sleeping."

His eyes widened. "Wait, I wasn't there? I don't remember, but just assumed I was. Oh man, he's going to fuck me now."

I felt a guilty pleasure in breaking the news to him. Up

to this point, he had been oblivious to the fact that he was going to get shafted. "Still at least you can fuck something!"

Nigel laughed. We caught up for another few minutes before setting off. I had some things to do in my hotel, and I didn't want to be anywhere near Nigel when Damien caught up with him, in case some of his punishment happened to get sprinkled in my direction.

For me, the rest of the week continued without a hitch. It was pretty much rinse and repeat. Nigel and I had to attend a few rehearsal sessions for the rep's cabaret, and we needed to learn some dance moves for the other nights, but they were simple enough. Most of the routines were the same as the year before, so we picked it up pretty quickly.

Good job really, because the rest of the guys weren't in the mood to help train us and so rehearsals were half arsed affairs carried out as fast as possible. As far as they were concerned, having to teach us when to step left and when to step right was eating into time they could be smashing guests or grabbing a sleep. And I couldn't blame them. Laura had effectively handed over all the guests and duties to me for my units and we were approaching changeover when the last of the guests she'd initially been rep for were leaving, meaning I was effectively fully in charge of my units.

She popped over to say goodbye to those she started with and made apologies again for leaving midway through. Thankfully, she was told I'd been doing a good job in her absence and the guests had had a good time regardless. Ever the team player, Laura gave that feedback to Damien in front of me, so it also helped to get me some brownie points.

Nigel was doing airport duty again for the second time in a row, and was due on again the following rotation for missing the sales meeting. This irritated him, but made me chuckle. I sensed Damien was trying to make an example of him and nip in the bud any lax behaviour. Nigel wasn't surprised he wasn't getting a break from it and wasn't particularly bothered. He'd gotten lucky the past couple of nights and managed to score with a couple of girls from his hotel. One of them was decent, too, so that perked him up.

Sales figures across the board were good. Nothing stellar — we were on target or thereabouts — but that wasn't enough for Damien. He was a good sales person himself, having been born with the gift of the gab, and he was hungry for us to have the highest figures in resort. He was very good at motivating people and fine-tuning his approach accordingly. If he thought you were capable, you'd see carrot. If he thought you weren't, it'd be the stick. I say the stick, it should really be the dildo, because you would be repeatedly fucked by it.

Case in point with Nigel and I. I hadn't been on an airport run yet, and my first would be when Jess arrived in a week's time. Nigel had been on twice already and would be doing a third and possibly even a fourth. At times I did feel for him, because as much as we ribbed each other, he did get the rough end of the stick most times. Thing is, it wasn't that he couldn't sell. He just couldn't be bothered. I think Damien knew this deep down and that was the primary reason he rode him.

By the time we were a couple of days in, pretty much all the team had bonded with us. Nigel and I weren't really thought of as outsiders now, or at least we didn't feel it, and everyone was pretty much just getting along. Everyone apart from Frank and I.

Although I never mentioned anything publicly, Frank continued to get on my tits. He was continually trying to act up and prove himself as some alpha male, but you could tell it was an act. He didn't let up once. It reached the point where I couldn't stand being in the same room as him, let alone having to talk to him, but I bit my tongue and tried to be as civil as possible. The girls seemed to tolerate him, and Nigel didn't seem particularly bothered by him, but he continually grated my carrot.

Just having to interact with him was like putting salt in my Calvin Kleins. It just fucking irritated. I think Nigel didn't have a problem with him because Frank would continually kiss his ass and hang off his every word. I don't think I was jealous of this, I just thought Frank was a 24-carat penis. Even some of his guests thought the same. Numerous complaints were made about him, ranging from pressure selling to general offensiveness. I think Damien pulled him up a few times, and at one point even reduced him to tears but, by and large, tolerated him because he was pushy. He would always try and sell, and if he couldn't make it, he would go back again and again to try and make something happen. Damien valued this effort.

CHAPTER 10
JACK-IN-A-BOGS

True to his word, Damien had engineered my first airport to coincide with the flight that Jess was arriving on. My sales figures had been good from the start, and he'd basically shielded me from nights of zero sleep, choosing to keep me fresh for the big sell the day after. Besides, Nigel and Tony were more than capable of taking my place given their revenues.

I was excited to see Jess and even managed to nip off straight after work the night before, meaning I was somewhat refreshed and ready for action. After all, it'd been a good month or so before I'd seen her, and I was horny. I tidied the place up and tried to make the apartment look like it could actually support a couple and not just a randy bachelor. First impressions would be key, so I made sure the sheets were clean, the place was tidied, and I had some food in the fridge.

I was tasked with picking up the Gatwick flight. Jess would be on a similar timed flight, and Damien told me I could wait for her as long as the flight wasn't delayed. It was changeover night for us, so half the guests were staying in the resort on a bar crawl, the other half were going to be swapped out at the terminal.

Laura took my lot into town on the piss. I rounded up everyone onto the coach as we stopped at each hotel. Thankfully, everyone was present and accounted for, so it made my life much easier. We made our way to the airport and everything went smoothly. I dropped the guests off at the check in desk and then made my way behind the scenes to a small breakout room that the reps could use to rest and relax in between flights.

I say breakout room but it was more like a breakout cupboard. It was on the first floor of the airport and there were barely enough chairs to sit on and most of the time people ended up sitting or laying on the floor trying to catch a bit of sleep, knowing full well they wouldn't be sleeping much once the guests arrived. Every rep had a portable alarm clock with them, and these would be going off continually through the night so you never really got a decent kip in. If you were unlucky, you'd be dropping off at, say, 10 or 11pm, but your incoming flight might get delayed, so you would have to wait until say 4 or 5am. Then, by the time you've dropped everyone off, it's 6 or 7am and you need to be up and ready to go at 8.

It was harsh. On this night, I dropped my outgoing off at just before midnight, my incoming was coming in at 01:00 and Jess was due to land at around 01:15. All things being equal, she would probably be out at the same time as the others, so it would be easy to get her on the coach as well for the ride back. I basically had an hour to kill before the flight, so I didn't bother trying to sleep. Jack was also with me at the airport, with Nigel due to come in later on at around 2am.

Jack and I paced the terminal for a bit, and sat and had a drink. It was probably the first time we actually got to know each other. He was a good lad. He'd played semi pro football in Kent prior to coming out and hoped to resume footie when he got back. He'd been doing alright with the girls on the quiet, and also told me that he found Frank annoying at times, so I was naturally becoming a fan. He quizzed me on my first season and asked if it was better or worse. I told him it was just different, but again, too early into this season to draw conclusions. Some of the things he came out with regarding his exploits had me welling up, he was really funny. His flight was due in from Manchester about five minutes before mine, so when he needed to go, I went with him.

The pair of us stood there at the end of the airport with big signs above us. Jack had actually brought the big foam hand along and was waving it like a tool, but it did the trick. Soon enough, holiday makers were pacing towards him like moths to a flame. "What flight love? Manchester or Gatwick? Gatwick? Oh, that would be the handsome gentleman on my right," as he directed them to me.

He had plenty of banter, in fact we both did. Within a few minutes we were surrounded by the herd and we were playing off each other. We had to quickly check the guests in and then point them to the coaches, where they were to wait until we counted everyone off. Only then we would leave.

My lot were still coming out in dribs and drabs, whereas his were all pretty much done. Just as the last ones for him were coming through, I was aware there were a couple of girls hanging around him. I didn't know if he knew them, or they were lost or they just wanted a chat. I had a brief space where I didn't have any guests—half were on the coaches, half were still to come through—so I approached him and the girls.

I couldn't believe what I was hearing. This girl was basically coming on to him in the airport. I don't mean teasing, I mean hot-to-trot, 'where can we go now to do it' type of thing. Her mate was just giggling. He looked at me, gave me his clipboard and foam hand and asked me to check the rest of his flight in.

Before I had a chance to answer, they were off. He had her by the hand and they were walking towards the bathrooms. I couldn't believe it. I covered him, making small talk with the mate in between checking off the guests.

Within a few minutes his coach was full and they were ready to set off. I was still waiting for a few more guests and of course Jess. A few more minutes passed, and all mine were checked off too. I was running out of small talk with the mate, and I kept looking towards the toilets waiting for Jack to reappear. We also had two coach loads of guests anxious to get to their hotels and either sleep or go straight out, and I could feel the pressure mounting.

All of a sudden, I saw a smile that changed everything. It was Jess. I left the mate on her own without so much as a word or a glimpse and walked over to her. She was pleased to see me and gave me a big hug and a kiss. I gave her the foam hand which she looked puzzled at, and I took her suitcase. You'd think the suitcase belonged to Fred West; it was that heavy and bursting at the seams.

We walked back over to the mate who just smiled. I stood the mini tardis upright and took back the clipboard. Jess looked puzzled.

"We're just waiting for one or two more guests," I confidently put forward. I tried to feign annoyance to keep it all on track. Just as Jess was beginning to nod in understanding, the mate spoke up in the thickest Mancunian accent you can imagine.

"Yeah, she's probably sucking off his mate in the toilet. She's such a minger!" With that she started to giggle.

I couldn't believe it. I was gutted. Jess looked at me, eyes wide open, and I just shrugged. Before I got a chance to say anything else that would only serve to put my foot further into my mouth, I heard a familiar "Oi Oi," and turned around to see Jack striding across the terminal like Connor fucking McGregor.

As he got close, I tried to give him a bit of a glare to encourage him to reign it in, but I failed abysmally. Not only did he high five me, he winked at Jess and then followed up with this immortal nugget: "Ah the joys of being a rep. It's a thankless job, but someone's gotta do it!"

The girl was only a few metres behind him. As soon as she got close, she just giggled and fell into the arms of her mate, clearly discussing what had just gone down. Jess looked far from impressed.

"Jack, this is Jess, my girlfriend."

Jack's broad smile suddenly shrank by about 75%. "Oh, er, pleased to meet you. I'm Jack."

Jess held out a hand and replied, "nice to meet you too. I see you're coping with the arduous demands of being a rep."

Jack was squirming. On the surface he was confident, but we all knew deep down he was uncomfortable as hell. "Hmm, yeah, just about. Sorry, you'll have to excuse me. Catch you later guys. Come on girls, coach 12."

With that, he grabbed the two girls, who hadn't stopped clutching each other's arms giggling, and disappeared out of the terminal. I looked at Jess trying not to smirk, but it was useless. She shot me an icy glare, but I couldn't help it. I started to laugh. She hit me in the ribs. "You better not be doing that in airports" she scowled.

"Definitely not," I replied. "He only had one of them in there with him!" She hit me again. I picked up her suitcase and led her onto the coach with the others.

Thankfully, by the time we got on the coach, everyone was relatively relaxed and not too stressed. When we pulled out of the airport car park, just before 2am, I figured we had an hour to drop everyone off, tops. 15 minutes going through Jess and I'd be in bed for 3:30, all in all not a bad result, as I needed to be up at 8 anyway to prepare for the welcome meetings.

I immediately got on the mic and started the usual welcome spiel. Everything ran like clockwork. I think I managed to get the guests in their hotels within the hour. I was fortunate, because there were a couple of large groups all staying at one hotel, so with one drop I practically cleared half the coach.

I made sure our last stop was my hotel bar. I showed Jess this would be where she could eat and drink and where she'd be finding me most days. We then walked to the apartment which was literally a minute away.

I don't think we even managed to open her suitcase. She managed to get one quick look round each room in the apartment and I was on her. I hadn't seen her in a month and, well, living in Ibiza and being faced with temptation, it kind of gets to you. Much to her annoyance, as soon as we were finished, I was asleep. There was no time to hear about the UK, what she'd been up to, how her flight was. I was already in the land of nod. Unfortunately, this would go on to become a common theme for us both.

When the alarm went off a couple of hours later, I sprang into action. Though I was tired, and could have gone in for round two, I was mindful that Damien knew she was on the island and felt I'd be under scrutiny initially, so was keen to get the welcome meeting on time, with good attendance and good sales figures. I knew he'd be on my case regardless, and didn't want to give him any real excuse to cane me. With Nigel and Tony by my side, I felt like I had some cannon fodder anyway, but still.

I let Jess sleep in, left her a key, and a note. By the time she made it out of the apartment and actually reached the hotel, we had already finished the welcome meeting, had sorted cash and paperwork, and the reps were moving en masse to Nigel's hotel for his meeting. Ours had gone like clockwork. 100% attendance, 100% sales. Damien was happy, and I was determined to bring the same energy to Nigel's meeting.

Jess walked in just as we were literally walking out. I managed to grab Damien to make the introduction and told her this was the man who sorted the accommodation. She graciously thanked him and gave him a big smile. The big man softened for a moment, but immediately fired a warning shot. "You're both very welcome, and it's lovely to meet you. I see Luke is punching far above his weight. You can stay there as long as you want, as long as he hits the targets we've agreed on. Don't tell anyone else about this, and don't cause any issues for him or me, otherwise we'll have to revisit the arrangement. Okay?"

Jess was a little bit taken back. Before she could say anything, Damien continued, "But now that's out the way, give us a hug. Welcome to the family." He leant in and gave Jess a hug and she reciprocated. This was typical Damien, tough but fair. You always knew where you stood. I gave Jess a sly kiss on the cheek, mindful of guests about, and told her I'd meet her here later. With that, we were off.

By the time we finished all the welcome meetings and paperwork, I got back to the hotel just after 4pm. I was starving. I managed to eat a bag of crisps for lunch and needed some substance. Jess was on one of the sunbeds listening to some music when I walked over. I could tell she was a little off with me initially. I guess she expected to have seen a bit more of me in the first 12 hours she'd been on the island, but I had made it perfectly clear to her that I was going to be busy. I reassured her that 'welcome meeting day' happened on Thursday and Sundays and were the most important days of the week due to sales, so this was just the way it would be, but the rest of the week should be easier. She softened.

I introduced her to Pepe and the guys in the bar. It wasn't a big public thing; I didn't want the rest of the guests to know that I had a girlfriend here. It just complicated things. I needed to be able to behave without distraction, and if that meant flirting outrageously, so be it. I also didn't want Jess being hassled by the guests if there were issues to be solved. They dealt with me or Laura if they couldn't find me. Obviously over a few days they'd see us and guess, but that didn't mean I wanted to make an announcement.

CHAPTER 11
THE AIR BED

Initially, everything went smoothly. I'd slowly managed to build on the momentum Laura had achieved and the hotel was running like clockwork. The official sales target of 70% participation on trips was being continually smashed. Most weeks if it wasn't 100% it was 90% or higher.

Having everyone on the trips and in the bars together made my life much easier. I would continually play match-maker and throw groups together helping them make friends and creating a good atmosphere. The new arrivals wouldn't just see it but would feel it as soon as they arrived. The guests were drinking more than before, which Pepe attributed to me, so he was pleased as bar takings were continually climbing. Despite the odd breakage here or there, there were no real incidents or anything notable to recite. That was until about three or four weeks in.

One particular group of degenerates decided after a night on the sauce that they were going to launch their bed off the balcony into the pool below. Now, I'm not just talking about throwing the mattress down one level. I'm talking the bed frame, mattress, sheets, pillows. Yep, the whole works ended up being jettisoned from the fifth floor.

What was going through their mind at the time I don't know. I wasn't there when it happened, but apparently the bed was tossed out around 4am. Security saw the bed go in but didn't see which room it came out of. Instinctively, they then went knocking room by room until the culprits were caught.

Now clearly it was going to be pretty obvious who the dickheads were as there would be a massive hole in the room where there used to be a bed. These imbeciles clearly didn't think that far ahead when they were hatching their master plan to recreate Atlantis one item of furniture at a time. What it meant was that, until the culprits were found, every room needed to be tossed prison style to find them, with guards banging on each door, batons drawn. If the door wasn't answered they let themselves in anyway with skeleton keys, much to the annoyance and fear from some of the guests. On they went, room by room, floor by floor, until they found the headquarters for Mensa.

When faced with the reality that they had been caught without a bed, the group of lads did what any lads do when faced with accusations in a foreign country. They denied it. The guards unfortunately possessed neither the subtleties of the English language nor the patience. The conversation, I can only assume, went something like this.

"Where bed?"

"We don't know, we found it like that."

"Ask again, where bed?"

"It wasn't us! Someone stole it."

At that point, the one nearest the main security guard will be getting walloped around the legs with a baton. He'll edge towards the door followed by the second security guard who is also using his baton to round up the other bed tossers. Once out of the room, the guys will be marched down the stairs in an abrupt manner and thrown out of the hotel. At which point, they'll phone Pepe to tell him what has happened, and he'll call me directly or the office, who in turn will get on to me.

By the time I got the call, the sun was already up. I wearily made my way to the hotel to find a thick, wooden bed frame next to the pool, with a full set of linen and a mattress laid out next to it in the sun. Pepe was there and was not impressed. Frankly, neither was I.

This was a real dickhead thing to do. Someone could have been killed if they'd gone for a swim, or if they'd missed the water and it had landed on someone poolside. Instinctively I apologised to him. He replied that it wasn't my fault, but he wanted these 'coños' out of his hotel.

Now, this was going to be an issue for us. It was peak season, and every unit was basically running at full capacity. If we take them from this hotel, we would still have a duty of care to place them elsewhere and I didn't really have the time to try and place them, and I know the office would have zero interest in spending too much effort trying to relocate twats, so I chose a slightly different approach. Bearing in mind these guys hadn't been allowed back in the hotel yet, they were keeping a low profile.

"Pepe, is there any damage to the bed?"

He replied no, and that he bought only the strongest furniture for his hotel, because it saves money in the long run and he knows the sort of wear and tear the units go through.

"So, if there's no damage, do you think there should be a charge for cleaning the mattress, the linen and for having someone do a safety check on the bed and to put it back in the room?"

Pepe saw where I was going with this. I continued, "We

could potentially ban them from the hotel until tonight. Say 11pm? Which means not only have they lost a day, but they'll also pay the charge to you for organising the replacement and cleaning. I'm sure they'll be good boys going forward. If they misbehave after that, we use the Guardia Civil. What do you say?"

I was hoping he would agree. This would punish the boys for something stupid, get him some cash, which hopefully would reflect well on me, and I would be saved trying to find these wankers a new home.

My idea worked. Pepe agreed. I went off to try and find the lads. We'd agreed on a fee of 50,000 pesetas which at the time would have been about £200. This was small enough that they could pay, but large enough that it would probably clip their wings and damage their holiday fund.

One of the guests told me they'd seen them hanging out in Savannahs near Café Del Mar, so I trotted down to see them. They were easy to spot. They were the only ones wearing jeans (from the night before). As I approached them, they both looked shameful.

"What have you dickheads done then?" There would be no salvation with me. "Why did you do it?"

One of them just outright apologised, told me they were pissed, and thought it would be funny. They realised how dangerous and outright stupid it was, but didn't know what to do next.

Once he'd finished, the second one owned up and said they shouldn't have done it and wanted to know what would happen to them now. I told them Pepe had been persuaded not to go to the police, but to give them a chance to say sorry and pay for the damage they'd done. The charge was £200 between them, and they were not allowed back to the hotel until 11pm as punishment. If they so much as turned their music up loud over the remainder of their holiday, they were out. If they didn't want to pay the £200 charge, then they could deal with the police where their passports would be handed over.

I didn't go easy on them, and nor should I have done. One of them started to moan about the fine saying it was just a bed. I nipped that right in the bud and told them he's lucky it's not £1,000, and they're still allowed to stay in the hotel. If they were kicked out it would cost them double that to find a new hotel and they wouldn't be getting a refund due to the bullshit they'd caused.

I told them to sit and think about it. I would be back in an hour to collect the cash if they wanted to do it, or take them to the police station to try and get their passports back and deal with the cops. I turned to walk away, and got about five metres. They called me back, told me they would pay, and asked where the nearest ATM was.

Once they handed me the money, I went to see Pepe. I told him they'd be back at the hotel at 11pm to apologise. I gave him the cash and apologised again on their behalf for the trouble. He did what Pepe did best: poured a pair of shots.

"Please, no hierbas!" I pleaded.

He laughed, no, this was something stronger, this was an Ibizan whisky. We knocked them back. "It's settled, " he said.

He asked me if I wanted any of the 'fine', which I declined, asking him to just put it towards my tab. He smiled and left me to it.

That night, when we were all gathering in the bar for drinks, there was still an air of gossip about what had happened, so I decided to put an end to it. I brought everyone together and told them I wanted to say something.

As the room fell silent, I pulled up a chair and beckoned everyone closer. "Guys, listen, I want to say something about what happened last night. Firstly, I want to apologise if the security guards woke you up, or frightened some of you by entering the rooms. This isn't normal practice. They wouldn't normally do that unless there's a good reason. As you know the lads in room 511 threw their whole bed including the frame off of their balcony. That could have killed someone. This was extremely serious, and the security, in my opinion, were absolutely justified in their actions. If you disagree with that, then I am sorry. If people are going to act like that, then they're the ones to blame for the situation.

"That being said, I've spoken to them both. They have apologised profusely. They're not being kicked out, they'll be allowed to return later, although they've had to pay a large sum for damages. Let's not mention it again. I have a couple of bottles of booze here kindly provided by Pepe, to say sorry for the whole affair with security. So, let's get this show back on the road and have a good night."

I'd lied. The booze hadn't been given by Pepe. It was a few bottles of schnapps that I had in my room left over from one of our bodega runs. I figured it was a nice way to try and put it behind us and to remove any ill feeling the guests might have had towards security. Thankfully for me we were about to take the guests to Es Paradis, which was a great venue, so after a few shots and a couple of bar hops, all was forgiven.

By the time the sun had begun to slowly rise, the battle-weary were wandering back into the hotel having had a great night.

CHAPTER 12
CARRY-ON COACH

Early on in the season, we were taking the guests to the water park for their day out. It was the day after a big club night and everyone was feeling a little jaded. We were there for a few hours and everyone was beginning to come round, myself included.

As we left the waterpark, we were taken to the Bodega (distillery) where the guests then had 15 minutes to drink as much as they wanted for free. It was usually carnage. Once everyone had had their share, we were then taking them to the go karting track back in San Antonio. This was a fantastic day out and everyone loved it. It was the highlight of the week for me.

Now for some reason, rather than pair up with Laura and her guests, I ended up being on the coach with Nigel and Frank. Don't ask me why, I can't remember the reasoning. Nigel sat at the front on the mic doing his usual routine and within minutes had the guests pissing themselves laughing.

Frank was standing up in the middle of the bus keeping a close eye on the guests to make sure that no one was looking to puke and also trying to hit on anything that even remotely resembled a human. On this occasion I felt like a bit of a fifth wheel, so I sat down at the back of the coach in the middle alongside a good group of lads and some girls we'd all been flirting with.

Nigel started a conversation about oral sex. Everyone was tittering. He was going off on a tangent here and there, but basically was describing what he liked to the coach and then asking what was he missing. The guests would then be shouting out stuff they liked or didn't and everyone was giggling along. It was pretty comical. Of course, it was childish, but good fun.

I don't exactly know what happened in the build up to what happened next, but at some stage, Frank started to get a bit big for his boots. He started calling Nigel and I out in front of everyone, and generally being a prick. I had a thumping head and couldn't be bothered to deal with this asshole but Nigel decided he was going to teach Frank a lesson. I zoned out for a bit, chatting to the guests in my vicinity.

After a while, the next thing I hear is Nigel daring Frank to lick his beanbag, declaring Frank too chicken. Everyone roars at this, and starts making chicken noises to Frank. I couldn't stop myself. I was crowing like a cockerel at him too. I don't know why, really, because there was absolutely no way I was even coming within arm's reach of Nigel's plums and I was pretty certain 90% of the coach felt the same way. Undeterred, I pressed on. In fact, given my feelings for Frank, I was probably the biggest Rooster on that fucking coach.

Anyway, after a minute of being buried by his guests, Frank says he'll do it. Much to my and most of the guests' surprise. Nigel stands up to face the back of the coach, mic in hand, and stands on the inside edges of the seats on either side of the aisle. Up until this point the driver hadn't really paid much attention to us, and just focused on driving, but even he was getting a bit arsey with Nigel standing on the chairs.

The whole time Nigel remains on the mic, teasing how Frank wasn't man enough and is too chicken. Frank begins to sheepishly approach Nigel. The guests are falling silent. Even I stop crowing, intrigued to see what happens next. Nigel adjusts his shorts and pulls them to one side, holding his old boy up and dragging his bean bag out to the side for all to see. The guests make a collective 'oooh' sound with tittering in the aisles.

"I dare you Frank, you've not got the guts. Everyone can see that. Go on just a little lick."

"I'm going to do it! I'll do anything me," replies Frank. You can tell he is praying for Nigel to back off and save him from his fate, but Nigel holds fast.

Nigel begins to berate him further, reducing his voice to a whisper. The whole coach falls silent until you could hear a pin drop. Frank refuses to give in. He ducks down, but tilts his head up so most of the coach can actually see what's about to happen or not happen. Nigel is in full control and sounds like a pervert on one of those 0898 numbers you used to see advertised after midnight.

"That's it Frank, you can do it. We knew you weren't chicken. Lick my balls Frank. Lick my balls."

With that, some of the guests started softly chanting "Lick his balls, lick his balls," and within seconds every single person on the coach, bar the driver and Frank, was baying for Frank to lick Nigel's balls.

Not wanting to disappoint the crowd, Frank reaches up and pokes his tongue out, hoping to make contact in the slightest of ways. Just the tip of a stray pube would be enough. Just the lightest of brushes.

He edges closer. Clearly, he didn't want to be chowing down, but at this point Frank's pride and ego are in control of his body. He nudges ever closer to Nigel's scrotum. The coach falls silent, you can almost hear gasps. Nigel is still there, ever on the mic.

"That's it Frank, prove everyone wrong…"

At this point, Frank's tongue is approximately a centimetre away from Nigel's sack. Without warning, Nigel leans forwards, twists his feet inwards and just drops. He plants his genitals squarely on Frank's face causing poor Frank's tongue, lips, nose and chin to make full contact with the whole package. He effectively dragged the whole of his sweaty undercarriage down 70% of Frank's face. If I were a betting man, I'd say even part of Nigel's shaft might have gotten involved.

Frank recoils in absolute horror, his legs buckle beneath him and he lands a few feet back on the coach floor. This is one of the funniest things I've ever seen, and the fact it happened to Frank makes me cheer from the heart. I'm in hysterics. The whole coach is in hysterics. Nigel is in hysterics.

Shall I tell you who's not in hysterics? The driver.

Nigel is still roaring with laughter when the driver slams on the brakes. Nigel is immediately lifted from his feet, goes vertical, turns briefly horizontal, before coming to rest at the base of the coach next to the gear stick and entry steps. The driver swerves onto the hard shoulder of the motorway and gets out of his chair.

Nigel doesn't even get a chance to protest. The driver hits the button on his dash with a closed fist and the front door swings open with a loud hiss. Nigel is forcibly rolled down the stairs out of the coach and lands on the dusty gravel in a heap.

The guests are speechless. No one, including myself, is

saying a word. The driver is angry. His Catholic faith clearly being tested. Further down the coach, Frank just about gets to his feet but the driver is too quick. The driver grabs Frank by the scruff of the neck with one hand, t-shirt with the other. Frank tries to pull back, but rage beats fear every time. Frank is almost yanked out of his shoes, and within moments, he too is bundled down the steps to the entrance. He lands somewhat better than Nigel, but not exactly cleanly either. The driver shouts something in Spanish to them and slams his fist back on to the dash. The front door swings shut.

No one else on that coach says a word. With that, the driver starts to move off, leaving these two perverts to fend for themselves. Sensing that I need to do something, I stood up and walked towards the middle of the coach, gesturing to the driver with hands open hoping to signal that a) I'm not a threat and b) I am not about to lick anyone's nuts. He just glares at me. I pick up the mic and then turn towards everyone on the coach, who at this point are shell shocked.

"Ladies and Gentleman, if you would like to turn your attention to the right side of the coach, I want you to give a big Ibiza wave to your reps Nigel and Frank."

At that point, everyone stands in their seats, starts to laugh and waves madly at the pair of them. Both are clearly somewhat perturbed about being dumped on their ass out of a coach, but Nigel manages a little wave back. Frank looks genuinely disheartened.

As we reach motorway speed, I try to pick up the tempo again.

"Who's having a good time?" The coach roars back into action. "Hands up who thought Frank was actually going to do it." Only about three hands are meekly raised in the air. I press on. "Hands up who thought Frank enjoyed it, and had done it before." The whole coach raised a hand.

This in itself was funny. In fact, we were laughing about it for the rest of the journey. We pulled into the go-karting track about 20 minutes later and the guests were buzzing. A mixture of all-you-can drink at the distillery and the chance to tell everyone that Nigel tea-bagged Frank.

By the time Nigel and Frank had managed to get to the venue, everyone had already departed, meaning they had to move to the last stop of the day: the beach party.

Damien was waiting for the pair of them. As soon as they walked in, they got a cheer from everyone. Nigel again chose to wave and smile, but Frank, fearing that his new nickname was going to be Teabag, elected to look sheepish. Damien tore into the pair of them out of sight, but definitely not out of earshot.

The pair of them had to go to the office to kindly ask one of the office girls to write them a letter in Spanish to the coach driver apologising for their behaviour. Picture yourself having to ask a polite young lady to translate a letter of apology to a traditional Spanish coach driver asking for forgiveness for licking a colleague's apples in front of a coachload of holidaymakers. Can you imagine yourself making that request? At least Nigel could say Frank wanted to do it. What can Frank say? He dared me? How stupid would that look. Priceless.

This wouldn't be the last time Nigel would become known to the coach company. Later on in the season, after a particularly bruising session at the distillery, the atmosphere turned somewhat more feral than normal. Rather than trying to cop off with each other or touch each other up, the whole thing took a turn for the worse. The behaviour became more like you'd expect at a football match. Guests were chanting at each other in hotel rivalry, arms outstretched.

As reps, we loved this. If your hotel guests were continually shouting your hotel name, it meant there was a unity among them, and that they liked the hotel they were defending. In other words, you were doing a good job and they were enjoying themselves.

Things could quickly change, however, as some guests started to rock the coach from the other hotel, complete with those guests still in it. Sensing things could get silly, we immediately pulled the coaches out of the car park and headed off, hoping to allow some of the guests to calm down.

That didn't mean the action stopped there though. We would continue to keep them entertained on the coach using any means necessary. 'Drive by' mooning was a common one. You'd encourage the driver to overtake the other and, as we went past, everyone would have their cheeks pushed firmly against the glass for the occupants of the other coach to see. Much to their annoyance, but our delight. Other times we would sing rugby songs, or just generally banter on the mic. Sometimes it wasn't just the guests getting out of control, but the reps too.

On this particular occasion, Nigel and I had led the coach onwards, belting out some rugby songs. The mood was electric—you'd only have to fart and the whole coach would cheer. We'd managed to cobble together some tips for the driver as a way of saying not just 'thank you', but mainly 'sorry' for the pain he was enduring.

Well, this time, as I was handing the driver the cash we'd collected after the whip round, Nigel was asking on the mic, "what shall we sing next?"

One rowdy guest at the back hollered, "The driver takes it up the ass." The whole coach roared with laughter. I pretended not to hear it as I was standing next to him. Thinking Nigel would do well to do the same, he surprised us all by launching into it in full voice:

Oh…. the driver takes it up the ass, doo-dah, doo-dah,
The driver takes it up the ass, oh dah-doo-dah day…
Doo dah-doo-dah day, doo-dah-doo dah-day,
The driver takes it up the ass, doo dah-doo-dah….."

He never made the last day. The brakes were firmly applied and we both went flying. Nigel hit the front, I landed mid aisle. The door swung open. Within seconds, the driver launched Nigel off the top step onto the gravel by the side of the road.

You see, the driver spoke English. Or at least enough to know when it was suggested that the driver might be a keen recipient of rectal loving.

Thankfully for me, the driver left me alone, otherwise I might have found myself joining Nigel by the side of the road. I just did what I always did, and picked up where he left off.

"Coach, if you'd like to extend a warm Ibiza round of applause to my friend, and your rep, Nigel." The whole coach clapped him as we disappeared into the distance.

Again, Nigel got ripped into by Damien when they eventually met. I think Nigel was given a record number of consecutive airport runs and had to face the girls in the office again. Once more, he had to ask for forgiveness in a letter, translated by the ground staff, apologising for his actions on the coach line. Between this latest episode and Frank's tea-bagging, for the next month or so he was genuinely nervous about getting on the coach in case he was going to get beaten.

On the whole he got away with it. There was only one time when he actually managed to bump into this driver again and that was at the airport. Despite Nigel extending a further apology, the driver simply refused to take him. He ended up having to switch with another coach, much to the bemusement of the new arrivals on both buses.

CHAPTER 13
THE NAUGHTY STOWAWAY

Working in a hotel means you come across all sorts of sights. I've seen people sleeping overnight on a lilo fully clothed. On sunbeds, in broom cupboards and on the floors of the toilets. I've seen people fast asleep stretched out in the corridor, presumably because their key didn't fit any of the doors on the wrong floor.

I've also witnessed my fair share of stowaways. Often, you would walk in and see an extra body. It was normally a stray that had been brought back by one of the guests, or could be a friend who decided to stay over for a night as this hotel was closer than theirs. On occasion you would also find arrangements had been made that were designed to be—how can I put this—something more than just temporary.

One time I knocked on the door of a room. I'd come to deliver some club tickets and event wristbands that a pair of lads had bought. When they opened the door, I immediately saw there was a third there, and he had practically made himself a camp bed. They regretted that I saw it, but I quickly put their minds at ease.

They revealed their mate had decided to get a flight over from Germany where he'd been stationed, but couldn't afford separate accommodation. They were all squaddies, and I decided to do them a favour. I made them a deal. I said that, as long as he behaved himself, the third could stay there all week with them, and that I'd even get him some fresh linen, but I had an issue with him going on the trips for free. The other two had already taken out the full week's package, and as the tickets were numbered, and the clubs had their own security, I wasn't going to be able to just smuggle him through. I said the only way this worked is if he bought a package for himself, which is already far cheaper than hotel accommodation, and then they would all get to go out together without fear of being thrown out or not getting in. After a split second they all jumped at it.

I returned to the room with some fresh linen, and the necessary paperwork, and within a few minutes he was done too. I handed over some tickets, closed the door, and said we'd speak no more of it. What this had meant though was that, as I had 10 new arrivals in my hotel, and all had signed up fully to the entertainment package, I was currently sat at 100%. Now I had an 11th, it meant I was at 110%. I quietly had a word with Damien out of earshot, and he agreed with my approach and we just let the numbers sit. As far as anyone else was concerned, I'd sold the package to someone staying in a different hotel.

A couple of days passed. Everyone had been going out to the various events, clubs and bar crawls that we'd laid on, but this night was a themed night with free food and drink. It usually meant that the guests would get hammered and were more rowdy than normal.

We started off in the bar as usual, played some easy drinking games, and everyone started to unwind and warm up. The theme of the evening was Victorian London, i.e.

very much a Dickensian flavour to things. All the staff at the event were dressed up, Oktoberfest style, with big laced blouses creating ridiculous amounts of cleavage. They would be continually serving pitchers of beer and sangria or wine to the guests. Things often got messy really quickly, but to be honest it was all part of the fun.

On this particular evening, the squaddies were on fire. They were the first to volunteer for anything. The first to take a shot, the first to try and win another. You name it, they were on for it. They needed no encouragement. As time went by though you could see they were beginning to glaze over. Their chances of getting laid were disappearing at the same rate as the drink in their glasses. All the hotel guests were sitting on long banqueting benches and the whole venue was packed full. There must have been between seven and eight hundred people in there, all singing and swaying in unison.

At some stage in the evening, some of the guests started to get too carried away. Some would be falling backwards off their benches, or would just find a space outside in a bush and take a nap. This was common practice, and normally the security guards would give us a heads up, and we'd find them and put them somewhere more visible and let them sleep it off for a while. It was as if we had a designated pass out area.

One thing that wasn't tolerated, though, was if people started getting overexcited or aggressive. When you have that much alcohol involved with that many people, you need to act quickly and decisively as the slightest thing could spiral out of control and the last thing you want is a mass brawl on your hands.

The squaddies by now were battered. One was just sitting there singing to himself, the other — the stowaway — was trying to talk to any girl in a 25 metre radius and getting absolutely nowhere. His eyes could barely maintain focus, let alone hold a conversation. The other lad though, well, he was the issue.

Various songs would come on and the guests would all be singing along with them, but for some reason this squaddie kept climbing up onto the table and standing up above everyone to sing. It was funny initially, and we managed to get him down quickly and in a friendly manner before security got a chance to get involved, but they definitely clocked him. I think by the time he'd done it a second or third time, the guards directed him down. He did as he was told once he saw them, but no sooner had he sat back down, he then decided to stand back up on the table. We could all see what was coming next.

One burly guard grabbed him by the arm and yanked him down. He was being ejected from the venue. When his mate tried to intervene and reason with them—as well as you can when you're the equivalent of about 12 pints in— he too got too close to security and his card was marked too. The guards were escorting them outside the venue to where the coaches were, but the two Squaddies weren't moving quick enough for them. Batons had already been drawn and were now being prodded in the backs of the two guys, who to be fair to them, were walking in the required direction. They weren't offering any resistance, they were just super pissed.

I was walking alongside them trying to keep them calm. I was telling them that we'd take them straight to the club to meet the others in the hope they would leave without fuss. But out of the corner of my eye I suddenly see the stowaway come running up from behind, approaching security like a missile, with several reps trying to catch up with him. Thankfully I managed to intercept him. I didn't know what he was going to do, but in this situation any physical contact with the security was going to result in an immediate escalation, and by that I mean a proper beating.

I put my arms around him to stop him from chasing, and managed to stop him in his tracks. He was shouting at me and trying to struggle, accusing me of not doing anything to help or protect them. I tried to calm him down, telling him that everything was fine, they were too drunk to be here and that I was going to take us all to the nightclub to continue partying over there. He was incensed. He looked again at the two guys who were about 10 metres away, walking out of the exit. They both had their hands up and seemed to understand what was happening and didn't want to have any kind of altercation. When I pointed out they were fine and that nothing bad was happening, suddenly stowaway swung a punch that hit me clean in the temple, causing me to recoil a few steps.

I was shocked. I was helping these guys out, and numbnuts here decided to smack me! In a moment I regain my senses and position my feet to throw a punch back but find myself grabbed by one of the other reps who prevents me from making contact. I try and shrug the rep off, but a second has me by the shoulders and I'm effectively neutralised. I plead with them to let me go but it's no use. They won't. Damien had been called over and saw the whole thing unfold. Stowaway at this point had also left the venue and presumably was standing outside with his other two mates trying to work out what to do next.

Security had also seen me take a dig, and they came over to see if I'm ok. I'm fuming. Practically spitting like a petulant teenager after his first can of Diamond White. They see this. Damien sees this. Damien is trying to calm me down, telling me if I touch him and it's reported, I'll be off the island. I don't care. All I can see is red. I ask them to just let me go outside with them.

Clearly the whole thing is ridiculous. They're in the army, I'm not, there's three of them. I would have been pummelled easily. Security looks at Damien, they both look at me, and then they take Damien to one side. A few quiet words are exchanged, and then I see four of the security guards quietly exit the venue.

All reps are ordered back inside and I too am reluctantly dragged in with them. I'm made to sit in the corner like a dunce while someone pours me a beer. Laura is tasked with babysitting me. After about five minutes, I begin to chill. Damien comes over and asks me sarcastically if I've found my tampon. I'm not impressed.

Before I have a chance to tell him fuck off, he leans in and tells me that security took care of it for me and that I need to calm down. On hearing this, things suddenly fall into place. I slowly regain my composure, stand up and walk with Damien over to the side of the venue. As I am leaning against a column watching on, a big hand is laid on my shoulder. I'm startled and turn around quickly. It's the security guard. He asks if I'm OK. Before I get a chance to answer him, he just smiles and says, "You should see the other guy." Clearly an English phrase he'd picked up from somewhere. I thank him, and he moves on.

I go back over to the table and pretty soon I forget all about it. The rest of the guests are roaring, people are spilling over each other left, right and centre. The rest of the night goes off without a hitch. By the time I roll into bed about 2:30 in the morning I'm pissed. The first thing that reminds me of the whole escapade is Jess who moans at me for being drunk but then sees the lump on my head and asks me if I've been fighting. I told her it was a minor scrap and that there was nothing to worry about. I didn't quite have the ego to tell her I just stood there and took one.

The following morning, I woke up with a thick head. The lump is protruding like a third testicle and, with pride dented, I'm feeling aggrieved. I don't even stop for breakfast. I march straight up to the squaddies' room and bang on the door.

One of them opens it and, before he has a chance to say sorry, I barge past him and stand at the foot of the bed of stowaway. I kick his foot with mine to wake him up.

"You got an hour to get up and clear out or I'll have security back for round two. I was trying to help you last night, and this is the thanks I get."

He tries to apologise, but I don't want any of it. As he sits up, his face is partially illuminated by sunlight poking through a gap in the curtains. I can see he's got a massive shiner on his right eye, a sore looking cut across the bridge of his nose, his left cheek is swollen, and his bottom lip is cracked and angry looking. I look across at the other lads and they too are nursing various marks and swellings. One even has a thick dark yellow bruise across the top of his arm, presumably from a baton. He's still trying to talk to me as I leave the room. All I say before the door shuts is "one hour".

That was the last I ever saw of him. The other lads still came out for a drink and went on the trips they'd paid for, although they were more mindful when it came to their behaviour. We ended up laughing the whole thing off. I also brought a pack of beers with me the next time we went to the venue and gave it to that security guard to say thank you. Luckily, none of them had to get involved again with me but it was nice knowing they were there, just in case.

CHAPTER 14
THE TEMPORARY GROOM

Predictably, as the season got into swing, so did the other reps. If it wasn't Jack getting blown in the airport toilets, it was Frank boasting of his threesome with "two models." No one could ever verify the existence of these so-called stunners who were desperate to compete in a single bed for Teabag's attentions. If they were indeed models, we just assumed they were foot models.

Nigel had a surprisingly slow start. Given the strength of the emails he'd been sending me when back in Blighty, I thought he was going to take off when he arrived but it took him a couple of weeks to get back in the saddle.

I sorely missed competing against him for girls and the hilarity which often ensued. If anything, I enjoyed the banter and the war stories afterwards more than the actual conquest, so while I might have been missing out this year, what with Jess being out with me, I still made sure I was getting a regular debriefing from him.

Nigel always liked the forbidden fruit, so it came as no surprise to either of us when he started to show interest in a bridal party that had arrived in my hotel: six girls away for a week on a hen-do.

It was your stereotypical hen party. All chilling and sunbathing during the day, followed by all going out at night on the piss. The bride would be wearing an old wedding dress every night they went out, the others wearing t-shirts with her face on the front of them. For variety, she would rotate between a sash with 'bride-to-be' on and a full veil on top of her going out gear. I don't mean to be down on them—they were a great group of girls and had a lot of fun—but the whole bride party had been done to death so many times it was almost boring.

That didn't stop them from having a laugh. The party was from Sheffield and they were very comical. Initially they would start off shy, so would avoid volunteering for anything —unless they were pushing the bride up for it—but once they had a few drinks inside them, they would go wild. More often than not they'd end up having a row in the group, there'd be some fireworks, they'd patch it up with tears, and the next day all would be forgotten and relationships would be reset. Like I said, very stereotypical. What they didn't count on, however, was the small stature of a man with a penis that was all head and no shaft, and who oozed charisma.

Nigel first laid eyes on my lot at the welcome meeting when he was presenting one of the nights out. I could tell he was interested because, rather than stand back with the rest of the reps when he'd finished his part of the presentation, he chose to wade into the crowd and sit in between the girls. He started to appear at my hotel more frequently, and I often caught him looking across at the girls. The thing is, the one he liked was the bride-to-be herself.

It started with harmless flirting. Nigel and I would both be around the pool, talking to all the guests, but we would often end up sitting with the group and getting to know them a bit more than the others. You had the bride-to-be who was sweet, with mousy brown hair, a cute little nose, and a seriously attractive smile. The maid of honour, presumably her best mate, was also good fun but not in any way interesting to Nigel. She got the nickname Nice-but-no, and then there were a couple of ushers—Usher 1 and Usher 2—plus the sister of the groom. I think they did the best to include her, but you could tell she wasn't part of the core crowd and was more there out of politeness. For that reason, we nicknamed her Token. Then she too had a friend who presumably was there to keep her company, so she was (somewhat predictably) named Token's Mate.

They were out for a week and partied pretty hard throughout. On their second or third night in, Nigel had come sharking and managed to find them in one of the bars. He made a beeline for Bridey. Any attempts by Nice-but-no or the Ushers to cock block were soon shrugged off, and he ended up slow dancing with her for most of the evening.

There was no way that the girls were going to leave her there dancing with him, so they stuck around and eventually convinced her to leave him. The thing is, they took her away from him in such a manner that it was almost like they'd stolen her from love. It was so funny, in that being heavy handed about it unwittingly contributed to what happened next.

Nigel met up with me at my hotel for breakfast. Jess was with me at the time so he couldn't speak freely. He was trying to give me signals but they weren't working, and ultimately he got frustrated and left.

Next, I get a call from the barman who says there's a phone call for me. It was Nigel, he was back at his hotel. "Mate, can you come over here? I need to talk to you. Couldn't speak freely with Jess."

This wasn't like Nigel at all. I finished my breakfast, made my excuses with Jess, and headed over to his hotel. His grumpy asshole of a hotelier was as thrilled as ever to see me. He just pointed and grunted like he always did.

"What's up mate?" I asked him.

"I think I'm in love with Bridey," he replied. I started to laugh. "The thing is, I think she feels the same." I laughed even harder.

"Don't be soft, she's getting married in a week. Did you kiss or something?"

He then went on to tell me the details about their slow dance and the deep and meaningful conversation they had afterwards. I could tell he was irritated by Nice-but-no and the Ushers for pulling her away from him, but understood why they'd done it. "You've got to help me!" he said.

"Me, how?"

"You need to set up Nice-but-no and the others with some lads so that I can get a free run at Bridey."

"How's that going to work, they're on a hen-do, and even if I do manage to somehow get you free of them, what about Token and her mate?"

"We'll think of something," he said. "Besides, since you've brought a bird out, it's not the same this year, this is the least you can do."

Before I had a chance to snap at him for that, he started to grin—which made me grin. We put our heads together imagining several scenarios.

In the end, we decided to wing it. Tonight was Porn Star Night, which was basically a bar crawl where they played super sexy/sleazy music in every bar we went to. All the reps were dressed as either strippers or whores or both, depending on the look.

For Nigel and I, we would go out as strippers. We both cut the collar and cuffs off from white long sleeve shirts, and wore those with a black bow tie. We'd smother ourselves with baby oil and then either wear black jeans or, sometimes, just black boxers if we were feeling brave. On many occasions, both Nigel and myself had been rugby tackled to the ground and had our undies forcibly removed by female guests leaving us truly starkers, wandering around the bar trying to hide our modesty with a serviette.

Usually it was the female guests who were the most aggressive. The lads would laugh at us, but you'd often be met with comments like 'fair play lads' or 'I couldn't do your job' sort of stuff. The girls, on the other hand, would basically assault us right from the first bar we walked into. If our nipples weren't being tweaked, then they'd outright just put their hands down our boxers. The more drinks they had, the worse it got. It never bothered us and we'd just laugh it off. Different times, eh?

That night, I decided to play it safe and go topless with the black jeans option. For this bar crawl to be a success we needed to pair people up pretty quickly. As far as drinking games went, we would start in the swimming pool, early doors. We would do some couple oriented activities where I would basically pick out a guy and a girl and throw them together to compete against another couple. It could be anything from piggyback wrestling in the pool to a relay race on a lilo or even a swimwear swap. It was imperative that there were lots of touch points between the groups.

By the time we met in the pool bar that evening for our warm up drink, you could tell there was already an air of expectation. The guests were still flirting and many of the people we'd been placing in couples were still talking to each other. This was a good sign.

Another game I liked to play to kick things up a notch was to buy a bunch of roses from the street sellers. We would place everyone in a circle, boy girl boy girl, etc., and then proceed to hand the rose from mouth to mouth without using hands. Once you were handed it, you'd remove a small piece of the rose, either from the stem or the petals, pop it back in your mouth and then transfer it to the person next to you.

Initially it was easy, but after a few goes around the circle, you were soon basically French kissing your neighbour and hoping that the remnants of the stem would end up in their mouth so you didn't have to do a forfeit. If you dropped the rose, you took a shot. If you used your hands in the process of transfer, you took a shot. If you backed out because things were too raunchy, you took a shot. This game was played several times and always got a great reception.

Once the roses were done, we would play Never Have I Ever. You would make sure that everyone had a long drink, then in turn, guests would stand up and say something they had never done. If someone had indeed done that thing, they would have to take a drink. For example, 'I've never slept with a member of my own family.' I guarantee you, someone in that room would have been taking a drink. Of course, you'd be relying on people's honesty, but even if someone was shy with the truth, their mate would normally stitch them up. I've lost count of the number of times a friend would bellow out "…why aren't you drinking, you've done that!" much to the laughter of everyone else. This game was always sexual in content, and again kept things going in that direction.

Once done with the hotel bar, we'd make our way along the strip to the first of our haunts. There would be some more drinking games, but the music would immediately go slow and sexy. It was a far cry from the 'throw your hands up in the air' blaring from every other bar in that strip.

We would immediately start dirty dancing with the

female reps. Nothing was too much. Laura would be dressed as a stripper. We'd be grinding up and down each other. Nigel, being the smallest of the guys, would end up getting doubled over and spanked across the cheeks by one of the female reps. In fact, I think every female rep would basically grab him, pull his trousers down and just spank him, much to the amusement of the guests.

Next, the DJ would put something a little faster paced on, like a salsa number, and the reps would separate and grab the nearest girl or guy out of the crowd and proceed to dance with them. We'd then grab more and more and before you know it you've got a hundred guests doing a mixture of salsa/dirty dancing with each other.

The longer it went on for, the more they were likely to hook up. Sometimes, couples wouldn't even leave the establishment. People would be banging each other in the toilets or sometimes even under the stage!

Now, Nigel had been very clear in his objective for this evening, in that he wanted a clear run at Bridey. Despite my misgivings about the fact that she was due to be married soon after, I had Nigel's back. I made sure to partner Nice-but-no and Token with a couple of good-looking lads from Nigel's hotel. Nigel had even told them that the girls had taken an interest in them, so for the next hour or so they were occupied. Token's mate had already found a dude she was dancing with and so that just left the Ushers who were guarding Bridey.

Bridey was wearing a full wedding dress, complete with L plates, so she was dancing with anyone and everyone. Ushers 1 and 2 were sipping their cocktails from the side, so I challenged them to a game of limbo. Both were fit and slim and were infinitely more flexible than me, so I tried to make it a little harder and more drawn out.

They had to do it with a full shot glass in their mouth.

Any spillage and they were downing it. No spillage and I was downing it. They loved this and, together with another couple of guests, we soon had a little conveyor belt going. As expected, I was complete crap at limbo and ended up just doing shots, but they were genuinely competing. With their eyes off the prize, this gave Nigel all the space he needed.

Nigel sneaked through the dance floor with the intentions of a fox but the grace of a yak. Having bumped into about 10 couples who were doing some version of salsa, he eventually started dancing with one of the guests right next to Bridey who was already dancing with someone else. At some point, Nigel shouted "switch" and engineered a swap. As soon as Bridey's hands came free of her suitor, he pounced.

For the next few minutes, Nigel was dirty dancing with Bridey. I'd like to say it was less dirty, more tender, but this was Ibiza, and this was Nigel, so they were both thrusting the fuck out of whatever song was being played. As the DJ started to fade in the next one, Nigel took Bridey off the dance floor and towards the back of the bar. I don't know what he said to her, but the next minute they were gone. Even when we moved the guests on to the next bar, Nigel was nowhere to be found. Damien asked if anyone had seen Nigel, I just said that one of his guests was puking up and he had to take him back. That got him in the clear.

Predictably, after an hour the other hen party girls found me and asked me if I'd seen Bridey. I replied that I'd seen her earlier when everyone was dirty dancing, but hadn't seen her since then. Nice-but-no and one of the ushers decided to go back to the hotel to look for her while the others stayed out in case she was still in the bar.

I didn't see any of them again for the rest of the night. I

just hoped Nigel hadn't gone back to my hotel with her, because he was going to be in trouble if he did.

The following morning I had breakfast with Jess, then shot over to Nigel's hotel to get the lowdown. He sat with some guests and seemed calm but cheerful. It turns out that, the night before, Nigel had done the unthinkable. He'd fucked her mind, not her body.

He went on to tell me that as soon as he had her alone, he got her out of the bar and took her to a bar at the complete opposite end of the strip. It wasn't clubby or loud. It was a mellow place, where people could come to enjoy a cocktail and actually hear each other speak. It had a Mayan theme and so was a little out of the ordinary. It was quirky and a bit of a hidden gem. If you wanted to romance someone there or just get away from the crowds, this was the place to go.

He and Bridey spoke for hours about everything, from her upcoming wedding to peace in the galaxy. I asked him if he did anything with her. He said no, he didn't even try. The most he did was hold her hand as he walked her back to my hotel. He didn't even hang around long in case the others caught him. He knew as well as I did that Bridey was going to be in trouble with them when they saw her. He didn't seem put off at all, intending to see her that evening.

I said he'd better have his wits about him tonight, because the girls would be on the defensive. He just laughed.

"He who dares, Rodders, he who dares."

This made me chuckle, but I couldn't help feeling that I was going to be faced with a load of aggravation in the hotel at some point over the next few days.

I got back to my hotel just before lunch. I saw Token's mate and the Ushers having a drink by the pool. I asked how they were and if they had a good night. They all replied they had a great night, but that it had ended rather badly. I inquired as to what went wrong, and they told me that because Bridey had disappeared, they thought something bad had happened to her. Nice-but-no was angry at her for leaving, Token was pissed off because she thinks she might have cheated on her brother. I feigned shock.

"Well, where was she then?"

They said that she was having a drink with another group in a quiet bar and just wanted a quiet night. They seemed quite puzzled, but didn't really read too much into it.

"Fair enough. It happens. She's probably got a lot on her mind with the wedding and you guys have been hitting it pretty hard out here." They nodded.

With that, I left them to it. I had been having my own dramas to deal with. Things between Jess and I were becoming strained. We weren't really seeing much of each other because I was always working, and whenever she did see me, more often than not I was shattered.

I had hoped that she would get a job—working in a bar or ticketing for some club promoter or something—but nothing had materialised. I don't think she wanted to be working in the evenings, and in the daytime she was happy to sleep and sunbathe. That was all good, but it was the evenings that I needed her to be busy. My hours were 9 in the morning until 2 at night, Monday to Sunday. Wednesday and Sunday were airport nights, so I could finish anywhere between 1 (unheard of) to 5 or even 6 a.m., and there were no days off. It was brutal, but I loved the job. And though pretty much everyone knew who Jess was in the hotel, and though she would make friends with some of the girls there, and would know the bar and restaurant staff so had people to talk to, I guess it wasn't the same.

As the weeks went on, I was becoming more and more exhausted. All the reps were. The rest of the team knew Jess, and she was always welcome to attend one of our club nights or catch a lift on a coach somewhere if we were going to the waterpark, etc., but there's only so much of that you can do before it gets repetitive. Besides, as she was on her own, she was normally pestered by guys, or wound up by the girls chasing me, so after a promising start she started to avoid our events and bar crawls.

That meant she would plan things for us to do after work. I would try and endure a dinner with her at half past two in the morning to try and give her the attention she deserved, only to have it thrown back in my face because I would fall asleep at the table before the bill was brought out. I hadn't seen intimacy in weeks because I was either too tired or we were rowing. Coupled with the fact that all the other male reps were absolutely ploughing through their hotels meant I was beginning to feel resentment.

I tried to set her up with a couple of bar roles and even found her some work at the venues we hit. They knew me, and most knew of her. She was a good-looking girl, comical and smart to boot. It was all cash in hand, so no paperwork, just work and collect. Whenever I brought the subject up, she would just react angrily, saying she'd find a job herself. The thing is, she didn't.

I didn't mention anything to Nigel or the others at the time. I think I didn't tell them for a number of reasons. Firstly, I didn't want them to hit me with "I told you so," and secondly, I didn't want them to encourage me to do something that I would later regret—after all, I'd been seeing Jess for almost six months, and I really liked her, or at least I liked what we had. I had been totally faithful and hadn't messed about out here or at home so I wasn't ready to give up yet, but things were beginning to get to me.

I hit the pool in the afternoon. Laura was already there as we were due to do some pool entertainment. She was sitting on a sunbed with the bridal party. They were all there apart from Bridey.

My mind was racing. Surely Nigel isn't on the case? I thought at first to give them a swerve, as they knew Nigel and I were thick as thieves, but curiosity got the better of me.

"Alright girls?" I said as I approached. They didn't look happy. "What's the matter?"

Nice-but-no piped up. "It's all gone to shit. We can't find Bridey. We've had a massive row, and we think she's been seeing someone."

I didn't really know what to say, and didn't want to say too much through fear of incrimination. "That's a shame, it always happens on holiday. Am sure she hasn't gone too far. You'll sort it out by the evening." I looked across at Token who looked like she was chewing glass. I thought best to make my escape and went over to talk to some lads about how they got on the night prior.

When Bridey did finally resurface she looked troubled. I caught her coming through reception and approached her, wanting to give her the heads up about the rest of her group. "Hey, how you doing? Your friends are worried about you. I think you might be in for a bit of a chat when you go up. Are you OK?"

I was somewhat taken back by the ferocity of her response. "They can go and fuck themselves! I've just spent a lovely afternoon with Nigel and nothing they can say can spoil it. I also want to thank you for what you did last night. Thanks to you helping him, we managed to have a lovely evening together." Shit. Nigel had squealed.

I immediately dropped the act. "Sure, look, you're welcome. I know he likes you, and from the sounds of it you might like him too, but you can't let on that I know about that, or am involved. Your mates will smash me and cause trouble. I just thought the pair of you could do with some time together without others putting their oar in."

I added that last sentence in the hope it would soften my demands for silence. She gave me a big hug and told me not to worry, no one knew about my involvement, and the others didn't even know about Nigel. She thanked me again, and then promptly headed off to face the music.

I popped over to Nigel's place. I was desperate to know what had gone down, and was keen for him to play this cool so that I didn't get royally ass fucked by having the bridal party suffer a complete breakdown causing me no end of issues or drama.

As soon as I walked in, he gave me a cheeky smile and greeted me. "Hello Luke, how are you this fine day?"

I started to grin. "What the fuck have you done? Did you smash her?"

"Why, has she said something?"

"No seriously, have you two had cuddles? She just told me she spent the afternoon with you, it was lovely, and the rest of her friends can, and I quote 'go fuck themselves'"

"Did she really say it was lovely?"

I could tell he was pleased with himself. Nigel went on to detail how he'd arranged to meet her by the sea front and they went and had lunch and had a nice relaxing time for a few hours. He said he hadn't slept with her, but they did share a kiss and a cuddle at some point in the restaurant. He also detailed how he was hoping to meet her tonight. I asked him to go easy on her but he just smiled and said if she fancied a slice what could he do? I know he wouldn't cause issues for me on purpose, and I also understood the power of the "kitty" so I didn't blame him. Ultimately, they only had a few nights left anyway, so if anything did blow up, it would be done and dusted by the weekend.

I met Jess for lunch and made the mistake of telling her about the dilemma. I'm not sure why I thought to share it, as normally I kept that sort of stuff quiet so as not to highlight the fact that the reps were actually messing around with the guests. I think it was because it was the first time Nigel actually showed real interest in a girl and wasn't just trying to hit it and quit it. I thought she would be interested too, but she of course blamed Nigel for leading this poor girl on.

When I politely pointed out that it took two to tango, she became cross with me for sticking up for him. This irritated the hell out of me. Bridey was older than all of us and clearly had been making her own choices. Now, whether this would turn out to be something more meaningful, like it had been for Jess and I, only time would tell. Maybe this would fizzle out as soon as she got on the plane home and she would end up marrying her beau after all, who knew? I wasn't going to just sit there and listen to this one-sided crap though.

I think seeing Nigel happy and excited to see Bridey only helped to remind me of how difficult things were with Jess. I was still determined to see things out, but this was yet another thing that we didn't see eye to eye on.

We had a pool party in the afternoon. Laura and I had spread the word, and the pool was packed. The hen party was absent though. At one point I popped back into the hotel and knocked on the door to see how they were getting on. One of the ushers opened it. Bridey and Nice-but-no were sitting there. Bridey had been crying and it looked like Nice-but-no had at some point seen some tears. I went there under the guise to ask if they were going to the pool party, but once there I asked if everything was ok. Apparently, Token had blown up at Bridey and accused her of cheating on her brother, which frankly, wasn't far off the mark. They'd all had a massive row and Token and her mate had left to go for a walk, and I was witnessing the aftermath. I couldn't get out of there quick enough. I made my excuses and went back to the pool. Nigel would have loved all this drama.

That evening was the Rep's Cabaret night. We gathered in the hotel bar as normal, and everyone was having a few drinks and generally socialising. The hen party was there, but were hardly talking to each other. I'd had enough of the drama for today, so I gave them a wide berth. Jess had come to the bar for a drink. She was coming to the cabaret with us, and so while she was mixing with the various guests and just being social, I didn't want her speaking to the hen party so I kept well away.

An hour or so later, Laura and I put everyone on the coaches and we made our way just outside of San Antonio to the venue. Everyone was in high spirits except the hen party. Clearly there were frictions. Bridey had a face of defiance, Nice-but-no didn't look particularly comfortable, and Token had a face like a slapped arse. In fact, the only ones that didn't seem particularly bothered were Token's Mate, who was happy doing shots with some other guests, and the two ushers. They seemed to be more intent to pull than play happy families. As we all gathered outside the venue with the other coaches for a welcome drink, Nigel approached Bridey. Her mood lifted immediately, much to the absolute disgust of Token. I think the penny finally dropped who the mystery man was.

No sooner had Nigel said hello than he had to leave to get ready for the show. Token immediately kicked off and Nice-but-no was caught in the middle of a slanging match. Jess had already gone in to get her seat, thankfully. Like a true coward, I sent Laura over to have a word. I went inside to get ready myself.

Now, for those of you that haven't read my previous book, Ibiza '98, the Rep's Cabaret was a night out where the guests would be entertained in an amphitheatre. We'd start with a comedian then progress to a hypnotist. This was no mainstream hypnotist, though. It was very adult themed and, frankly, hilarious. The rest of the evening would involve the reps from the various hotels then doing short performances for an hour or so before the venue turned into a bar with a dance floor. Afterwards we'd take all the guests to a proper night club back in San Antonio. It sounds cheesy as hell, and truth be told, it was, but the guests always loved it. We always had positive feedback.

The sketches were pretty much the same this year as the year before. Instead of doing a Spice Girls dance like the year before, the girls would end up doing a striptease to some Britney Spears medley. For the guys, we always ended up naked on stage doing a Full Monty strip with a plate dance at the end. Thankfully the closest thing you got to a smartphone was a Nokia 3210 so our modesty remained pixelated and unidentifiable.

Everything had gone as planned. We were all well-rehearsed and knew our places. The girls had just finished their strip and were getting ready to go back out onto the floor with the guests. The DJ was playing some music for the short intermission before the main event. The boys were all amped up backstage. This was our time.

The Full Monty strip was where you really separated the men from the boys. Numbers at the venue could be anything from 600-800 on a big night. That's a lot of people that potentially get to see your brooch and earrings. Some of the male reps would be backstage attempting to bring some life into it, either manually or with the use of elastic bands.

Nigel and I would be taking shots. I could never bring myself to start warming up through fear of taking it too far and getting a spontaneous boner on the stage. Oh, the drama of that. Four lads all dancing in sync with the fifth standing to attention. That's the sort of shit that will see you on the therapist's couch. Nope, far better to drink tequila. Nigel was amping himself up, telling me that tonight was the night and that Bridey was going to get some loving. This made us both laugh. If Token or Nice-but-no could have seen or heard this, we'd be dead men. They didn't, so we toasted.

The lights went down, the music faded out, and that was our cue to take our places on the stage. For the next five minutes no one spoke. We just pranced around on stage trying to be as seductive as humanly possible and over-egging everything. There was more pout on that stage than a Queen concert. As we were reaching the crescendo of the performance, all the girls were going wild. All of us were proudly standing there, in banana hammocks, shielding the pork chop with only a police-style hat. The thongs were carefully ripped off from the back so as not to give yourself a paper cut between the cheeks, and for a few seconds we stood there holding only this peaked cap. As the audience whistled, cheered and jeered, the lights would strobe and we would frisbee the caps into the audience and sprint for the back curtain.

The thing is, we didn't all go at the same time. Nigel decided he wanted to make a gesture. He was next to me and he threw his cap at Bridey. She clasped it like a trophy. Such was her state of mind that she spent more time on the cap and the fact she felt chosen than she did looking at Nigel's helmet shining in the spotlight. He stood there smiling for a whole five seconds before the lighting changed and we followed suit. Everyone was already laughing at Nigel and, when it was our turn, the whole place went up. We raced off stage where Damien was waiting for us. He laid into Nigel about what he just did. Nigel didn't care. Besides, he'd been to the airport so many times this season already, it wasn't even a deterrent now.

Nigel and I had just enough time to take another shot of tequila before we had to go back out to finish the routine with a plate dance. This was the Greek style dance we all performed, only this time we were naked from the start. Our modesty was protected with only a pair of paper plates. We'd stand next to each other and time it so that when Nigel put his hands up, I would already have my hand in front of his meat and two veg.

Theoretically, the audience wasn't supposed to see the real Nigel. In reality, everyone sat there for a few minutes watching several pricks bob up and down in the air like buoys in the sea. We were all at different heights, so how was I supposed to gauge how far up or down Nigel's plums are when I'm told to stare straight into space?

Jess found it pretty amusing. I could see her sitting with some of the female reps she'd got acquainted with and it was nice to see her smile. She hadn't been doing too much of that of late. I glanced across at Nigel and there was only one person he was looking at. I then clocked Bridey who was smiling continually at him. Token was nowhere to be seen. Presumably it was all too much for her to see Nigel in the buff.

As soon as the show was over, we quickly got changed back into our normal clubbing gear and made our way back out to the guests. Bridey was waiting for Nigel by the stage, under the pretence of handing back his peaked cap. As soon as he saw her, he basically jumped on her. She reciprocated and the pair practically fell through the curtain. We all left them to it as we had guests to talk to.

Another hour passed, and we were on our way back to San Antonio to a club called Summum. This was a pokey little club off the beaten track. It wasn't flashy and didn't have the big headlining DJs, but it was a suitable end to a less fashionable night. The drinks were cheap as hell, and the DJs played pure party music. It was also a place where you could get lost in if you really wanted to.

I think at this point Nigel wasn't even attempting to work. As soon as we were in there, he grabbed Bridey and they went and hid in the club. Jess was having a few drinks herself and looked a little wobbly. I was caught in the middle. I was trying to keep an eye on Jess, who was clearly the worse for wear, as well as look after the hotel guests who were also getting smashed. To top it all, I have the hen party continually pestering me searching for Bridey. I couldn't wait for the night to finish.

At two o'clock I filed outside, had a quick debrief, and was off. Nigel didn't even bother going to the meeting. At this point I assumed he was already knee deep or he was about to be. I went back inside to grab Jess. By the time I found her she was ruined. It was as much as she could do to stand up. We went outside, the fresh air hit her, and predictably she threw up. If that wasn't enough, she didn't want to take a taxi, so I had to escort her along the whole strip. She then turned on me and got pissy because I didn't spend more time with her in the club, despite me working. I couldn't win.

I woke up the following morning with a clear head. Thankfully, Jess had a hangover from hell, despite jettisoning her dinner the night before. This was karma. Did she apologise? Of course not. Served her right, miserable mare. I went to work and hung around the pool with the rest of the guests though the hen party was nowhere to be seen. This suited me.

I had a swim, some breakfast, and hung out with Pepe. It was a very low-key morning. It wasn't until just after lunch that I saw Bridey walking in through reception. She was clearly on the walk of shame. I casually acknowledged her as she disappeared up the stairs. We had a sales meeting at 2 and I figured I'd get the lowdown from Nigel.

I got to the sales meeting a little late. I wasn't in a rush, and besides, I had the best numbers in the area meaning any of Damien's normal pressure or threats weren't applicable. I strolled in, made some half-assed apology, and sat there listening to Damien rip Tony a new one because he'd lost some paperwork. He'd already chewed Nigel out for missing the sales meeting last night, and I think Nigel had been given some chores to do as punishment. He didn't care, though. He was sitting there pleased as punch. I looked at him and he just gave that proud nod. He'd clearly got into Bridey and he was happy with himself.

As soon as we were dismissed, we were giggling like teenagers. Nigel told me he didn't even wait for the meeting. He grabbed her and took her home practically as soon as we got into the club, as he feared there would be issues with Token and the others. In retrospect that was probably a wise move. I couldn't believe how focused he'd been. I asked him if it was a good cuddle. He joked, saying he was great, she was average, so between them it was above par. He went on to say that they were due to meet again this evening and though I didn't tell him at the time, I doubted it was going to be so plain sailing. I figured Token would have something to say about her brother's wife-to-be getting drilled by a rep a week before the impending marriage, but didn't want to burst his bubble.

I went back to the hotel to find there'd been a complete

blow up with the hen party. I found Token in tears outside, being comforted by one of the ushers and Token's mate. Bridey, Usher 2 and Nice-but-no were sitting in the corner of the pool area clearly deep in emotional conversation. I just kept a low profile and decided to take a walk. They only had one more evening here and I was tired of the dramatics.

I decided to go and find Jess and popped back to the apartment. She was on the balcony reading a book. I asked how she was and was met with short one-word answers. I guess she was still pissed with me for being tired all the time, or not having enough free time to spend with her. I asked her if she fancied anything to eat or drink and she ignored me. Rather than risk another bust up, I quietly left and went back to the pool. I got chatting to a group of lads who'd come out to stay, and they suggested we go to a bar by the sea front to have a few drinks. I thought that was just what I needed.

We went to Savannahs which is a sunset bar down from Café Del Mar and Mambo. It was a cool place, less trendy than the others, but ultimately felt a bit more up market because of it. We all got a beer in and just spent an hour or so getting to know each other. The boys were from Wigan, and while they were happy to get on the piss and have some fun out here, they were also laid back. Their aim was to just relax and recuperate from the stresses from home. If they got laid, they were happy, and if they didn't, it was no big deal. They didn't set out to drink themselves into a coma but would have one or two to loosen up. It was a mature but rare attitude to have out there at that point in time, and it was the kind of balanced thinking I needed to surround myself with.

After a few pints, I started to loosen up and the topic of conversation had turned on to relationships. They knew of

Jess. I think everyone in the hotel knew of Jess. It was funny actually, out here it was a complete role reversal. Most of the guys out here were kind enough to give her a wide berth, knowing she was with me. Whether they thought there was no point, or whether they were just being respectful, I'm not sure. Probably a bit of both.

The girls, on the other hand, made no effort to tone down their attempts. I would continually get propositioned, albeit in a jokey type of way, and whenever I made the point that it wouldn't go down well at home, they would respond by saying she'd never find out. Naturally, some of them would be bluffing, but Ibiza '98 taught me that the majority weren't.

One of the boys asked me what was going on between us, as he'd seen me looking a bit stressed and I confess I was a little taken back by the directness of his question. I managed to say something along the lines that we were serious but having a bit of a tough time out here of late. I think they could tell the gravity of the situation by the way I swallowed half my pint the moment I stopped speaking. Unexpectedly, one of the other lads managed to sum up the problem we were facing in one or two lines. I was shocked by his eloquence.

"I can imagine it must be tough on you," he said. "You're working all the hours God sends out here, and while it might look like the best job in the world, you're under a constant state of pressure. Whether that's physical stress of not having enough sleep, coupled with the pressure to get sales and keep the guests happy and safe, or the mental stress of trying to keep her on an even keel. She probably doesn't appreciate that, and just thought she'd fly out here for the summer, have a nice life with you in Ibiza, all paid for, but without any expectation of how demanding the job would be on the pair of you. She's probably pretty moody about it all, which in turn is adding further pressure on you and adding to your stress." I could have hugged him. He had single-handedly hit the nail on the head.

Before I had a chance to even respond, one of his friends chimed in, albeit with a lesser degree of mental clarity. "And knowing every other bird out here wants to bang you must piss her right off." I couldn't help but grin at that.

"Yeah, it's not helping things between us, that's for sure."

The first one regained control of the conversation. "Is she making you happy though? Is it worth all the additional stress?" The silence was deafening. I'm not even sure I managed to reply before he added the cherry to the top of his counselling sorbet, "And there's your answer." With that, everyone looked deep into their pints of San Miguel.

It was almost as if we were at my relationship's wake, and someone had just finished the eulogy. I changed the subject to something lighter, and began to prod the group on their performance to date on the holiday. Pretty soon the focus was on one of the other members that was yet to get laid, and he received some gentle ribbing and banter.

Despite having a few more beers and generally enjoying the time with the lads, it was something of a mask. I couldn't get the situation with Jess out of my head, and started to wonder if I would be better off without her.

Later on that evening, everyone met in the bar like always. It was the last night before a rotation, so half of the place would be going home the following evening and determined to go out with a bang. On the face of it, the hen-do looked like they'd put a lid on most of their woes, but the atmosphere was still pretty frosty. However, some kind of fragile peace accord had been struck. Of course, I knew it would go to shit the minute Nigel appeared, all confidence and smiles.

My sixth sense was spot on. Once we got to the venue, all the hotel guests merged with one another. Nigel walked in, calm and grinning like the 15th Dalai Lama. He shot me a glance. I indicated to him where Bridey was and got comfortable, ready to watch the fireworks.

As soon as he walked over to greet the girls, Bridey blushed but started to grin. She was hanging off his every word and everyone including Nigel knew it. Token didn't take her eyes off Bridey once. You had to respect her intentions; I mean, her brother was getting screwed here, metaphorically speaking.

Nigel made some corny joke, Bridey burst into laughter as if he was Will Ferrell, and that was it. Token stormed out the room. Her mate rolled her eyes—undoubtedly bored of the drama by now—and begrudgingly followed suit. The Ushers looked at each other but stayed put, and Nice-but-no just reached for her glass. I became distracted but it wasn't long before Nigel snuck out and went back to hers.

This was a bold move, even for Nigel. By all accounts, it was (at least, according to Nigel) a very romantic shag. Thankfully, he had the decency to hop out quickly afterwards so as not to get caught by the rest of the party. He even made a brief appearance back in the club. I'd like to think he was trying to put the rest of the group off the scent by being seen there working, i.e. not ripping through Token's brother's Fiancé, but I suspect he was still horny.

I was determined to get home early that night. I caught a glimpse of Damien and asked him if he'd mind me nipping off a bit early as I was tired. He asked me what my figures were and then let me go, telling me to keep up the good work. When I got home, Jess was there. She'd been out for a drink with a girl she'd made friends with. She was surprised to see me home early, but wasn't exactly warm in her mood. I thought some cuddles might help to bring us closer.

I couldn't have been any more wrong. It was robotic and cold. I tried to make conversation afterwards but she seemed very cross with me, and all I kept thinking about was what the Wigan boys had said earlier. I asked a seemingly harmless question about what she was going to do the following evening, reminding her I would be at the airport, and she snapped back at me with some sarcastic comment. I bit my tongue as I could no longer be bothered to argue, preferring sleep, but I remember it as the turning point in my mind.

As for Bridey, well, no one knows if she ever got married that following week. Needless to say, her relationship with Token would have remained frosty for a long time to come. I heard that Bridey reported feeling confused as she left. As for Nigel, he never mentioned her again for the rest of the season!

CHAPTER 15
SLEEPY TITS

I was tired. No, scratch that. I was fucking exhausted. I could practically fall asleep standing up. When was the last time you were able to lean against a pillar or a bar in a club and have a quick snooze? I mean, so tired that you don't even hear the music or people talking. This isn't being hammered drunk. This is getting to a point where, for a split second, you can feel something supporting your weight and you just nod off.

The guests found it hilarious. Some would try and take photos. Others would be scolded by other guests who could see we were working our bollocks off.

A lot of the other reps would go and hide in the toilet cubicles for a nap. Some would even pair up in a cubicle. They'd sit on the floor, backs against the wall, and drift off together. They did that so as not to cause any drama. One toilet out of order for the evening was just an annoyance. If two or more were commandeered, then security or the bar staff would get involved because the resultant queues would be going out the door in no time.

I never kipped in the loo. Not because I was above that, but because I knew if I dozed off there, they'd be waking me up the following day and it would cause no end of grief. I'd be accused of banging someone. Damien would be pissed at me for going AWOL. It just wasn't worth it.

In a funny way, it was actually the booze that kept us going. The minute we found ourselves flagging, we'd grab a drink. Didn't even matter what it was. The more tired you were, the stronger you ordered. It was the only way to counteract those heavy eyelids.

It was of course a vicious circle. You'd begin to get tired, so you'd have some more drinks. You'd naturally start to get merrier, and maybe you'd party harder. You'd go dancing or you'd do silly shots. Rinse and repeat. Other reps would go on the smash and take home a guest or a worker.

What this actually meant in layman's terms was that you were getting even less sleep. Rather than finish work at 2am and get a solid six or seven hours of sleep in, you'd be on the piss until 4am. Or you'd be leading the charge up the West End with guests in tow looking for another place to go dancing. Of course, they were happy to continue—it was their holiday and they only had to max it out for what, one or two weeks? Try doing that for one or two months. Or four months! I often joke with Damien and Nigel now, some twenty something years on, about the pace we maintained while there in the 90s. I'd be lucky to last three days if I attempted it now, such is the blessing of middle age. Nigel wouldn't even last the first night!

Back in resort, not everyone managed to save themselves from the sleep demons. One rep from Hertfordshire had come out for his first year with the company. He was on fire. He'd been on the piss pretty much constantly and had found himself showered with various females right from the get-go.

There's a popular expression called 'burning the candle at both ends.' Well, in his first six weeks, he'd not just burned that candle but put a light sabre through it. Unfortunately, what he didn't bank on was the fatigue. He'd peaked too early. He hadn't even made it through to peak season and already he was starting to fall from grace. He started oversleeping. He missed airport runs, causing no end of chaos for the rest of us who were trying to cover his lapses. People started to fall out with him because of the workload, his behaviour adding more and more pressure to his team, and a lot of the reps were already at breaking point.

He was sharing a room with another first year. The rep apartments were a complete dive and pretty much all were situated towards the back of San Antonio, behind the West End. Some were housing three or four reps—a far cry from my sea view palace I shared just with Jess.

Now, whenever Sleepy Tits wasn't working (or attempting to work), he was sleeping. He had no time for anything else. No laundry. No cleaning the flat. No buying groceries. No replacing or repairing clothing from the continual abuse it was getting, day in and day out. In essence, he'd become a dirty bastard. The other reps by comparison weren't exactly housekeepers themselves, but at least they managed to organise a once-a-week wash between them and managed to change some sheets.

Not Sleepy Tits. If I had to hazard a guess, I think he probably cleaned his sheets once a month, if that. Given these would have been especially soiled from various drink fuelled encounters, not to mention the heat from living in the Balearics in the summer, you can imagine the state of them. His white sheets were in fact more of a mushroom beige, and if you dared hold them up to the light, they'd appear to glisten like oil on water. That's not all. Given the fact that he never went to the laundrette either, it meant his clothes were practically moving on their own.

We were issued with company trainers to complement the uniforms we had to wear. Well, they went in and out of the swimming pool almost daily—bear in mind this was long before Havaiannas became a thing. Most of the trainers had to be jettisoned after about six weeks. Not Sleepy Tits. He hadn't had time to find a replacement, so three months in he was still wearing them.

This caused no end of argument with his flat mates, such was the condition of his clogs. They stunk out the whole apartment. They were purely rancid. One of the reps who shared a room with him got so annoyed, he actually launched them over the balcony in anger. These things were so bad, no one even stole them. Even wild dogs gave them a miss, meaning they were soon found and brought back into the room. I can't remember whether Sleepy Tits had picked them up or whether they'd walked back home by themselves.

It wasn't just the stench that was causing issues in that apartment, it was also the ants. His clothing lived in a heap in the corner. There was no effort to try and separate the pieces or give them an airing. Everything was just screwed up and launched into a pile every day and night. When it came to choosing what to wear for that day, it was a case of the sniff test, or whatever pair of underwear was the easiest to catch.

The thing is, the whole heap had become infested with ants. They treated the pile like it was some modern eco-friendly colony. You would watch them stream in and out of the pile in long orderly lines. All going about their business. If you were lucky, occasionally you would see a leaf or piece of bread get moved along the line with military precision. Again, this was playing havoc with the other flatmates, particularly the one that had to share a room with him. Ants aren't content to play on their side of the room, they want to explore. At least once a week the other flatmates would pour boiling water all over the floor in an effort to encourage them to move out. None of it worked.

One day, Sleepy Tits had decided he was going back for a snooze. It was under the pretence of getting some paperwork from some sales he'd carried out earlier in the day, but it was a blatant lie. As soon as he got in, I can only imagine he made a beeline for the bedroom. Even if that wasn't his first thought, as soon as his ass would have felt the mattress, he was done for.

Thing is, his flat mate had just put fresh sheets on. Now, compared to Sleepy Tit's sorry state for a bed, this proved too much temptation. Again, whether he just wanted to feel a little luxury for a minute, or fully intended on passing out there, we will never know, but that's not all. Not content with lying on his roommate's freshly made bed, Sleepy Tits must have been overcome with emotion, because not only did he kick off his rancid footwear, but he also pulled his shorts and pants down too. These were so grimy, they would have been biologically fused at this point, so it wouldn't have been an easy task. I can only imagine the excitement that would have washed over him, feeling that crisp, fresh, white linen against his skin. Within moments, he was stroking himself off.

The first I'd heard of all this was when I was downstairs in another apartment. I'd gone back with Tony and Laura. We managed to grab an hour off and I couldn't face going to see Jess, so I nipped off with them. They had some errands to run, and we decided to grab a quiet beer away from all the guests off the beaten track. Tony wanted to grab his dirty laundry so he could drop it off on the way. Laura and I were waiting in the communal area in the heart of the development. We heard some commotion above, as we looked up, there were a few other reps gathering. They beckoned us up but motioned to us to keep quiet.

Intrigued, we walked up to the room, to find the reps stifling laughter. I asked what was going on, but was told nothing, they just said go through there. Laura and I wandered through a crowd of giggling but quiet bodies. Everyone continually gestured to go through to the bedroom. I wasn't sure what to expect, but such was the laughter, I knew I wanted to see it.

As I poked my head round the corner, Laura started to giggle. There was Sleepy Tits, flat out on his back, snoring and wheezing like an asthmatic bulldog. He had his pants and shorts pulled down to his knees, and his t-shirt half way up his midriff. His flaccid Brighton laid alongside his outstretched hand like a tortoise's neck. If it wasn't apparent to anyone that he'd blatantly just knocked one out on his room-mate's bed by now, then the pièce de résistance was the little bit of man mustard that was adorning those once crisp, fresh, white sheets. On seeing this, Laura's smiling face turned to disgust as she left the room shaking her head. I stayed to see what was about to happen next.

No sooner had Laura left the room, the flatmates walked back in. One of them had a little cardboard sign that said "Open All Hours" which he neatly propped next to Sleepy Tits, who was still oblivious to his audience. The other flatmate, who until now had considered himself unfortunate to have been given the sofa bed in the lounge, then proceeded to fire off some shots with his disposable camera. Despite the audible click, followed by the ratchet winding noise of Kodak machinery, Sleepy Tits didn't stir once. Not even the noisy arrival of Tony asking everyone if they'd seen Laura and me managed to raise him from the land of nod.

Eventually, when everyone had taken their shots and had a good laugh at him, it was time to wake that dirty bastard up. All the reps, male and female, had gathered around the bed, and on the count of three cheered surprise in unison.

To this day, I'd never seen such an enthusiastic hurrah. You'd think it was someone's 50th birthday. Sleepy Tits was ripped from his dreams like pubes on a waxing strip. He looked bemused, startled, and to some degree terrified. So much so, that it wasn't until one of the girls told him to put his cock away that he even realised he was out at half mast for all to see. Roomy confronted him immediately, accusing him of wanking on his bed, much to the titters of everyone else in the room, but Sleepy Tits denied it. Despite being faced with a mountain (well, spoonful) of evidence, he continued to deny it until he was blue in the face. When questioned as to why he was asleep on Roomy's bed and not on his own, and why his cock was out, he continued to deny it. Even when another rep pointed out the little deposit of sleepy soldiers he'd left behind, he was absolutely adamant that nothing like that had happened.

You can imagine the absolute caning this kid got for the next few weeks. Where's Sleepy Tits? He's probably knocking one out. Has anyone seen Sleepy Tits? Yeah, he was behind the bar ripping one off. Sleepy Tits, what are your performance figures for this week? 2 sales, 3 sleeps and 15 wanks. We were merciless.

Despite our ruthless caning of this little masturbating menace, he didn't change his ways. He was never able to make up enough of his sleep deficit, and his performance hit the skids further. Without wanting to elaborate on the details, he was eventually removed from duty due to some irregularities over paperwork. One of the last things he apparently said to his team before he left for the airport was that he really hadn't sorted himself out that afternoon, despite photographic evidence and about 11 witnesses proving otherwise!

CHAPTER 16
THE TWIN DEFENCE TEAM

J ess and I were still not really getting along, the times when we enjoyed each other's company being few and far between.

We were in peak season at this point. The whole island was rocking. In fact, the only place that wasn't rocking was our bedroom. I was either too tired, or she didn't want to know. She became harder to live with and moody. She'd gotten herself a job handing out flyers for one of the local promoters and had made a few friends there, so she had more of a social life now and also something to do during the day rather than just work on her tan and be pissy with me. I was hoping this would help things between us.

It didn't. Every time she snapped at me, rather than try and build a bridge, it was easier to just walk away and ignore her, which I know isn't the healthy approach now, but in the beginning of your twenties, few people are blessed with such relationship wisdom.

One of the final nails in the coffin was a plane load of arrivals we had just received. I had a great bunch of guests. My hotel was full, everyone had taken the entertainment package, so I was running at 100% with one of the best figures on the island.

So much so that Damien had asked me to spend some time with Tony in his hotel to try and get his numbers up. I would go and spend an hour with him, talking to some of his guests to try and get them interested or motivated to sign up, but it was infinitely harder there because his hotel lacked momentum. I don't know if it was because the pool was small, or he didn't have the right mix of groups, but when you went in there the atmosphere felt flat. It was a cheap and cheerful place, where people who were on a budget went, but everyone was pretty much keeping to themselves. Now contrast that with our hotels, and it couldn't be any more different. Our place was like a community centre. Everyone knew each other, everyone was friendly. Half the hotel guests were banging each other and the rest were happy to just drink and socialise. It was perfect. In fact, I was having such a good time at work that I didn't want to leave early.

When it was time to finish work at 2am, Laura and I would organise a party in another bar with our guests, or we would stay out with them until the morning hours. I'd often tell Jess but she seldom joined. Whenever I would get a potential hour or two to myself, I would spend it lounging in the pool at the hotel with the guests rather than trying to find Jess for lunch. I was having a genuinely good time. I also think it was masking my disappointment in what was happening at home.

One particular group of guests in my hotel were girls from Nottingham. There were four of them. They were really good fun and down to earth. Typical girl next door types. Nothing seemed to faze them, and they were always up for a laugh.

There were two identical twins and their friends.

Charlie and Anna (twins) were both extremely fit. In fact, they were all really attractive, but they just carried on like normal, as if they weren't, which made them even more so. Right from the start, every guy in our hotel and most of the hotels around us were on their case. Even individually these girls would have attracted attention, but when you stuck them together, all done up to go out, well, you can imagine. It was every man's fantasy. Whenever we would go out down the strip or into a bar, there would be queues of guys lining up to shoot their shot. It wasn't just the twins getting the attention, their friends were also attractive, and also getting noticed.

I remember one night the girls were getting too much attention from some local guys who decided to throw the dice. The girls weren't interested in the slightest and so made it politely and abundantly clear that the conversation needed to stop. Undeterred, the locals continued to press for engagement until the girls started to feel uncomfortable.

One of the guests witnessed this and came and found Laura, who then came and found me. We were in one of our regular bars, so I knew I had security on my side if anything was to develop. When Laura told me, I had been deep in conversation with a group of Welsh lads who were also in the hotel. They too came with me to the front of the bar. It's not that I was spoiling for a fight, but I equally didn't want any of my guests to be hassled.

When I arrived on the scene, the twins were just looking at each other awkwardly trying to ignore the guys who were asking why they weren't talking to them and why they were being rude to them when they were on their island, etc. Without thinking, I walked up behind both girls and put my arms around them both, standing in between them like some pimp. The only thing missing was my purple fur coat and matching hat. I looked at the guys and just smiled. The girls instinctively put their arms around my waist and turned to face the locals too.

Their main guy said something in Spanish. I didn't catch exactly what it was, but I knew it was offensive. I just smiled wider. At which point, the Welsh lads seemed to fan out behind me and the girls. They didn't say anything either but just watched in silence.

The main guy spat on the floor just in front of me. I didn't take the bait. I pulled the girls in closer and smiled harder. He called me a son of a bitch in Spanish, to which one of the Welsh lads finally lost his composure, filling the air with his melodic Welsh accent.

"Fuck off, Pedro, and take your boyfriends with you."

I tried hard not to laugh and risk provoking a fight, but it didn't stop the rest of his group from cracking up. I think a couple of the girls started to laugh, too, which definitely poured a little extra piss on their Spanish pride. Thankfully they didn't take the bait either, and just left us to it.

Once they'd gone, Laura appeared and began fussing all over the girls. "Oh my God, are you alright? Did they hurt you?" She couldn't get her questions out quick enough. I remained still through all this, but it became apparent to me that while one of the twins had let go of me to turn and face us to talk, the other (Anna) still had her arm around my waist. As I looked down, she noticed that I had noticed, and we kind of stopped motionless for a brief moment. She blushed. I smiled. Laura got everyone involved a round of drinks and I thanked The Boyos for the backup.

The rest of the night proceeded as planned, with no additional stress. The Boyos took it upon themselves to defend the girls, and stuck quite close to them for the rest of the evening. I think the girls liked this. There didn't appear to be any romantic interest from either side in each other, it was more a brother/sister kind of thing. It was as if the

Welsh lads were there to hold back the hounds, and the girls were genuinely funny and had a good laugh with them.

This was typical of the feeling and mood of the hotel at the time. I would go back over to check in on them from time to time, continually inquiring if everything was OK and if they would fancy meeting any more locals. The banter would only increase. At one point I was bringing over barmen to the twins offering them up as some kind of man candy. The barmen knew me, and knew I was taking the piss, but they were happy to play along. By the end of the evening, I'd noticed that one of the twins, Anna, kept looking at me, and truth be told, I kept looking at her.

This was pretty much the pattern of behaviour throughout their first week out there. Everyone was having a great time. We would continually flirt with each other, and every time a guy other than myself came near them, Welsh reinforcements would appear and do their best to cock block. It was really funny to watch, and at one point I think one of The Boyos even christened themselves the Twin Defence Team, which made everyone laugh.

They would even cock block the male reps from the other hotels who would of course come sniffing like jackals. While all this was going on, things between Jess and I hadn't improved. She'd come to the hotel a few times during the day and we'd have lunch together, or she'd just chill on the sunbeds while I would do the pool entertainment with Laura. Sometimes Nigel would pop over for some antics, but she never really seemed happy. I'd go over in between games to see if she was alright or to bring her a drink, but I think at this point I was probably annoying her more than anything. And if I wasn't annoying her, she was definitely annoying me.

Some of the guests picked up on the negative vibes and would ask me about it. I'd be constantly fielding questions like, "what's up with the wife?" or, "you had a row with the missus?" I'd always just roll my eyes and come up with some lame excuse, answering that it was just her time of the month, or I'd come home drunk yesterday and broke a chair or something equally as ridiculous. I was initially embarrassed but, as time went on, I would become resentful.

Once the new arrivals came through and we were done with welcome meetings, I had to drop tickets and various receipts and things to each room. If people weren't in their rooms, I'd just slide it under the door. I always preferred to hand it to them, because I wanted to make sure no one had any second thoughts or doubts about the trips, and also to remind them what time to meet in the bar. The quicker I could get them into the spirit of things, the quicker they'd be part of the community and my job would be easier.

On dropping off the last tickets, I was walking along one of the corridors when the twins passed me. They invited me in for a cup of tea. I accepted and we sat and had a long chat. The sort that you often have with relative strangers on holiday that can leave a lasting impression.

Out of the blue, Charlie asked me what was up with Jess. Why was she always snapping at me? I wasn't prepared for that one. I explained how we'd been having a tough time of late and things weren't really working out. Before I knew it, I was literally pouring out my thoughts on a platter. Within a few sentences, I was admitting that the relationship had run its course and we needed to break up. It was the first time I'd actually spoken those words, and I was somewhat surprised to hear them come out of my lips. Anna remained silent during this little outburst. Charlie didn't though.

"Sounds like you need to get rid, and quickly. If she's

not making you happy, there are plenty of others who will. Especially out here."

I was beginning to squirm. I wasn't prepared for this matter-of-factness, and to have Anna looking at me directly opposite, whom I fancied the pants off, made me even more uncomfortable. I think she could tell I was looking for the exit.

Anna tried to ease things by asking if there was any way back for the pair of us. I meekly offered an "I'm not sure" before making my excuses and heading out.

On the walk back to the hotel, I was conflicted. Part of me felt a weight beginning to lift, having come to the realisation that Jess had to go, but the other part of me felt sad at the same time. I was really disappointed. I had some idea in my head about how it was supposed to be, but the reality was nothing like it. I felt down. It's a natural feeling to have unless you're a stone-cold bastard, or your partner is a complete asshole that needs to be pushed off the side of a cliff.

I got to the apartment and found Jess was getting ready to go to work. I asked how she was. She just snapped at me, telling me nothing had changed in the last three hours since she'd seen me. I decided I wouldn't bite my tongue any longer. I told her to fuck off. Plain and simple. She was taken aback by this but I didn't let up.

"I'm sick and tired of you snapping at me all the time and constantly being on my case."

"Well, I'm fed up with you always spending so much time at work and putting your guests above me."

She had a point, but this had been well and truly fleshed out before we agreed to come here.

Things quickly deteriorated; within moments it was a full-on slanging match. She called me a variety of names used to describe the male genitalia, and I told her to effectively sling her hook. Doors were slammed and I made my way back to the hotel.

As soon as I was there, I used the phone to call the office, and asked one of the girls to put me in touch with travel. I bought Jess a refundable ticket to the UK. I had a couple of days to decide, and the cost would be taken out of my salary. I was embarrassed to be asking this from the company as it was effectively letting everyone know what was happening, but I was determined.

I guess word got round pretty quickly, because the next thing you know I had Damien call the hotel and ask if I was OK. I was feeling sad inside, but managed to swallow the lump and just said, "Yeah it's fine, all part of the process." He knew it was a front but decided not to press it. Just told me he'd see me later and we'd have a drink.

I put the phone down and decided I needed somewhere to hole up for 20 minutes to get my game face on, ready for the guests. I thought I'd go and find Nigel. He would cheer me up. He'd tell me some stories about his hotelier hating him, and how he'd caught crabs or something equally unpleasant, and all this mess with Jess would be forgotten about, even if only temporarily.

As I moved away from the bar, I turned around to leave the hotel and literally stepped on Anna. I hadn't seen her and my mind was elsewhere. We both apologised in the way that only awkward Brits do, but I guess the anguished look on my face gave me away. She didn't say anything but gave me a hug. It was exactly what I needed, even if it was a little twisted to be coming from her. In my head, I went from comforted to sexual in the space of about 5 seconds. Thankfully, one of the other guests shouted "get a room" which killed the thing entirely, otherwise I think my waist-band would have come under pressure! We both pulled back. I went to find Nigel. She went back upstairs to get ready.

That night we went out on a bar crawl prior to going to Eden. Everyone was looking their best. The new arrivals were keen to get on the piss and have fun, those that had been out already were slightly less keen to get smashed so early on, but they were also livening up.

We went to a bar on the corner of the West End. It was one of my favourites. Behind the bar, there was an English barman called Richard, or Rick. He was a legend. He would wear funky rimmed glasses and weird and wonderful items of clothing. He pulled it off well though. In fact, he was a big hit with everyone, especially the girls. Damien knew him since he'd been repping as a junior when Rick had been there a few years already, so they'd both kind of gone along at the same time together.

Damien took me to one side. We had a big hearty shot of sambuca and then he whispered something into Rick's ear. Rick shoots off to find another barman and within a minute returns to us. Damien and I are taken to the back of the bar and through a side door out back. We pass along a dark corridor before we're in what looks like a recreation room. I can only assume it's where the staff came to relax before or after their shift, or where they counted the takings at the end of the night.

Before I get a chance to say anything, Rick goes over to this big chest in the corner. It looks old. He proudly puts it down on the middle of the table in front of Damien and I. Damien knows what's coming next and is smiling at me. I'm at a complete loss but keen to find out.

The chest is opened and Rick leans in to pull out a big square tile. On it is a little white mound of cocaine. He puts it down carefully and squarely on the table. On the tile is a small pair of miniature spoons, presumably to snort from. "Tuck in guys."

Damien doesn't wait a moment longer. Within seconds he's doubled over this tile, spooning gear into his beak. You'd think he was sponsored by Dyson. He let up just to replenish himself with some air before diving back in. I, on the other hand, was massively out of my depth.

I'd never done drugs in my life. The closest I'd come to doing anything was trying a cigarette when I was 16. I took one puff, nearly choked, and never tried it again. I didn't want to let them down but I knew drugs were a slippery slope. I politely declined, telling them it didn't agree with me while trying to act as if I'd seen it all before.

I'm not sure if Rick believed me, or indeed even heard me over Damien who was doing his best impression of Henry Hoover. Rick pulled out several heavy looking books, carefully placing them down before producing a bottle of something dark from the bowels of the chest. He grabbed me a shot glass and promptly filled it to the brim. He then proceeded to take what I can only assume (and hope) was sugar and began to stir it into the shot. He handed it to me.

As I looked at it, Damien surfaced again for air, giving Rick the opportunity to sample some of his own marching ants. Damien looked at me, his top lip glistening with powder and told me to get it down me. I did as I was told.

As the liquid hit my throat, I immediately felt my body recoil. Neither my body nor my brain knew what it was, only that it shouldn't be in there. I looked at the bottle more closely: Absenta (i.e. absinthe). I knew the taste as I'd had it before at university, but this was far harsher.

Rick straightened himself out, giving Damien the chance to do another lap in the powder pool. "That's the real shit right there. None of that crap you find in the UK."

He then proceeded to budge Damien over so he could dive back into the white. It was like watching two puppies fighting over a bowl of pedigree chum. I took a seat and tried my best to forget the shite that had just rolled down my throat. The only thing worse than this that I'd tasted previously was Hierbas.

Once Rick and Damien had had their fill, they too sat down around the table. Damien went on to tell Rick that I was having bird troubles. Rick knew of Jess and immediately piped up, "What, the fit one? Ah, sorry to hear that, but you're in the best place in the world to fix it."

I just smiled and nodded. Didn't really know what to say, and didn't like the idea of baring all across the table from the fruits of Pablo Escobar's labour.

Without a word, Damien picked up one of Rick's thick books and handed it to me. The words Ibiza '96 had been stamped on the cover. I opened it.

It immediately hit me that these weren't books but photo albums. I pulled back the first blank white sheet of paper and was immediately confronted with a photo of a smiling girl's face and someone's cock. Somewhat surprised, I chuckled and turned the page. Guess what. Different girl's head, same cock. I turned to the next page. It was the same modus operandi. The same length hanging out of a different girl's mouth.

I flicked another couple of pages forwards and realised they were all basically the same. I then handed that album back and picked up the next one. Ibiza '97 was scrawled across the front of that with a gold glitter pen. I pulled back the blank sheet and, guess what. Something was different though. Obviously, it was a different girl's head, but something looked different with the pipe. Ah, it's now pierced.

I looked up at Rick. Rick was kicking back in his post Colombian slumber. He just smiled.

"I got the piercing done out here in my second year. Hurt like hell but the girls love it. They all want to see it."

It suddenly dawned on me that this was his thing. He would ask girls if they wanted to see the piercing. The girls would say yes, he'd take them somewhere discreet, and a few moments later, it was subway time.

I mean, it was an impressive collection of albums. He also had several further volumes, where the girls had taken photos of him repaying the favour to them. He asked me if I wanted to see them, and Damien encouraged him, in between rubbing his gums, but I insisted I was good. Last thing I wanted to look at was Rick's smiling face hovering over a badly packed kebab.

We kicked back for a short while longer before Damien decided it was time for us to move on. At their insistence, I was given another shot of Absenta while they got on the spoons for one last round of sherbert. Rick carefully packed away his vices and placed the chest back over in the corner of the room. He escorted us both out to the main bar area and it was man hugs all round. Damien told me that if I needed the time off to fix things at home, I just had to ask. He also told me not to bother going to Eden either if I didn't want to. He'd make an excuse with the others. I thanked him and told him I'd probably take him up on that offer. With that he left the bar, and I went back to the guests.

I fully intended to leave the party directly after the bar. I wanted to get Jess after work and try and sort something out. I mean, I hadn't told her I'd bought the ticket, and even though I was sure it was over, I didn't want to part on bad terms. A small part of me was even hoping there might still be a way back.

Absenta had different ideas. About 20 minutes after saying goodbye to Damien I was in the zone. I was on fire. I had successfully managed a stage dive and had motivated security to intervene to prevent an encore. I had been dirty dancing with anything in a 15m radius. That included the twins, although apparently, I had sought the permission of the Twin Defence Team first, who required me to complete a challenge. The challenge was to drink vodka and orange up your nose through a pair of straws.

Being a total exhibitionist, I seized on the chance to up the ante. I made them a bet that if I could do it while doing a headstand, every single guest in my hotel needed to do two shots of tequila with me. After they managed to get all the guests together, the deal was on.

The guests from other hotels looked on in bemusement. The vodka and orange was poured and two long straws were placed in it. I lightly bent the straws at one end so that they would be able to fit in my nose while inverted. I could tell that security were getting a bit rattled with me, but Rick soon put an end to any concerns.

I took off my t-shirt, using it as a mat for my head and did a headstand. One of The Boyos held my legs, the other crouched down next to me with the vodka and orange, and carefully placed the straws into my hooter. I could already see quite a crowd forming and this served only to encourage me further.

After a brief countdown, I was off. I inhaled that sweet orange water as hard and as fast I could. Initially I started to splurge, but once I relaxed and eased off on the pressure, it started to go down with ease. Maybe I'd found my new talent! A few seconds later and we were done. Everyone cheered, I was put back upright with the help of the lads, and I was given a bar stool.

I felt like a general ordering people to get their shots. As agreed, every single guest, including the twins, took their shots of tequila. Laura, who had been missing until this point, appeared out of the crowd and made tracks to move people on. She saw the state of me and laughed.

"Damien tells me you're not coming to Eden tonight? All ok?" she asked.

"Yeah, something I need to take care of."

She already knew, and so wished me good luck and gave me a tight hug before leaving me to it. She took the vast majority of the guests onwards to the club, and I was left to make my way home.

Any thought I had of finding Jess at work evaporated the moment the fresh air hit me. I was hammered. Not just talking shit to strangers hammered, I mean Spiderman hammered. I had to cling on to any vertical surface I could find to maintain balance. Didn't matter if it was a wall, a window, a car, or a signpost. If it stood still, I held on. I had a few offers of help from several Samaritans who were out and about, but I declined.

Eventually I managed to make it home and managed to drink several pints of water before crashing out on the sofa. It wasn't even midnight. By the time Jess came in, it was 3:30. Apparently she'd gone to Eden after work to find me, but was told by one of the guests she recognised that I didn't come to the club, so she'd been out looking for me.

Of course, this wasn't my fault at all—we'd never arranged to meet after work—but that didn't stop me from getting an earful. Clearly, I'd had a drink, but having had a few hours of sleep meant I could think (and talk!) straight. I tried to calm her down, but she was still angry having spent an hour walking in and out of most of my usual haunts looking for me. She continued to push.

Rather than soften, I hardened. I don't know if I was just emotionally exhausted, or the Absenta hangover was increasing in intensity, but we had a huge row. You know the sort, when you feel you need to apologise to the neighbours the next day. She told me in anger she wanted to leave, at which point I broke the news that I'd already bought her a ticket for the end of the week. It took the wind right out of her sails. The look on her face instantly made me regret the argument and the manner in which I had told her. We both sat down and began to talk more rationally. It was tough, we weren't making each other happy, but neither of us wanted to move on. After about an hour of emotionals we both crashed out.

The following morning, I left before she woke up. I had a bit of a thick head but thankfully nothing too dramatic. I hate to think what would have happened if I'd engaged in the Colombian. Given I'd never done it before, I'm sure I would have overcooked it.

My hotel was a ghost town. Laura used the opportunity to go and get some laundry done, so I went to find Nigel to fill him in.

When I got to Nigel's hotel, he was being shouted at by the Hotelier and security. Apparently, security had caught a girl leaving his room in the morning and grassed him up to the Pope. The hotelier was making all sorts of threats and gestures towards him. Nigel just kept repeating, "Lo siento, lo siento, no entiendo," which translated means, I'm sorry, I'm sorry, I don't understand. They weren't letting up.

"What's going on? " I asked as soon as I arrived. He didn't even finish listening to them telling him off, he just rolled his eyes, stood up in the middle of them moaning at him, and walked me to the pool area. He didn't give a shit that he was in trouble and we had a good laugh about the situation. I told him about Jess. He was kind but intimated that he thought this would happen.

We sat down on a pair of loungers and talked it all through. Suddenly, a thought hit him like a bullet.

"You know what this means? Oh my god, it's really

happening! Get in!" Nigel's mind had clearly gone into overdrive.

"What are you talking about?"

"We're going to play knock-a-door smash finally. We're going to go on the smash together, and it's going to be like old times."

It took a minute for it all to sink in. I was emotionally drained and the last thing I wanted to think about was to get into any more situations with girls, but Nigel was so encouraged by it, he started to instantly reminisce about our season previously, and all the things that had happened to us while on the hunt.

By the time he finished, the mill stone around my neck felt lighter. I mean, we still had just under two months of peak season left, and a lot of damage could be done in that time. I start to feel my spirits lift. Sensing this, Nigel thought he'd try and seize on the opportunity.

"Actually, while you're here, why don't we pay a visit to one of the rooms. I know there's a couple of girls who would love to get to know us."

He had a mischievous grin on his face, and I know for a fact that he'd 'been' to this room already, so what he was actually suggesting was me going up there, sitting on the sofa with the mate awkwardly, while he got his nuts in again. With any luck and a bit of charm, I'd be horizontal too. Had he asked me this last season, I'd have been climbing up the balconies, but this was too much too soon.

He just laughed when I refused and we continued our conversation over a pot of tea. The hotelier continued to stare at us both the whole time. We ignored him. The only time I even thought to look was when Nigel mentioned it. "Look at that miserable cunt staring at us both," he'd say. He'd smile back and offer a small wave, much to the annoyance of the Cardinal.

I headed back over to my hotel shortly after lunchtime. Some of the guests were coming round and I still wanted to see how Jess was.

When I got there, she was already sitting down having some lunch. I cautiously approached her, unsure as to what her reaction would be. She was actually nice about it all. She'd had time to think last night and this morning, and also agreed it would be for the best. Ibiza wasn't making her happy, she was bored, and she understood that things between us weren't right.

I felt instantly happier after talking to her. Sad as a break up is, at least it was better than fighting. I reconfirmed the ticket with the office and, well, that was that. She had two days left and then would be gone.

I went to find Damien to find out how he was. When I found him, he looked rough. He'd barely been to sleep. When I asked him how his night was, he just gave me that look. I thanked him for the drink at Rick's but I didn't mention the drugs. In fact, it was never brought up again. I updated him on Jess, and told him that she was going. He offered his sympathies, but then sharp as a knife issued me an ultimatum.

"I tell you what, if you manage to increase your hotel sales figures from here, and keep them above this level for the rest of the season, you can stay in the apartment on your own. You can do whatever you like, with whoever you like out there, and nothing is going to stop you."

Shit. I hadn't even thought about the prospect of having to share again. I didn't need any time to think. "Deal!"

I left him to it. He looked like he was going to fall asleep at the table. For the first time in ages, I started to feel lighter, more positive. Things were looking up.

The next few days went quickly. Things between Jess and I remained friendly and civil. We still slept in the same bed and we'd still make each other drinks or food. On her last day, I left her to it. I managed to get the evening off and told her I'd be back at around 9ish to pick her up and take her to the airport.

Up until this point, I'd been ok. I'd felt better about things but was dreading this. I never was very good with goodbyes, and despite everything that we'd been through over the last few weeks, this was still going to be a killer.

I picked her up in the office Jeep and drove the short way to the airport. We conversed lightly but neither of us really said much. I knew most of the staff in the airport anyway, and was still wearing my rep's clothes, so we didn't have to queue anywhere. I literally abandoned the vehicle opposite the terminal and took her inside.

The girls on the counter were kind enough to get her checked in, and I skipped the line to push her baggage through. We then went and got a cup of tea. Shared a few laughs, a few tears, and with that she was gone.

I felt empty, directionless if you will. I hung around the office counter that we had at the airport and made polite conversation with the staff there. It was obvious what had happened, and one of the girls gave me a big hug, then another did the same, and before I knew it I'd been embraced by everyone there. I think even one of the lads got in on the act. One of the girls quipped that I wouldn't be single for long, to which I replied, I'd hold her to that. It destroyed her, she blushed massively, everyone whooped, and she scuttled off behind the counter.

The drive back felt really weird. I felt free, but also sad. The easiest thing in the world would have been to park the car, go down the West End, grab a few beers and fire into the nearest girls I could find, but I didn't want that on my conscience and didn't know how I would react the following day. Though I felt instantly better overall, I still wasn't 100% sure I'd done the right thing. I guess only time would tell. Not only that, but it was a rare occasion when I hadn't had a drink and actually had some time to get some proper shut-eye, so didn't want to waste it on a cuddle. I got back to the apartment, which suddenly felt large and empty, and hit the sack. Not that I had much time to reflect on anything. I was out like a light within seconds.

The following morning, I woke up late. I guess my body had finally managed to catch up on some quality sleep and was reluctant to let go of it. I'd totally blown it with the hotel. I should have been there around 8-8:30, and the clock was now reading 11. I hate oversleeping, because no matter how much sleep you've had prior, when your body is forced to wake up quickly you spend the rest of the day chasing yourself.

I got to the hotel, clearly dishevelled because the guests immediately started to cane me. I didn't even have time for breakfast. It was changeover day, and I needed to make sure all the guests who were leaving knew what time their pickups were for their various flights, and also to check through the incoming guest manifest with the hotelier, as I always did, to make sure there were no surprises. I didn't even have a chance to dwell on Jess's departure. I just got on with it.

Once finished with the errands, I managed to grab a quick bite by the pool. I practically inhaled the meal. It wasn't until one of the twins told me to slow down that I realised I was practically gnawing at my fingers. I told them I hadn't had a proper dinner and had missed breakfast.

Right on cue, Charlie asked me, "So, what's going on with your bird then?"

I looked at Anna. She didn't give anything away.

"I dropped her off at the airport last night. It's done." I looked back at Anna.

"Well, good for you!" she said. "I think you've done the right thing. She clearly wasn't making you happy."

I just kind of nodded. I wasn't really sure what to say, and with Anna sitting two feet away from me, I didn't really want to be having this kind of conversation. I quickly changed the subject. They were going home that night, and so I asked them if they'd had a good time, and asked how the last night was? I asked them if the Twin Defence Team performed ok, they both laughed.

Anna, who until now had remained pretty low key in comparison to her sister, suddenly piped up. "It's a shame there weren't any fit guys about to get into trouble with."

A little taken back, I decided to tease her a little. "Am sure you could have found someone? Were The Boyos that strict? Maybe you were just dancing funny and no one wanted to know!"

She playfully hit me on the arm. Sensing her cue, Charlie went back to her sunbed, leaving Anna and I alone. "It's a shame we're going home tonight," she said. "Could have done with a bit more time out here, especially now that you're single."

It was lovely to hear. Anna was lovely. Super fit, friendly. I definitely would have been involved with her had I not been attached. I just replied to her calmly with pure cheese. "We'll always have Nottingham!"

She laughed. I promised her that I would go and visit them for a weekend when I was back in the UK after the season finished. We talked a bit more before she left to join her sister.

I didn't get a chance to see them again until we were at the airport. I was on an early flight out and had to wait for the incoming one. I knew what flight they were leaving on, so I wandered down from the breakout room when the rep who had taken them to the airport appeared.

I surprised them in the check in queue. We exchanged hugs, and I reiterated my promise to go and visit them in Nottingham once I was done with Ibiza. We exchanged contacts, and with that, they too were gone.

Part of me was gutted. I would have loved to have spent more time with Anna out there. She was great, but also given the situation at the time, I'm glad nothing actually happened. I wouldn't have wanted to do the dirty on anyone, nor make any cheap propositions.

CHAPTER 17
BLITZKRIEG!

As I alluded to in Ibiza '98, we weren't just selling resort entertainment packages to the guests. We were also selling tickets to a weekender that the company would throw back in the UK later on in the year.

This event was simply incredible. It was always held in a Butlins or a Pontins style holiday camp. The rooms were atrocious. Military style blocks of apartments with worn out carpets, mouldy showers and thick plastic sheets. Despite being heavily chlorinated by the army of cleaners, you still felt you could get pregnant just by sitting on them.

The thing is, none of that mattered. This two day bender was a chance to meet up with people you'd been on holiday with. There would be coaches picking up from all over the country, hauling horny teenagers away for a weekend of absolute debauchery and mischief. There were thousands attending. The company would break out some bigger DJs and turn it into one big festival. You'd drink, dance, fuck, drink some more. Rinse and repeat. It was an amazing trip away, normally held in November when the UK is nothing but grey, wet and miserable.

The cost to go on this trip was normally about £80, give or take. To qualify, though, you needed to pay a deposit in resort. The deposit was £15. Nowadays that's a couple of pints in a poncy bar, but back then in '99 it still represented a decent amount of money for our guests, and it wasn't handed over lightly.

In addition, this was the only thing we sold where we actually got a hard commission back from the company. For every £15 deposit I collected, I retained a fiver. This was paid cash at the end of the season. Just before we would be due to fly home, we would be given an envelope with all of our commissions for the season. This was decent. If you had a big group of, say 8-10 lads, and you convinced them to put down their deposit, well that's £40-50 in your pocket. At the grand age of 19-20, that's decent cash to be had.

The prime time to try and sell this weekender was normally after the full day out or a big clubbing night. The guests would be on a high, some would have copped off with each other, and so the thought of meeting up with your holiday romance again in November was an easy sell.

The first weekender I ever went on was in the autumn of '97, with my best mate at university Mike. It was so good. I got laid twice. Mike lost his virginity, and I ended up successfully interviewing for this rep's job. So for me, selling it was a cinch. It was the mutt's nuts of a weekend. My passion for the event surpasses anything I could ever put down on paper, try as I have.

My second weekender was in the autumn of '98. It was after my first season, so it was lovely meeting up with all the guests again and sharing some fun times. It was great just getting back in with everyone. So, if I couldn't sell it quite so well in my first season, by the time it came to my second season, it was game, set and match. It was this simple: if you stayed in my hotel in 1999, you paid this deposit. In fact, even if you didn't stay in my hotel in 1999, you still might have paid your deposit!

There was no pressure selling involved at all. I wasn't about that. The thought of forcing someone to pay for something they didn't want was abhorrent. All I had to do was detail what happened at the events. The look on my face and the overall vibe did the rest.

This was one of the only situations where I actually got out what I put in. The more I tried, the more money I earned. And the deposits weren't pooled. I was making hundreds of pounds a week cash on top of my regular salary and share of the entertainment packages we were selling. In fact, sometimes, I was so successful that Damien would send me to other hotels to have a go if their reps were struggling.

At that point, any deposits taken would be under my name, so my commission. This would be a sticking point with some of the other reps, as they would see it as me taking food from their plate. More often than not, Damien would use it as a threat—a form of motivation to get their act together—but on other occasions he actually went through with it, and I would go in and book their guests on the trip. I don't think it made me particularly popular when I did it, but they also understood they weren't having any luck, and it was always a last-ditch attempt at the end of the holiday.

One time during peak season, I had a stormer. Most of my guests were two-weekers and they'd all decided to go for the entertainment package. I was sat at 100% participation. Despite Damien's best efforts to annoy me during sales meetings, it was water off a duck's back. Once they'd been there for a few days, and we'd taken them out on a few trips, I'd then wander round with my bag and clipboard and ask them if they were interested in signing up for the reunion. Needless to say, they did. They ALL did.

So, there I am sitting at 100% participation on the entertainment package, and 100% participation on the weekender. I've now got nothing to do. Damien was busy digging out some of the other reps for being way below the 70% target he normally set. Tony for instance was languishing around 30-40%, Nigel would have been mid to high 50s, and Laura probably 70% or thereabouts. Me? I'm sitting there like rainbows are flowing from my ass at 100%. In fact, I'm so cocky at this point that I just ask Damien if I can go, half way through the meeting. Rather than snap at me, he encourages me to go and grab a sleep or catch a beer on the beach. I don't need to be told twice. I nip off and chill out for the rest of the afternoon, allowing the rest to continue to be berated.

The following day I had no one left to chase. Everyone had paid up, everyone had signed up, and everyone was pissed up. The pool was rocking. There was a sales meeting again later on in the afternoon, but I had zero interest in being there on time and, with the current state of everyone else, I doubted I'd be missed.

I was organising various poolside games. Belly flop competitions, lilo races, water fights. You name it, we were doing it. Someone even brought out a yard of ale, so we all had a go at that. At some point though, I wanted to go and buy some music from the CD store in the West End. So I made my excuses and ducked off for some retail therapy.

As I walked through the West End, proudly donning my rep's tags, people would say "hi" to me. Naturally I said hello back. Some of these were workers, some were guests from our hotels, others were just randoms. I passed a big group of lads who were just sitting down having a beer in the sun. They seemed to be watching the girls go by and some of the world in between.

"Alright lads, having a good day?" I say to them, or words to that effect. They acknowledge me and ask how I'm doing. I reply, but I don't stop.

I pass into the CD shop and grab one of the latest albums that had just come out. The Ministry of Sound Ibiza Annual I think had just dropped. I pop back out and bump into a couple of girls who were in our hotels. I flirt outrageously with the pair of them, and one of them gives me a kiss on the cheek before the pair wander off giggling. I even get a look back and they laugh even more. Unbeknownst to me, this big group of lads had witnessed the whole thing and, as I turn around looking pleased with myself, there's 20 odd pairs of eyes looking at me smiling.

"Bloody hell, you must get loads of puss out here mate!" one of them asks.

I just smile and shrug. "What can I say?"

They laugh.

I stop again to talk with them. I ask what hotel they are in, are they having a good time, who's getting laid then etc. They invite me to take a seat with them, so I do. One calls for the waiter to bring out a beer.

We continue to make small talk. Mainly about the place, the bars, the girls. When the waiter brings out the beer, he sees it's for me and sees the tag. One of the lads tries to pay for it, but the waiter sees me and just smiles telling him it's on the house. I knew the waiter. It was one of the bars we went to regularly with the guests, so we shook hands and I said hello. He disappears back inside. If the guys weren't impressed before, they certainly were now.

Suddenly I'm hit with a barrage of questions. How do you get to be a rep? Do you not pay for 'owt? You get free food and booze? I do my best to answer the questions, but I don't want to look like I'm showing off, nor that this is an easy life. As time goes on, we share another beer and we start to bond. I can tell instantly who the ringleaders are, everyone is quick to point out who had gotten laid, and who hadn't, and there's some gentle teasing and banter forming. They were from the North. I was from the South, and that also cropped up a few times.

So, basically, they were a rugby squad that were looking to come away together. They originally wanted to go to Greece because it was cheaper, but one of the mums was a travel agent and had managed to snag them a deal to Ibiza. They were staying in a rival tour operator's hotel but, by all accounts, it was pretty tame. Their rep hadn't really sold them a package of entertainment or been around to see them, or done anything really.

Their experience stood in stark contrast to my lot. It's not that they weren't having a good time on their holiday, more that they had just been left to it. As we drank more, everyone started to really relax and we had a great laugh.

At one point, one of the main guys says, "We wish we were in your hotel. You're a great laugh, not like our cow of a rep."

I was flattered, and told them that if they wanted to come out with us, or stop by and party in my hotel, they were more than welcome. I pointed out how to get there, and told them which bars we frequented, so if I saw them out I'd try and chuck them some tickets. They seemed grateful.

While everyone was gelling so nicely, I couldn't help myself. "So, I don't suppose your rep has told you about any weekenders in the UK, has she?"

The rival tour companies all did their own versions of the weekender as it was big business. Fortunately, their rep hadn't gotten round to it yet (or didn't intend to). So, I took the initiative. I explained to them what it was about, how much fun it was, and went through the whole spiel.

By the time I'd finished, I knew that probably two thirds of the group were up for it, but I still had to convince the others. The north-south banter had suddenly become an obstacle, because every time I tried to close the holdouts, they kept teasing that £15 up North was a lot more than down South, and the rest would laugh.

I needed to think quickly. It wasn't the fact that if the entire group signed I'd get a £100. I already had more than that coming to me with my current guests. No, it was the accolades I'd receive. Not only could no one touch me on my current performance in-hotel, but if I then waltzed in having closed this lot, from a rival company, I'd be legendary.

I wanted this sale. I needed it. Time to kick things up a notch.

"Tell you what lads, you seem like good boys, and you're clearly sporting. How about a wager?" They leaned in. "You boys are in the rugby squad, right? So, you have rugby socials and you can drink?"

The mere fact I had dared to even ask such an obvious question provoked sniggering from the whole group.

"How about we have a little drinking competition then. Me against three of your best. Last man standing?"

I could sense the group were interested. "How's that going to work?" asked one of the ringleaders.

I went on to explain that we would buy a few bottles of spirits. We'd go halves on the booze so no one would be drinking for free. We'd keep drinking until people gave up. Last man standing wins. If I win, they pay for the deposits and have the option to go to the weekender. If they win, I pay.

The guys spoke amongst themselves but very quickly

reached agreement. The banter naturally followed. Apparently, I was a southern shandy drinking twat who was going to be paying for them all to go to this big weekender. The stage was set.

Before we agreed to go anywhere, I got the deposit form out. I needed two forms for 20 people as there wasn't enough space. I got everyone to fill in their name and address, and the whole form was filled out except their credit card details. I got one of the guys to agree that we would use his credit card for their payment, and that he would chase the others if I won; my credit card, which I showed them, in case I lost.

Once we were in agreement, we went to the local off licence and bought three bottles of booze. We had tequila, melon schnapps and a hierbas. As much as I hated that shit in a bottle, I knew it might come to my aid. I doubted these boys had ever had it before, so it would be a nice surprise for them. The boys then took me back to their hotel where the competition was due to take place.

I felt nervous as hell walking through the rival's hotel. I took off my rep's tags and just walked in amongst the rest of them. Thankfully they were such a big group, I just blended in with the masses. Even my branded rep's bag didn't give me away.

Once in one of their rooms, I decided to take charge.

"Let's be having you then. Who's got what it takes to challenge the champ?" My arrogance was there for all to see. "Which of you northern monkeys fancies losing to a sexy southerner?"

That was it, it all kicked off, the banter coming thick and fast. Every single one of them wanted to volunteer, but one of the ringleaders called for calm, and three were selected. They all stepped forward, and some chairs were pulled for us all. The rest of the group spread out around the room.

I sized up my competition. The first one was a lump. He was as wide as I was tall. If you'd asked me to bet which one would have been chosen, he would have been my first choice. Despite being relatively young in his rugby career, he already showed signs of a disappearing neck! We'll call him Mr Big.

Next one up was another stocky guy. He was more athletic than lumpy. The sort of person that only has to take a shit in a gym toilet and walk out with a 6-pack. One of nature's naturally fit ones. Doesn't put weight on, great at every sport, etc. We'll call him The Specimen

Finally we have this slim lad. He doesn't look like he belongs in the rugby squad at all. He's all ribs and dick, probably weighs half what I do, but he's tall and lean. Presumably the wing. We'll call him Streaky.

Streaky could be their secret weapon. You know what they say, you can never judge a book by its cover. He could well be like the short and skinny Asian guys who clean up in eating competitions. You know the ones, they're a third of the weight, half the height, and a quarter of the age of the supposed grown-ups in the room, yet they can swallow more hot dogs than Monica Lewinsky on coke. Yeah, I needed to be mindful of him.

I lined up the bottles and we opened them. I asked what they wanted to start with? The Specimen said the schnapps. I opened all three bottles and poured four shots of schnapps.

I repeated the rules. If you can't finish your shot, you're out. If you vomit, you're out. If you pass out, you're out. All shots to be filled to the top, and no one can help anyone else out. These rules might seem obvious to you reading this, but remember, someone's credit card was going to get done for £300 after this, so I didn't want there to be any mistakes.

My plan of attack was simple: I needed to scare these boys into submission. If we did this at a leisurely pace, there was a high chance that one of the three if not all of them might beat me. I didn't have the time, nor the energy to win by attrition. This needed to be psychological warfare. Blitzkrieg!

In Wikipedia, blitzkrieg is described as a surprise attack using a rapid, overwhelming force. Basically, I needed to scare them into submission and get the hell out of there before I fucked myself.

We all took down the first shots. Some of the others slammed their glasses down aggressively in a triumphant display for their team mates. Not me, I was already pouring the next shot. I chose tequila. They were taken aback by my haste.

"Come on lads, stop peacocking, more drinking!" Within ten seconds, the four shot glasses were lined up again. "Cheers!" I threw back the tequila.

At this point, I was pretty much numb to the taste of it, I'd had it that much. But it didn't follow that my drinking companions had endured the same resistance training. Streaky started to pull a face, much to the amusement of his mates. Again, we went. This time hierbas (aka liquid dog shit).

I immediately poured and shot. I didn't even wait for them to finish their own shots when I started refilling mine.

"Bloody 'ell, he's a lunatic," was muttered somewhere in the room.

I just smiled. I didn't want to slow down at all. This was max speed, or "Pooooooower!" as Jeremy Clarkson would holler. Even Mr Big couldn't keep a straight face as the hierbas hit his palette.

"You alright princess?" I teased. He told me to shut up and just pour. "Atta boy!"

And so I poured. And I poured. And I poured.

After about the third round of the three bottles, i.e., shot number nine, The Specimen bailed out.

I'm not sure if it was the fact that he couldn't take the booze, or it was me reminding him that if he continued, he wasn't getting laid because he was going to be a dribbling mess. I suspect a mixture of the two.

One down, two to go.

I needed to try and faze them out. We'd only been going for a couple of minutes, and I knew that once the first shots started to hit, I'd start to slow and my advantage would be lost.

Only one thing for it, double up!

I asked one of the other lads to fetch some more glasses. He did as he was told. For the next pour, we each had two shots. One was always filled with schnapps, the other with either hierbas or tequila.

I was keen to take out the bottle of schnapps, because it was easy to drink and a refreshing change to the two drain cleaners.

The rest of the room started to babble at my new speed. Mr Big asked what I was doing. I told him to shut up and just drink, much to the laughter of his friends. Streaky looked unsure of himself.

"Make up your mind now, long legs, because there's no point you puking if you can't win."

I downed both of the shots in quick succession and began immediately refilling. To his credit, he took them both down, but waved the white flag as soon I refilled his glass.

I started to breathe easier, all that was left was Mr Big. He'd been matching me shot for shot up until now. While he didn't drink as quickly, he hadn't wavered either. Thank-fully, another few rounds and the schnapps was done.

I quickly poured out one of each now. One tequila, one hierbas. I needed to intimidate this big dude and I was worried we might finish the bottles before we got to that point. He was a good 25 to 35kg heavier than me, and that would begin to play a part, despite my perceived training.

I gave some pesetas to one of the lads and told him to go and quickly buy more bottles from the bar downstairs. The whole room cheered. They were enjoying the debacle. I sunk two more shots before he'd even left the room.

Mr Big paused. Bingo.

To quote Darth Vader; I have you now!

"Come on big lad, don't let the side down!"

I couldn't hear his response over the noise his team mates were making. They were bellowing at him to continue. Reluctantly, he took the shots. He turned around to his compatriots and started immediately complaining about the tequila and how it wasn't his drink and, if it was vodka, he'd be better.

By the time he faced front again, he had two shots looking at him and I was refilling my own, having just taken them without him looking.

"Fookin' ell. You're not messing around are you!" he said to me.

"Stop flirting, get drinking," I grinned.

He threw the first one down, but paused at the hierbas. "What is this shit anyway?"

"Spanish absinthe!" I replied, without the blink of an eye. "Get it down you, I'm already waiting."

While he was pondering the choice, I slammed both of mine. I held the shot high above my mouth and kept moving it up and down inverted, as if to take every last drop. I burped at one point and could feel sick in my mouth. I quickly swallowed, lined the shot glasses up and refilled them. I could definitely feel my head cloud over and my senses begin to numb.

This was not good. I still needed to finish him off and get the credit card details before pulling the parachute. So I started to tease Mr Big.

"Come on, soft cock, if you don't finish that and the next two, I've won."

He wasn't budging. He wasn't drinking, but he wasn't giving up. Every one of his mates was shouting at him to drink. He sat there motionless.

I couldn't afford to wait. If I didn't get this done and nip out quickly, I was in trouble. I could tell he was faltering, but couldn't apply enough pressure to get him to tap out.

I banged the other two shots in front of me in quick succession. "Right, I am now five ahead of you. Five. You need to drink that and two more pairs just to be level. You in or out?"

He raised the glass to his lips. His hand shaking, he managed to get about a third of it in, before putting the glass down. "I'm out, you mad bastard."

I was so relieved but my job wasn't done. I still needed the credit card details. I told the lads I had to go as I had a meeting, and thankfully they were decent enough to get their credit card out. I copied it.

One of the group signed both forms and I gave him the carbon copies. I asked to use the loo before I went, and they obliged. As soon as I shut the door, I stuck my fingers down my throat. I was practically masturbating my tonsils. I managed to throw up about 200ml of liquid. Nowhere near enough to undo the damage that would be coming. I did as best I could but needed to leave quickly. I grabbed my bag, thanked the boys for a good afternoon, and told them to stop by the hotel bar tonight.

As I was heading out, the other lad turned up with three bottles of schnapps. He was disappointed to have missed the ending. When he asked what should he do with them, I told him to pour everyone else a shot and enjoy them on me! This went down well, and everyone thanked me again. Now, though, I really needed to get out of there.

I began to feel unsteady on my feet. I managed to make it as far as the hotel reception when I began to feel the vomit building in my stomach. I started to get cramps. I made a dash straight out the hotel and without even looking, bolted straight across the road to the nearest tree. It was like I had tunnel vision. I threw my ring up. This was not just a liquid puke, this was a full on, booze/lunch/breakfast puke, and I had never been so relieved to have thrown up so violently. Not content with one round, I went again, and again.

Thankfully no one else was around to see me turn myself inside out. I quickly left the scene of the crime and walked around the corner. I sat on a bench for a while in an attempt to regain some composure. Thankfully there was a little supermarket just across from me, so I bought myself a ham sandwich and a litre bottle of sprite. I was still feeling the effects, but having removed most of it, began to unwind.

By the time I got to the sales meeting, I was hammered. Not can't walk hammered, but stupid, funny mood, idiot hammered. I skipped into the meeting like it was a playground.

"Where the fuck have you been? Look at the state of you!" Damien was taking no prisoners.

The tension in the room eased, as instead of the rest of the team getting chewed out for not selling, I was about to get royally butt fucked for turning up, five minutes before the end, pissed as a sailor.

Without letting up, Damien went on. "You better have

something for me, or a good reason why you're in this state, otherwise you'll be doing every airport for the rest of the season."

At this point, I stopped smiling and inverted my rep's satchel all over his desk and paperwork.

"Damien, what was my target this week?" I teased, knowing full well I was already at 100% and so there wasn't anything else I could do to it.

Damien, intrigued himself, decided to play along.

"Your target was 70% and you're currently at 100%," he said in a patronising manner.

"Well, what if I told you that I managed to find a few more?" I mused.

"Well, you have 20 on the board this week, so how many more have you got? This better be worth it. You're battered."

I handed him the two forms. Everyone could see there was a long list of names on there.

"There's 20 on here." His expression changed. "Where did you get them from?"

"I just blocked a Twenties hotel," I told him, and sat on Laura's lap, laughing. "I needed to go through a drinking competition to get them. Which is why I might be a tiny bit merry."

Damien was anxiously checking over the paperwork to make sure it was all filled in. Satisfied that it was, his whole demeanour changed. "You are a good lad!"

I wasn't done showboating though. "What percentage is that now?" I asked, knowing full well the answer.

Damien stood up from behind his desk and proudly announced that I was at 200% of my hotel capacity. Before I could do any more damage to his meeting, he told me to go and sleep it off, and asked Laura to cover the hotel bar without me.

I rose from Laura's lap, still a little unsteady, and tried to collect my things from his desk. Laura quickly stood up and shepherded me out the door, telling me she was going to collect my things and promptly put me on a sun lounger outside the office.

Apparently, by the time the meeting had finished a few minutes later, I was dead to the world and snoring like an animal. Everyone decided it was a good idea to let me sleep it off.

Nigel came to wake me a few hours later. It was already dark and the guests were already in the West End!

CHAPTER 18
SHOW US YOUR GIRAFFE

J ess had been gone a week. The twins had gone, and I suddenly found myself in my hotel without a particular interest. I'd yet to get involved with anyone out there, through fear of making a mistake and wanting Jess back.

Although, truth be told, Jess was long gone, and I was feeling happier without her already. Nigel had been begging me to play knock-a-door smash with him. He'd come over to me several times in the space of two or three days, trying to line up some couple swapping and even a random threesome at one point. When I found out the target of his desires I politely declined. She resembled the Honey Monster in a dress.

While he was comical, and at times annoying, he was right. I definitely needed to get back in the game. We had just over six weeks left and I wasn't about to let this season completely pass me by. I'd managed to get a little bit of sleep over the last few nights, so felt relatively well, and had just had some fresh laundry done.

I went over to Nigel's hotel to see how he was doing.

The Pope glared at me as I walked in to find him. He was talking to some guests in reception. I joined them and we all chatted for a few minutes before they went off somewhere. I asked Nigel if he had anything decent in his hotel worth a poke that he hadn't been through already.

"There he is. Welcome back. We've missed you," he replied. I laughed. He then led me to the pool to have a little gander.

His pool was much smaller than ours, and it was much easier to see everyone without you needing to basically patrol the perimeter. We sat down on a table near the edge of the water and began to survey the landscape. Nigel was giving me notes on who was single, who was taken, who he'd had a go at, who he thought would be game, and so on.

One girl walked over to us to say hello. She was cute, with dark shortish hair and an athletic figure. She looked good in her bikini. She asked Nigel something about what time they were due to meet in the club that evening, because her friends were going out for dinner and wanted to meet everyone there afterwards. She acknowledged me and I said "hi". She smiled.

Nigel picked up on that and introduced us. We made small talk for a minute or so before she stood up to leave. As she stood up, she dropped a spray she'd just bought and it began to roll towards the pool. Without thinking I stood up and stopped it from going in with my foot.

No sooner had I picked it up and begun to stand upright, when I felt a crushing force in my ribs and back. I'd been rugby tackled. One of Nigel's guests had caught me perfectly. His weight and momentum carried me clean off my feet and halfway across the pool. I think I even let out an involuntary yelp as the air was forced from my thorax.

I'd been winded. At least my guests had the decency to

tackle me from the side or front. This was a sucker punch. I got myself out and sat on the side. I couldn't really talk as I was trying to get the air back in my lungs, but just gave the lad a thumbs up. He felt bad that he winded me, but it was cool.

Nigel sat there laughing. I gave the spray back to the girl, who asked me if I was okay. I just nodded. I still wasn't quite ready to chat yet. She crouched down and pushed me forward and began to rub my back. I'm not sure if this was truly necessary but it felt good. Nigel gave me a knowing smile.

After a few seconds I thanked her and stood up, dripping wet. Nigel gave the fella who wiped me out an instant four-finger fine and went off to get a long glass of tequila for him. This allowed me a minute to talk to the girl on her own.

"I hope that spray is valuable," I joked.

"Just deodorant, I'm afraid."

"Well, out here that's invaluable. Can't have you kicking up in the club, you'll scare off all the boys."

"It won't make any difference, they're all scared of me anyway."

Here we go. She's got some chat. My interest level was turned up immediately. "Well, maybe you're playing with the wrong ones."

This was complete cheese, but I was out of practice and, considering some knob had just knocked the nuts out of me, it was the best she was going to get.

"Maybe I am." She smiled, unbothered by the corny lines that were escaping my lips.

"Just make sure you use your deodorant, and maybe we can fix you up."

She paused. I wondered if I'd pushed too far. This was the last thing I needed, I was trying to recapture my mojo, a knock here would set me back days. I didn't say another word.

Nigel walked back with a tall glass of tequila for the fly-half wannabe. Just as he approached, she turned to me and said, "I'll see you in the club and I'll wear the spray!" With that she scuttled away.

I was relieved. I thought I'd blown it. I sat back in my chair and watched Nigel bark at this guy to finish his drink. The guy did as he was told, apologised to me again, and then went back into the pool with his mates. They were all laughing at him.

"She seemed nice," I said.

Nigel just looked at me and smiled. "Luke, my friend. I'm going to give that one to you, because you need help and I want to get you back on the horse."

In other words, Nigel fancied a slice but it looked like I might have pipped him to the post.

"That's very kind of you sir. I think I'll take you up on the offer."

I laid my t-shirt and trainers out in the sun to try and dry. Nigel was excited as some of his mates had just confirmed they would be flying out from home to stay with him in a couple of weeks. He was sharing some more war stories from university. These boys were going to have a riot out here.

By the time I went back to the hotel for lunch, I was excited to meet the lads and had forgotten all about the girl at Nigel's place.

Laura was doing some pool entertainment. I wasn't really in the mood. I was more content in trying to dry my trainers out. Every time I took a step they squelched like an old growler getting battered.

We all met up in the hotel bar as per normal. I was feeling ready to party, and pretty soon the place was heaving. We had full attendance in the hotel, so the place was packed. We played a few drinking games including cocktail sticks. This always went down well.

I took several guests from their groups and organised a play off. The aim of the game was simple. We all sat around the table with pints of San Miguel poured and ready. We would then interlink our arms and basically tap our hands in turn going around the table.

The idea was to tap the table when it was your turn, but not lift your hands at all when it wasn't. If you didn't tap when it was your turn, you lost a point, and if you lifted your hand at all when it wasn't your turn, you lost a point too. If someone tapped twice quickly in succession, the direction changed immediately. If someone tapped three times it skipped the guy next to you. It was very funny to watch and quick moving.

Now, when you messed up, you were given a cocktail stick. You had to lightly jab this into your brow, in the fleshy bit between your eyebrow and your forehead. If done correctly, the cocktail stick will stick in there, leaving no mark and not drawing blood. It just sits there, sticking out above your eye line like a cat's whisker. Obviously if you did it too hard, it would be painful and you'd end up with a small war wound.

For every point you lost, you took a cocktail stick to the head. At the end of the round, someone would set light to the other end of the cocktail sticks and you couldn't remove them until you downed your pint.

You have plenty of time to drink because the cocktail stick doesn't burn quickly. The problem is, as you tilt your head back to drink, the flame on the end of the cocktail stick gets closer to your eyes. It's not going to burn anything, but it appears very close, so all you see is flame and feel the heat. It gets people panicking. People think they're going to lose their eyelashes or eyebrows, and they chug that beer down for dear life.

It's very comical to watch. Can you imagine seeing someone sitting there with five burning cocktail sticks poking out of their eyebrows, desperately trying to see off a pint. All the bar would be cheering them on and laughing. We'd do prizes for the fastest, and forfeits for the slowest. It wasn't just the lads playing too, the girls were equally as capable at downing pints and lighting their sticks.

After playing that, we would switch it up a bit and start to play things like Russian Roulette with vodka, hold court for any prior drinking fines that needed to be repaid, or sometimes we'd play spin the bottle, which was always good fun if you wanted things to get a bit spicy.

Once we were done, Laura and I moved the guests on in a single herd and took them to the West End.

We got them into the first bar. Nigel was already there with his guests. I don't think he cared about being the first ones there, he just wanted to dump them off and chase skirt. Laura and I never wanted to be first, because the atmosphere would be inevitably flat for the first arrivals. Far better to bring the guests into a place that already had people there.

I didn't waste any time. "Where is she?" I asked Nigel, still not convinced I hadn't blown it earlier.

"She'll be here, don't worry. She didn't come to the bar," he replied. "Besides, look at everything else that's here."

As I turned around, two of his guests walked past me and smiled, "Hi Nige', hi Luke!" I didn't even know who they were. We just smiled back.

Then another one of his guests walked past me, with legs up to her armpits. "Hey Luke." I looked across at Nigel. I had no clue who she was either.

"What's going on mate?" I was puzzled. He started to laugh.

It turns out, a few of the guests who had been by the pool and on the balconies earlier had seen me get wiped out. A couple of the girls had asked him if I was okay. Nigel seized on the opportunity to then tell them I'd mentioned to him how cute they were, and had been asking after them later in the afternoon. He basically repeated that to most of the girls in his hotel in an effort to jump start my new campaign. I now had randoms smiling and giggling at me.

Bless his balls. I could feel myself grow in confidence. Even if Deodorant Girl doesn't show, someone will be getting to know me tonight. Of course, he didn't tell every girl in his hotel. He had a few he kept for himself, but it was a nice touch to help the Luke relaunch.

He didn't stop there. Next thing you know, he's lined up some guests in a boy, girl, boy, girl sequence and started to play pass the rose. He planted me next to a fit girl with him on the other side of her. By the time the rose came to us, I don't think we even bothered to try and pass it. We basically both snogged her, and then the girls either side of us.

Wasn't just us, either, the guests took our lead and before you knew it, everyone was making out with everyone else. Laura saw this and just shook her head. She knew I'd kept myself under wraps so far and that I was a shadow of my former self last season, so while she might not have approved, I think she was pleased to see me finally relaxing into it. Nigel then asked who wanted to play pass the ice cube, but I think this was a bridge too far, and the line-up started to disperse.

I went over to talk to a couple who were staying in my hotel. They were quite a bit older than all of the other guests. I'd guess he was possibly late 30s, if not 40, and she wasn't much younger. Turns out they had kids at home but were dying to come out and party. The fact they were surrounded by teenagers and young twenty somethings didn't bother them in the slightest. They'd been out every night since they had arrived. Nigel liked them too, he referred to them as Auntie and Uncle. They didn't mind, and in fact I think they found it quite endearing.

The nickname caught on and a few of the guests started to use it. This couple were popular. If there were drinks or dancing to be done, they were right in the epicentre. They bought me a shot. I didn't know what it was, but it looked a nice chemical blue. Perfect, I thought, I'll be passing sapphire turds for the rest of the week. I necked it with them. Curacao. Wasn't the worst taste in the world, but not the first choice to chase down my vodka redbull.

They were having a good time. They'd been laughing about some of the antics the other guests had gotten up to, and she was teasing him about her fancying Nigel. He didn't care, he just thanked me for putting him next to a nice bird to pass on the rose to. I just winked, she dug him in the ribs.

As we were talking, Laura brought over a tray of schnapps. We all took a shot. She took the last and we sank them in unison. Just as we'd finished, a familiar voice appeared behind me.

"You started without me then?"

It was the girl from the pool. I couldn't help myself. "Hello stinker, fancy a drink?"

She bit her lip and shook her head. "Don't you dare start with all that. I'll have whatever you're having, but make mine man size, I need to catch up."

This was music to my ears. "Don't look at me. Nigel's your rep. Nige', get stinker a drink."

Nigel just stood there with Auntie and Uncle, watching

the banter unfold. "I told you don't start with that. You need to get it. I want to see that you're useful."

Uncle started to "woooooo…", but Auntie soon put a stop to things with an elbow to the waist. I smiled and went off to get her a drink. I bought another round of schnapps and brought them back for everyone.

She was disappointed it was schnapps and called me out on it. "Is that it? Thought you could take stronger?"

It was Auntie's turn to get in on the act now. "She has a point?"

I scowled at Auntie. "You can behave yourself. We don't want anyone getting too drunk. Besides, she'll be needing her strength later."

Auntie almost blushed. Uncle stared into the bottom of his drink, smiling, and I shot Stinker a glance.

"We'll see," and with a cheeky smirk she finished her schnapps.

I didn't even have a chance to look at Nigel, when she took my shot out of my hands and finished that too. We all had a laugh about that. Nigel put his hand on my shoulder and whispered "my work is done" before disappearing into the crowd.

I formerly introduced Stinker to Auntie and Uncle. We continued to chat for 20-30 minutes, after which point I got the nod from Laura and we started to round the guests up. We were moving on to Extasis which was a small club next to the Ibiza egg, just a few minutes away from the West End.

Now, this club was a health hazard in every way. There were raised podiums everywhere, a sunken dance floor in the middle, and wholly inadequate ventilation. It would have been the perfect place to hold a weed party, as it was one big hot box. A lot of the reps didn't like this place due to the heat, and due to it being quite claustrophobic in there.

Nigel and I were big fans from our first season. It was easy to get lost in there, and plenty of corners where you could misbehave without being visible. As reps we had to get everyone going, so as soon as we got in the place, we had to head straight to the dance floor and drag a few with us. They'd normally squirm a bit, but within a few minutes the dance floor would be full and people would be partying. Once the floor was full, we could then disappear and mingle at a more relaxed pace.

My guests were having a great time, everyone was dancing and smiling. I bumped into Nigel. He was happy. He'd just lined up a lay back at the hotel and was just biding his time. We shared a beer at the back of the club and started to fool around with some of the nearby guests. We were encouraging them to randomly grab passers-by and to hit them with the lambada, and see how long they could last with the stranger.

Girls were great at this. Any guy that got randomly grabbed by a girl and danced with tended to hang around for a bit. Most of the time when the guys did it, the girl would run a mile. Sometimes they'd stick about and that was that for the night, but most of the time it was a break for the border.

At some point, Stinker and her friend appeared. Her friend had apparently tapped off with one of the guys in a neighbouring hotel the night before and had been spending time with him and his mates. Stinker, however, wanted to spend time with us.

This was fairly standard practice. One of the pair goes one way, but the friend wants to take a different direction. I said hello to her friend, but the friend was clearly preoccupied with what was going on with her beau and his mates.

We'd been talking for literally two minutes when her friend pulled the chute and disappeared into a sea of sweaty bodies on the dance floor. Even if you weren't dancing, the place was so humid, you were sweating like you were anyway. I had a bead on, and Stinker looked flushed. I decided to take the initiative.

I leant in and smelt her. She wasn't expecting to see my beak an inch from her shoulder and recoiled.

"What are you doing?"

I grinned and told her that I was checking the spray I saved in the pool was still working.

"You cheeky bastard." She started to smile. "Well, is it?"

"I couldn't tell, I need more time."

She smiled, grabbed me by the hand and took me on to the dance floor.

Normally, I would have been reluctant to be so close to a guest so publicly, but right then, the stars had aligned. There was no one else in my hotel I was messing with. My sales figures were through the roof. I was newly single and willing, and to top it off, the place was so dark and steamy, you couldn't even tell what was going on from the outside, unless you were right in the thick of it.

We danced and had fun for an hour. Any opportunity I had for a close up, we were pinned to each other. If the DJ decided to even remotely play anything latino, it was an invitation to press up on each other, salsa pose at the ready. I was horny as hell. Any thoughts about behaving professionally went out the window.

She must have been feeling the same. Aside from the random touch ups we were exchanging on the dance floor, it wasn't enough. Eventually, some threshold level was met, and she suddenly stormed off the dance floor clutching my hand. She made a beeline for the bathroom, with me in tow like a parachute at the back of a drag racer.

As we turned the corner, reality hit. The queue for the girls' toilets was spilling out the door. No time to stop now, this was happening.

I pushed her straight past the queue and we made our way over to the opposite side of the bar where the gents' was. She pushed open the door with such force it shook on its hinges. There were a few lads loitering around the urinals, chatting with the guy who was trying to sell them aftershave and chewing gum. She blew past them like something out of a comic book.

We hit a cubicle and it was as much as I could do to lock the door before I felt my belt go, then my zip. She pinned me to the inside of the door and plunged her tongue into my mouth. I pushed her off me and repaid the favour, pinning her to the back of the toilet wall. I lifted her onto the back of the cistern. She had one foot on the seat, the other wrapped around my back. She yanked my trousers down in one go, and stopped to adjust her own outfit. She was sexy as hell, and just looked at me without saying a word.

She got down from the cistern, turned around, hitched her skirt up and leant forward, pushing against the wall. I had to focus so as to not drop the rubber I was rolling on.

Within moments, we were going at it like a couple of drunk teenagers. It was hot, it was rough, and it was loud. We didn't care. I can't even remember who was making the noise, was it her? Was it me? Was it both? After all the stuff that had gone on recently, I needed this.

We were going at it for ages. Totally oblivious as to what was going on around us. Occasionally we would swap round. She would sit on the back of the tank and I'd be standing, straddling the seat, but more often than not we would revert to both standing.

After a while of this, I started to become more aware of

my surroundings. For instance, I hadn't noticed previously that the cubicle doors were saloon doors. Thankfully they were low enough that, unless you were on your knees outside you wouldn't have been able to count the number of pairs of shoes underneath. The wooden slats in the doors were also at such an angle that you couldn't see through them, so we were all covered there. No one could see my little white ass moving like a bee's wing. There was just one caveat.

The height of the doors. If you were six feet or taller and you stood right up to them, you could pretty much see everything. We didn't think about this at the time, nor did we care at the time. It was only when something caught the corner of my eye that I decided to take stock.

I turned my head to the side while I was hanging out the back of her to see Uncle's head above the doors. I was a little taken aback. I looked at him, he looked at me, and he quietly mouthed, "Go on son," while nodding with encouragement.

As much as I appreciated the gesture, I was somewhat preoccupied. Not wanting to let go of her hips, I shook my head and tried to shoo him away with my neck, much the same way an irritable giraffe would fling its head at a competitor or annoying fly.

Uncle could sense I didn't like being disturbed on the job, put his hands up as if to say sorry and disappeared. Stinker was none the wiser. I ploughed on.

Whack, whack, whack…

A few moments later, something in my head told me to turn around again. I did. This time it wasn't just Uncle. He had pulled Auntie into the gents and lifted her up so she could get a good view too.

I couldn't believe it. She gave me a big smile and a thumbs up. The sort of thumbs up you give your 7-year-old on sports day. Again, I appreciated the gesture, but I was knee deep here and needed to concentrate. Last thing I wanted to do was lose wood.

Again, I initiated the annoyed giraffe followed by me pleading with my eyes for privacy. They took the hint and Auntie disappeared below the door line like a submarine blowing its ballast tanks, and Uncle just gave me a double thumbs up. Within seconds they were gone, leaving me to pound in peace.

Post-cuddle, Stinker suddenly became aware and self-conscious that she was in the gents. We both wanted to try and escape with as little notice as possible.

Unbeknownst to us, Uncle and Auntie had arranged a welcome party. They had gathered a few of the gang and had a couple of cold beers waiting. Ignorant to all of this, we'd agreed I would leave first, and then she would follow a few moments after.

As soon as I opened the door to the cubicle, the restrooms were empty. Even Mr Freshen-up was nowhere to be seen. I quickly called her and we left. We both thought we'd gotten away with it.

The moment we left the toilet, dishevelled but relaxed, we could see that we hadn't. Uncle let out an "oi oi!" with such gusto you'd think it was Brandon Block at a Bogota pool party. Everyone tittered. The game was up. Stinker didn't even try to hide it. She sheepishly grabbed the two bottles of San Miguel from Auntie's hands and handed me one of them. We toasted each other, before toasting the group and proceeded to drink.

I didn't mention to Stinker that we'd had an audience earlier; it was my little secret. We would continue to pay each other visits for the remainder of her stay on the white island, but nothing ever quite topped Extasis.

CHAPTER 19

A NIGHT OF FIRSTS

For the next few weeks, I was on fire. Like an eagle, there was a good chance that if it moved, I was interested. Nigel and I were tag teaming in bars and clubs like a couple of wrestlers. If he had a nice one in his hotel, I'd get the shout for the mate, and vice versa. We reverted to our first season antics that had been so effective in '98.

Knock-a-door smash was played with gusto. If anything, we were even more confident than we'd been the season prior. Not only had we more experience under our belts, but more successes. We knew the game, and we both knew how to play.

After about a month post Jess, I think Nigel had basically shagged himself out. He started to tire. There were repeated incidences of us pairing off with friends, only to find out that he'd been unable to perform through drink or fatigue. Either way, it wasn't good. He needed to slow down and catch up on sleep, otherwise there was high chance his season would suffer.

Damien had already moved to a position where he was riding both Nigel and Tony with equal frequency due to lacklustre sales performance in their hotels. As much as Nigel was key to the team, and everyone loved him, he still had a decent sized hotel in resort and questions would start to be asked about the low figures. If they weren't asked of Nigel directly, they'd be asked of Damien, and as we all know, shit rolls downhill.

At one point, I was even going around with Nigel to help him catch up and sell extra tickets to some of the guests that had declined the entertainment packages. I never took the credit for it, handing the paperwork to Nigel to hand in, just so he'd get some breathing room. It didn't make that much of a difference overall, but helping to keep him out of airport duty once or twice a month meant I had a more effective wingman with me.

Eventually, the inevitable happened. Nigel found a girl. I think at some point he'd decided he didn't have the energy to hunt and have sex, so he decided to get involved with one of the female reps and have sex without the hunt part.

While I was disappointed, his decision did make sense. Now, though Nigel wasn't exclusive with his new belle, I don't think he was playing away. He would choose to go back for a quick bonk and then get some sleep. This left me at somewhat of a loose end for a few weeks and so I decided to throw myself into the guests—quite literally.

As soon as the 2am sales meeting was finished, Nigel would head back with Kate, and I would go back into the club or bar. I started to arrange after-parties and then after-after-parties. My alcohol intake increased, and I started to become a bit of a handful at times. I'd find myself in weird places and in various states, sometimes with girls, sometimes on my own.

There was one time in particular which stuck out in my mind. We had a large group in my hotel from Northern Ireland. They were all school friends and had decided to come away for a boys' holiday before they headed off to university. Despite them only being a year or so younger than me, they seemed frightfully naïve and inexperienced.

If there were any scams to be had on tourists, it happened to them. If anyone was to be ripped off in a bar or club it was them. I felt for them a bit. They didn't really have a pot to piss in between them and yet people were taking advantage left, right and centre. They were really good fun though, and so enthusiastic. They had the strongest accents you'd ever heard, and at times even I had to concentrate on what they were saying to each other.

It was cabaret night. We'd taken all the guests on coaches to a venue just outside San Antonio and we'd entertained them for most of the evening. We'd had the adult hypnotist on stage, and half of the group from Northern Ireland had volunteered.

Most of them were sceptical, only to find themselves a few short minutes later crawling around the stage. Half of them thought they were sex slaves in gimp suits, the other half thought they were lizards. By the time they were brought round they couldn't believe it. They had no memory of it. Obviously, with no smartphones or handheld video cameras, the only way they could relive it was to ask the rest of the group who spared no blushes when excitedly informing them of how stupid they'd behaved.

As we finished the final striptease of the show, the girls began to get the groups ready to move. We—the male reps —were getting changed into clubbing gear, while the female reps were beginning the task of filling the coaches. By the time I caught up with the lads, they were already merry, practically singing, and Laura was struggling to contain them. She asked me to help her out, so between us we managed to get them on to a coach headed to San Antonio. At one point, I had to practically lift one of them over my shoulders, much to the amusement of his mates, to get him onto the bus.

By the time we got to the club, the fresh air had hit a few of them and they were all in a pretty sorry state. Predictably, the bouncers at Eden refused some of them entry, meaning none of them were going in. Rather than abandon them, I asked Damien if I could take them back to the hotel to prevent them getting into any bother. He reluctantly agreed and sent Laura with me to help move them on.

As soon as we managed to pick them all up, we started to move them along the sea front back towards the West End. We would have to cross through the strip to get them to the hotel and, as we were walking along the seafront, I asked Laura if she wanted to go home or if she wanted to go to a bar? The reason I asked was because half of the lads were keen to bat on. They assured me they would get the few who had had too much to settle down and fall back into line. Laura agreed. She was a good laugh, and I think she was happy to be away from the others for an evening.

We decided to take them to some lower key places higher up the West End away from our normal haunts. Neither of us wanted to bump into any other reps or be crucified by Damien, and the main bars we frequented were full on, meaning the lads were likely to struggle inside.

As soon as we got into one of the bars the lads began ordering fish bowls. At Laura's insistence, they also ordered a couple of coffees and a few sprites for those that had been struggling. There were two that were particularly bad and unsteady on their feet. We would prevent them from drinking alcohol for an hour so as to help them come round. In actual fact, it was more like two hours, but every time they asked how long did they have left, we would say 20 minutes. They were none the wiser.

Eventually, the plan worked and they regained their coherence and more importantly their coordination. The guys were having a great time. Any girls that happened to walk in a 20m radius found themselves under attack from Belfast charm.

As time went on, the group became more and more mixed. Laura ended up turning in around 2:30am, but for me, well, I was out for the duration! By the time the clock hit 3am, most of the guys had managed a few snogs and we even had a few hangers on that looked like they were going back to the hotel with them afterwards. Normally I would take that as a good result for the guests, but this evening it wasn't enough.

One lad looked particularly glum. When I asked him what the matter was, I was slightly taken back by his response. "I'm alright. I've had a good night and all, but just haven't been able to find a girl."

Before I had a chance to console him or offer to go to a different bar with a fresh set of legs, his mate jumped in. "Aye, he's a virgin. It's his sole mission to lose it this week."

His friend nodded solemnly. "I have to get laid, I have to. I'm not going to university as a virgin. We all made a pact."

As he was telling me, more and more of his mates seemed to gather round and back up the story. A couple of them put their arms around him. It was quite heart-warming really.

That wasn't all. His friend went on, "he's even wearing his special underwear for the occasion." As the words left his lips, his mates within earshot started to laugh. I was intrigued.

"What special underwear? What are you packing?"

"Go on, show him," replied one of the crew.

With that, he pulled his jeans down to reveal a leopard

print elephant g-string, complete with big floppy ears and a pair of googly eyes. I pissed myself laughing. It was the last thing I was expecting. Even this downcast lad started to grin when he saw my reaction. Can you imagine turning up to your cherry popping ceremony wearing a trunk? I instantly admired the impudence of the young buck standing in front of me.

I tried to offer some support. "Don't worry, you've still got tomorrow night! I'll move heaven and earth tomorrow to try and fix you up."

I'd already begun to think in my head who might be a suitor for this young lad.

"No, it will be too late," he said, and I was puzzled. Was there a time constraint on this pact? "Tomorrow is our last night, and we are going to hit it big. We're starting at lunchtime and everyone knows that we'll be too pissed to even talk to girls let alone get laid. It had to be done by tonight."

His wingmen started to murmur, there was agreement in the ranks. One of his boys stepped forward and asked me calmly, "Luke, is there a whorehouse nearby?"

I was surprised at the request. Seldom had people found the need for that in Ibiza, or if they did, they hadn't asked me. I would have been happy to take them there, but given it was going to be his first time, I'd have preferred he got hold of a civilian rather than a professional.

As soon as V-man heard the word whorehouse, his spirits lifted. "Yeah, good idea, just take me to a brothel. That'll fix it."

Again, the rest of the mates were murmuring in agreement like a bunch of Stormont MPs. I confirmed that there was indeed a cat house only a few minutes' walk away from the West End, but their idea was still meeting resistance in my head.

The more we talked about it, the more the boys started to rationalise the idea. V-man was up for it, but having seen the place, I didn't really want to take them there.

In the end, we came to an agreement. I would take them to a couple more bars first, and if nothing materialised, I would take them to see the brasses. They reluctantly agreed. We immediately settled the bill and I took them down to the busy end of the strip.

We walked straight into Koppas, right on the corner. The clock had just turned 3am. Unfortunately, the ratio of guys to girls was about 3:1 meaning Koppas had already peaked. Most of the holidaymakers were already in Es Paradis, Eden, or on their way to the bigger clubs like Amnesia, Privilege, Pacha, etc.

We did an immediate about turn and walked a few metres back up the strip to Simples. If anywhere was going to be busy at this time, it was there. Simples was laid out with a decent sized dance floor, so for anyone too pissed to go to the bigger clubs, or anyone looking to party on, this was always a good shout.

Unfortunately, as soon as we walked in, hopes began to fade. There were slightly more people in here than Koppas, but it seemed like there were even fewer girls. Undeterred, I got the guys to grab a table and we bought a round of drinks. Most of the girls that had been attached to the group had dispersed already, and aside from one pair that looked intent on keeping their men, the group had become very male heavy again.

I grabbed a few of the lads and we did a sweep of the place, looking for any groups of girls that might be worth talking to or introducing V-man to, in case he still had some magic in him. Unfortunately, it was Lichtenstein (nil points).

Dejected, I walked back to the group. All of the lads

were drinking and chatting, but you could tell they were just waiting to go to the brass house. Again, V-man was being comforted and encouraged by the others, and his spirits seemed to perk up.

My offer to go to another bar or even try the club again was immediately and unilaterally declined. One of the lads piped up, "Just take us to the prozzies." Before I had a chance to reply, they started to stand and down their beers.

It still didn't sit right with me, but there were 11 of them, and this had been the most sober they'd seemed since I'd met them on their arrival. They were determined for their comrade to lose his V plates. If I didn't take them to the place I knew, they'd still find a way, and at least I would take them to the one near the hotel, which was actually a functioning place. God knows where a taxi driver would take them, or if they would inadvertently walk into an ambush somewhere.

Reluctantly, I agreed. We left Simples and walked up the strip which seemed to be getting emptier by the minute. We passed the Ship pub, crossed the square, hung a left and down there about 300 yards on the right was the massage parlour. It was actually on the way towards the rep apartments where I'd stayed the year before.

The working girls there were a real mix, with a heavy influence of African nationalities. I knew this because every night I used to walk past them on the way to the hotel and back from the strip, and I would see them and they would proposition me without question. They would recognise me and I would exchange a few comments. Occasionally you'd get one that was offended at me declining "sucky fucky" at seven thirty in the evening.

I was never honest in my response and I think this irritated them. It wasn't that I didn't want to plough. I was in my prime and continually wanted to get knee deep. It's just

I didn't fancy getting horizontal with someone who looked like the north end of a southbound elephant. The term wizard's sleeve wouldn't even do it justice here. There were smaller windsocks at regional airports. That said, the girls knew I was working there, and a few of them still recognised me.

Just before we got to the entrance, V-man was getting encouraged by his band of brothers. They were all chipping in telling him what to do, how to do it, what not to do. You could tell he was a little overwhelmed, but at the same time he was game.

I asked him, "are you sure you want to do this? Are you ready?"

"Luke, my friend. I was born ready. Someone's getting the trunk!" came the response. The team roared. It was like someone had just won the cup. Any thoughts I had of trying to help him cherish his first went out the window. Hell, I was encouraged.

"Attaboy!"

As we piled through the entrance, we were approached by one of the madams. She said it was 2000 pesetas each. There were 11 of them, plus me, plus two girls who were there for the experience. 2000 pesetas was about £10. No way we're giving that.

I played hardball. I told them I was a rep; I was bringing the group in for some drinks and to party. I said one or two want to get involved, but we're not paying a door fee, and frankly we could just go to the other one on the other side of San Antonio. I was bluffing, in that I had no idea where any other whore houses were, but I assumed the taxis did.

I said a couple of the guys wanted to take some girls, the rest of us wanted to drink. She tried to insist, but I wouldn't budge. I called everyone out and we moved towards the exit. She started to swear under her breath in what I assume was French or some other sub-Saharan tongue, but she stopped us from leaving and led us through into this bar and reception area.

V-man's eyes were darting all around the place. You could see he was wired. His mates were all chattering like monkeys in a zoo. As soon as we sat down, they were on us like a pack of wolves. I ordered 12 beers and a couple of bottles of water. They promptly came out, but not quick enough to deter some of the professionals.

Within seconds, half the lads in the group had women of all shapes and sizes on their laps, and I was getting an impromptu massage. It was only when I told my one in Spanish that I was a rep and these were my guests that she let go of me and went to another to try and ply her trade. The girls in our group who looked animated initially were positively uncomfortable after one of the professionals tried to insist that they all go for a threesome. The lads just laughed. The girls politely declined and then sat closer to the table trying to hide themselves from the attention.

The drinks were expensive, but that was par for the course. One of the lads took a quick whip round and paid for them. That at least put the barmaid at ease as she too was hovering around us. V-man was deep in conversation with one of his boys, trying to work out who he liked or what type of girl to ask for. I just sat back and watched the whole episode unfold. The guy, his wingman—the one who was doing most of the talking—stood up and went to talk to one of the girls.

I say girls, she was probably the oldest one there and couldn't have been far from knocking on 50. Clearly she had seen better years. They seemed to be deep in conversation about either the price or which lucky lady was going to get her world rocked by V-man.

At one point, Wingman was gesturing to V-man. V-man stood up to walk over, but as he got halfway across the room he was intercepted. One of the girls literally grabbed him by the hand and let him through an archway. V-man didn't get a chance to protest. He managed half a glance over his shoulder back at the group before he was pulled around a corner! And that was the last we saw of V-man. No one could quite believe how it went down. Like a coiled snake she sat there biding her time. She sensed an opportunity and pounced.

With V-man gone, Wingman's conversation took a different turn. Suddenly, Wingman found himself negotiating not on behalf of his virginal buddy, but himself. A few more moments of conversation and the experienced old madam put her finger to his lip and led him away down the same corridor. Just like that, we're a duo down.

My attention suddenly shifted back to the table. Some of the boys were handing over notes to the girls for the unsolicited lap dances or hand massages they had half-heartedly received. I think some even paid because the others were. Every time someone approached me, they were met with the wagging finger! And not the kind they got paid for!

We waited for a good 20 minutes before some of the group got restless. Morale was starting to take a beating thanks to the extortion that kept being applied to them by the girls from the sub-sahara. They decided to wait outside, along with the two girls who were getting fed up of being invited to a threesome, foursome, fivesome, etc. Fair play to them for sticking it out that long.

I and another chose to wait inside for our pair of deviants. We figured if there was any trouble, it was better to be in there and needing to be chucked out as opposed to outside needing to get back in. To tell you the truth, the security guard looked past his prime and I think half of the professionals there were more intimidating. Despite being pestered to bend over and pay triple the price for more beer, we managed to hang on to our existing ones and draw it out.

A couple of minutes later, they both appeared. Wingman looked sheepish. V-man looked dazed. I'll never forget the look on his face. I asked them both to check they had their wallets and keys on them and that everything was in order there. They both did as they were told and I led everyone out of the house of sin.

As soon as we appeared the chattering outside immediately ceased. The whole group, including myself, were keen to hear how V-man got on. Everyone was firing questions in quick succession.

V-man, still in a post-coital state of mind, struggled to answer them all. Eventually one lad stood tall and hushed the rest up. He brought some order to the babbling boys from Belfast. Rather than have V-man answer questions, he had him retell the story, front to back for everyone, ordering him not to leave out any detail.

As V-man recounted his tale, he seemed to come round and grow in stature as he progressed through the details. By the time he got to the point where he was actually copulating, I think he even used the verb "to smash" which had me chuckle to myself. This kid couldn't smash an egg, let alone a fortysomething old brass in Ibiza. It must have been like a pair of saloon doors. Not to mention it was his first time.

Still, I let him bathe in the limelight. The night belonged to him and as he went on, his friends threw more and more accolades his way. V-man shed not only his moniker that night, but also his innocence.

He was being heartily congratulated by his mates, and

at one point was also receiving the bumps like it was his 13th birthday. He was soaking it all in. He proudly proclaimed he was now ready for university, and that he was going to do some damage. The group grew more raucous with every sentence.

Things began to tail off though, as I led them in the direction of the hotel. It must have been approaching 5am, and the reality that we needed some sleep started to kick in. As we were taking the back roads to the hotel, everyone seemed to go quiet. We'd all had a good night, and it was time to rest and recuperate.

One thing that bothered me though, was Wingman. He'd been strangely silent.

"What happened to you then?" I asked.

Wingman froze. I think he thought he could just pass under the radar without sharing any of his details with the group, but seeing as this was a night of bonding, that wasn't going to happen. Some of the others in the group echoed my request for details. Eventually, Wingman started to talk.

It appears that Wingman had been presented with a full menu of options, starting with full sex, oral sex and then basically an erotic massage, and then just a cheeky handy shandy. I think prices were something like £100, 75, 40 and 15. He'd initially wanted a blow job, and they'd both agreed on it. However, as soon as they were in the room, no sooner had the condom gone on when the crafty old toad claimed she'd hurt her neck and offered the massage instead. When Wingman protested—as much as you can protest with a condom on, inside a whore house—she agreed to refund the difference. Wingman continued.

He expected to then get a massage and the rest of the treatment, but ultimately, had his shoulder rubbed with one hand while getting tugged off with the other. He had been jettisoned from the room along with his shirt, only to hear it being locked behind him. When he tried to inquire about the price difference from what he paid to what he actually received, he was met with a firm, "No refunds," and a "Go away am tired." Wingman had effectively paid £75 for a hand job from the old knacker.

This was hilarious. I wasn't the only one to find this funny either. His mates were creasing up. Even the girls that were still in tow were chuckling between themselves. As if his shame couldn't get any worse, even V-man couldn't resist getting in on the act. "Even I got a blowjob," he proudly proclaimed. Wingman shot him a look of daggers as that comment set the whole group off again.

I could tell Wingman instantly regretted going into the cat house, or at the least, nipping off for a naughty. What happened next though, totally changed the slant of the conversation.

"And that's not all," said V-man, everyone stopping in their tracks to look at him, waiting to hear what was going to come out of his mouth next. We didn't have to wait long.

"…I went down on her!"

The group stopped laughing.

"I beg your pardon?"

"Well, she did me, I thought I had to repay the favour."

Faces around the group started to contort. Just the thought of it made me shudder. The mood of the group changed. Wingman could breathe easy again. Getting conned by the oldest brass was a moot point when faced with V-man's need to muck out. I just kept thinking about all the things he might have caught in his mouth.

As we reached the hotel, I bid them farewell. They thanked me for a good night out and V-man gave me a hug. I jokingly told him to shower and brush his teeth twice. He just laughed. V-man didn't care. He felt like a man and was now ready for university!

I didn't see them surface again until lunch time. They were in a jubilant mood, with V-man looking every bit the picture of triumph. They did indeed carry on as planned, and proceeded to get absolutely plastered during the day. By the time the evening came, half of them didn't even make it out. V-man didn't care though. He'd done the deed and was already waiting for fresher's week!

CHAPTER 20
VOMIT PROVOCATEUR

For the next few weeks, I hardly saw Nigel outside of work. He'd been seeing Kate and I think they were practically living together.

Things out there weren't ordinary. Such was the pace of life, emotions were heightened with timelines and horizons dramatically shortened. Whirlwind holiday romances were started and finished within a fortnight.

This type of time scale wasn't just for the guests, it applied to the reps too. Kate was an attractive girl. It was her first year repping and she'd been doing a great job. She was initially sweet and kind but, as the season wore on, she began to change. Being one of the more attractive girls out there, she would fall out of favour with some of the other female reps, who were, to put it bluntly, jealous. Initially she was getting more attention from the guests, the male reps, the bar owners, even security. She'd already had a brief fling with one of the team but that didn't work out. I think she possibly may have had a cuddle with another, thus giving the necessary ammunition for the other female reps in the team to turn on her.

It won't surprise you to know that usually, by the end of season, most of the female reps ended up having two if not three relationships with other members of the team. Those numbers are probably an underestimate. For me personally, it was the last thing I wanted to do. It would just make things awkward when it would inevitably fold a few weeks after for one reason or another, and I couldn't be doing with the drama. That's not to say I didn't dabble, but it was strictly on a rent-a-length basis.

As the season marched on, what was once a confident and kind persona began to appear bitter and resentful. But I'm not surprised given how cliquey some of the reps could be out there. Kate would share a room with some of them which would only have made it worse.

I think one particular evening, Nigel had caught her crying outside of one of the clubs. He immediately approached her to see what was wrong and to provide comfort, and the pair of them basically ended up having a four hour drunken chat where they put the world to rights. I guess Nigel had been the first rep in a long time who'd been genuinely kind to her, and he had started to uncover some of that happy-go-lucky girl who had first appeared on the island several months prior.

It didn't take long for the pair of them to suddenly end up as cuddle buddies. By all accounts, she'd practically moved herself into his lair, despite his hotelier shouting at the pair of them every time they graced the main entrance of his hotel. Initially Nigel seemed happy. I was pleased for him, even if it did mean that I'd lost my partner in crime.

Our morning updates took a turn though. Whereas before we'd compare notes on who had done what and to whom, his daily report now consisted of how many more hours of sleep he'd had, and how she'd cooked him dinner. This pales in comparison with the week prior where he

would have told me how he got fingered behind the DJ
stand by one of his guests.

Nigel being unavailable as a wing didn't slow me down
in the slightest. As I said before, I was happy for him, but
having lost half the season's fun down to Jess, the last thing
I wanted to do was get back into a relationship. It did mean
though that I needed to change my tactics. Having a couple
of reps drinking and dancing into the early hours then
seeing what was on offer was one thing. They're considered
party animals, but when there's only one of you, well,
rather than seem opportunistic, it just reeks of desperation.

I started to hang out a bit more with some of the bar
staff and the ticket touts who we would see nightly on our
travels through the West End. I got attached to one girl in
particular who worked in one of the bars, Cara. She would
invite me out after work with some of her friends.

Initially, these friends would look down their noses at
me as a rep. To them, I was nothing more than a shepherd.
Herding guests around San Antonio and taking the holiday
makers to lame nights out rather than the big clubs. I could
see their point, I mean, as far as being on the cool scale
goes, I was probably on the same level as a pair of dunga-
rees and a Naf Naf jumper!

That being said, most of them had had some dealings
with reps and appreciated how hard we worked and how
crazy we were. That was another reason why reps and
workers didn't really mix. The workers would finish work
around 1am normally, then would head home to get ready
or would go straight to the big clubs outside San Antonio.
They'd spend the rest of the early hours dancing their bits
off in places like Amnesia, Pacha, Privilege, Space, El
Divino, to name but a few. Thing is, they would skulk back
at 8am, or even later, whereas I had to be at work by then.
They'd be able to roll out of bed at 3 in the afternoon bright

and fresh and ready to go again. There was no way I'd be able to do it.

Cara understood this from the beginning. She was under no illusions either. She knew Nigel and the rest of the team and had witnessed our antics many times over. She knew we were continually misbehaving with the guests and just having fun. Despite her mates always trying to drag her —and by extension, me—to Ibiza Town, we would often just go for a drink or a dance together somewhere smaller and more low-key.

Cara was super cool. She got it. She understood the demands of the job, the temptations and, more importantly, was just looking for some fun herself. I guess when you're spending every evening in the world's largest nightclubs surrounded with ecstasy, speed and God knows what else, it's not the easiest place to actually meet people or have a relaxing one. Besides, she was actually due to go back to the UK shortly, as she had a family holiday booked to go to Australia which she couldn't miss, meaning this whole thing was destined for temporary relationship status. The timing was perfect, and my mid-campaign intermission coincided perfectly with Nigel's hiatus from the cause.

One morning, I was sharing a coffee with Pepe when Nigel walked in for a chat. Pepe immediately invited my reprobate of a mate to join us, finished his espresso and went off to get a coffee for Nigel too. He looked like he needed it.

"What's up with you?" I asked him. He had a face like a slapped ass.

"I think I've got knob rot again," he replied. I started to laugh. Pepe was still over by the bar so he was out of ear shot.

"What's happened now? Kate?"

Nigel then launched into graphic details about how

aggressive Kate was in the sack. Even if Nigel was tired or unable to perform, she'd refuse to leave him alone. It was as if she took it as a personal snub to her attractiveness.

I listened quietly as Nigel revealed that she'd effectively tried to pull him off for approximately 90 minutes before getting frustrated and going to sleep in a mood.

"What's up, weren't you up for it?" I asked.

"No, I was shattered and not in the mood. She's still not speaking to me."

I started to laugh. At which point, Nigel cautiously surveyed the area around himself and then pulled his shorts down to reveal a rather sorry and red raw and sore looking appendage.

"Jesus, was she using sandpaper?" I asked, wincing.

"I don't think that she's working out, Luke," blurted Nigel.

This was a turn up for the books. Being treated like a joystick was only the tip of the iceberg.

"Go on, spill it…" I beckoned him to reveal more.

Nigel continued for what must have been a good solid 5 or 10 minutes. I had no idea that things had deteriorated between them to such a degree, or that he'd been feeling so unsure of himself. Kate had seemingly tried to take over pretty much all aspects of his life. She didn't like the way he was dressing, so whenever she could, she'd go into town on her own and buy him various items of clothing.

She didn't think he was trendy enough and managed to get him to cut his hair into a different style. She insisted on them cooking together rather than grabbing what they could at the various venues and hotels we operated in. This particularly grated on Nigel.

"Why the fuck would I want to cook in Ibiza?"

He needn't say another word. I was completely behind him on that.

"Have you actually spoken to her about this?"

"Well, I've mentioned I quite liked my old clothes but she'd already binned them."

I started to laugh. "Mate, that's one big red flag right there." That wasn't all though.

"She's practically a nymphomaniac, but not in a good way."

I looked at him, puzzled. "What do you mean, not in a good way?"

Nigel explained further. "You know when someone just loves or needs a bonk. You can tell they're really into it, and they're just looking for physical satisfaction? Well, this is different. We're always nailing, but I don't think she wants it that much, she's just paranoid that I'm going to go elsewhere. It feels almost charitable. It's as if she's scared of losing me!"

"She knows that you're not smashing around though, right?" I asked.

"Yeah, but half the time I don't even want to have sex. It's different when it's with the same person."

I nodded. "What are you going to do? You can't continue like this. She'll end up taking the skin off your gherkin."

Nigel laughed. "I think I'm going to have to give her the flick."

For all Nigel's indiscretions and lack of conscience at times, I could tell this was weighing on him. Now seemed like the perfect time to tell him about how much fun I was having with Cara. I started to tease him about how much she let me do, and how she didn't care what I wore, how I looked, whether we cooked, ate in a restaurant or just drank.

"You should try this kind of relationship mate, it's brilliant." Nigel called me a cock and started to laugh.

At this point, Pepe finally came over with his espresso. "Lo siento Señor Nigel! The machine is fucked this morning."

We both laughed.

"That's alright Pepe," said Nigel. "Thank you for the coffee. Are you happy with Luke as your rep? Because I'd be happy to swap with him if you feel he's letting you down in any way shape or form."

Pepe let out a laugh from deep within.

"Shut up Nigel, you rat!" I hissed.

Pepe joked he'd consider it, but only if Nigel could commit to being in a stable relationship with a nice local girl and leave the guests alone. Before Nigel could respond, Pepe winked at me, and disappeared behind the bar.

"I love Pepe. Luke, you have no idea how lucky you are to have him here. You're getting food and drink and having your mates looked after, while my one is working out what poison he can put in my bed that won't be detected by forensics."

It was at this point that Nigel returned to the subject of the inflamed and rather wounded looking member he was nursing in his rep's shorts. "Do you have any cream?" "What, for that? Not sure I have. What exactly is the problem? How long's it been like that for?"

Nigel detailed how he'd had an itchy flute for the past few days and it was getting worse. I couldn't help but smile as I confessed to him that I didn't have any cream that would help him, and that he would have to go and see the Doctor. Not only would that be embarrassing—not that Nigel gave a fuck—but everyone else would soon learn about him and his dirty todger.

Nigel still didn't care. He was oblivious to what people thought or said. For my final twist of the knife, I dug deep.

"Not only that, but people will assume that you caught it from Kate and that she has a dirty Mary hinge."

Bingo. Nigel stopped mid scratch and looked up at me suddenly. "Do you think they'll blame her?"

"Abso-fucking-lutely I do, and she'll think you're even more of an asshole than she does already once you've put her on the train to dumpsville." I knew it was cruel, but I couldn't help myself.

"Ah, don't say that, Luke, she's going to go mad when I tell her."

I didn't let up. "Well, at least you've got an excuse now. You can't be in a relationship where your penis is continually suffering physically."

Nigel started to laugh, before returning this gem. "You're right, it's not fair to the pipe. He just wants to be loved, not battered or attacked with fungus."

"Exacto-mundo, now get yourself down to the clinic, get some Canesten on it, and go and tell her how you're feeling. Every day with her is another day not playing knock-a-door with me!"

Nigel stood up. "You're right, it needs to happen."

With that, he thanked me for the chat, thanked Pepe for the drink, and disappeared out of sight.

"He's a funny one," joked Pepe.

"Yeah, he's the best," I replied.

I didn't see Nigel again until later on that evening. I needed to nip back to my room. We were going to Es Paradis and I had a load of unsold tickets that were given to me by Damien to try and flog on. I'd forgotten them in the apartment and, once I had dropped my lot off into the first bar, I shot back to get them.

This was another nice little earner which helped put us in the limelight. I had maximum attendance on this night. The area as a whole did. Damien would get extra tickets that weren't sold and would hand them to us on the night to try and sell discretely to people heading into the club. Obviously, we didn't want to take the piss directly opposite the door staff, but we would earn commission for every ticket sold which was added directly to our hotel figures. I wasn't taking anything from this personally, but knowing that I could sell most of these meant that the area was doing well which reflected better on Damien, and in turn I could continue to enjoy the soft perks that came with it (i.e. avoiding airports and not sharing my love pad).

I got back to the first bar just before they were all about to move on to the next one. Nigel was somewhere inside. I grabbed Laura and told her that if anyone asked, I'd gone to move these tickets on. I wasn't in the mood for entertaining at that point and wanted to sell the wedge of tickets and turn up like the golden boy at the door. She agreed, but before she left me, she mentioned that Nigel was absolutely battered.

"Really? Is he hammered? Is he sad?" I asked for clarification.

"Yep, he's off his rocker already. He's not sad though, he's having a whale of a time!"

I just smiled. "Look after him until he gets into Es Paradis," and with that I was off.

Technically, I should have been in the bar with my guests, but I fancied a break from it all that particular evening. I knew Damien wouldn't have been impressed, but if I appeared with a good percentage of the tickets sold, I knew I'd get a pass so thought it was worth the risk.

I walked across the seafront area to the small strip of road between the West End and the main approach to Eden and Es Paradis. I took off my rep's tags and tucked the lid of my company record bag into itself so no one could see any logos. I then started to approach groups at random, seeing if they were heading into Es Paradis that evening. I already knew which DJs were playing so it wasn't a difficult spiel.

Fortunately, given the proximity of the clubs to the West End, it was pretty easy to close. You'd ask the groups, are they going clubbing or on the piss? Most would say both. You'd then ask if they're staying local or heading out. Heading out meant going to Ibiza Town (Pacha, El Divino) or towards the airport (Privilege, Amnesia). Most would say local, so it was a simple choice of Eden or Es Paradis?

Hardly anyone had tickets, so I would just discount the face value of the ticket a little and, well, that was that. If you're not bothered which club you go into, or there's a high chance you'll do both if you're drunk enough, why wouldn't you take a discounted ticket? The tickets were all bona fide, printed full colour on decent paper, it's not like I was selling 10p raffle tickets!

I must have sold every ticket I had in a little over an hour. There must have been 60 or 70 of them. Perfect. I then took myself over the road to one of the bars to chill out. I would be able to see the reps and all the guests once they descended on the club. I sat facing the road and relaxed. It was a rare moment when I was on my own and was able to people watch.

I must have been half way through my second San Miguel when I spotted the guests. I paid my tab and finished the beer. If the guests and the reps were en-route, that must mean management were already at the door. They were always there overseeing the entrance and the queues. Presumably to make sure no one was being fiddled on admission stubs, etc.

I managed to get ahead of the crowd and spotted Damien talking to door staff. I managed to catch his attention and pulled him to one side. He was his usual charming self.

"What do you want, numb nuts?"

"You won't be calling me numb nuts when you see what I've got for you."

With that, I opened my bag revealing a couple of grand's worth of pesetas. Damien smiled and nodded approvingly.

"How many tickets you got left?"

"None. I did the lot."

"Seriously?"

"Yep. If you have more, I'll do them too."

Such was my confidence that he told me to wait and called the big man over. They had a few words between themselves and then someone was sent to go and grab another bunch of tickets. It was all done in a very clandestine manner. Not because anyone was stealing, but I guess because the company wasn't supposed to be hawking the tickets they had presumably bought at a discount on the street — they were for our guests only.

That being said, business was business, and within 10 minutes I'd temporarily swapped bags with one of the admin girls. Just before I left, I managed to extract a concession out of Damien. I had effectively 'bought' a pass for the evening. Not only that, but if I sold this new lot, then 'my boyfriend' as Damien liked to call him, was cut loose too. I told Damien that we wanted to chill out for the evening as we were both tired. I thought that was an easier sell than admitting that Nigel was, in all likelihood, blind drunk and liable to throw up on himself and others at any moment.

Off I went to the same stretch of road. Same M.O., ditch the tags, cover the bag. You'd think I was dealing weed the way I was circulating amongst the masses. It was even easier this time round. It was that much later in the evening and any crowds coming in my direction were 90% likely heading to Eden or Es Paradis. Within 30 minutes I'd done the hundred additional tickets I'd been given. I walked back to the door triumphantly.

The admin girl was still there talking to the others, so I casually walked up to her and offered her bag back. Without a word we exchanged bags and I went back over to Damien.

"All done?" he asked.

"Yep, not one left. You got any more?"

I was on a roll. Despite it touching midnight, I wanted to prove I could do more. Damien walked off for another quiet word in the big man's ear. He came back and told me that was enough for tonight. He said that they would make sure I had a proper number of tickets for next week and to keep up the good work. He then politely set me free. To his surprise, I began to head into the club.

"Where are you going? I thought you wanted the evening off?" he asked, bemused.

"I did, but am off to get Nigel."

Damien then remembered that he was part of the deal too. "Ah, forgot. Yeah, he's not in there. He didn't make it."

"What do you mean, didn't make it? Where is he?"

Damien went on to tell me how he'd apparently been thrown out of the last bar for attempting to get naked on the dance floor. One of the other reps took him back to his hotel as he was too much of a liability. He then alluded to the fact he was going to ride him rough like a beach donkey because of it.

I reasoned with Damien that he had some personal stuff going on and that's why he was out of character. I asked if he could go easy on him tomorrow. I then brought up the ticket sales and the smooth performance he was enjoying as a pathetic attempt to plea bargain. Reluctantly he agreed. With that, I made tracks, leaving him to enter the club.

I wanted to find Nigel to check he was okay, given I assumed he'd broken up with Kate. I went to his hotel, much to the disgust of the asshole behind reception. I banged on his door, but no one was answering. I managed to piece together—in between the Pope's venomous denunciations—that Nigel had come back drunk with someone, but had left on his own a short time later.

I went back into the West End. I surveyed a few of our usual haunts and even headed back to my hotel in case he'd somehow ended up there, either sharking or looking for me in his drunken stupor. I saw Pepe, but he just told me he hadn't seen him since this morning.

After another 20 minutes or so of looking, I gave up. I figured he must have copped off with someone and was probably sound asleep by now if he had really been that drunk.

I didn't see Nigel until about 11am the following day. He looked rough. He came to my hotel to tell me what had happened. It didn't take him long to tell me as he couldn't remember much of it.

He hadn't said anything to Kate, as he hadn't found the right time. He said he started drinking with some guests by the pool in the afternoon and had nothing to eat at all. This in turn left him feeling a bit under the weather and why he overdid it on the booze.

He said he just accelerated from there. He didn't even remember getting to Simples bar or why he was trying to take his clothes off on the dance floor. By all accounts, one of the reps had taken him home after he was kicked out of there. They essentially put him on his bed and left him to it.

Nigel said he must have laid there for 20 or 30 minutes but then decided he was horny and decided to go out into the West End to find a friend. He said he didn't really remember what happened next, and appeared to black out for the next hour or so. He said he came round sitting on the rocks outside of Café Del Mar talking with some bohemian hippies before deciding it was time to go home.

He managed to grab a kebab on the walk home as he was starving. Just as he finished it, he bumped into some guests who managed to catch him for a drink. Nigel said he didn't want any more to drink, but didn't exactly want to go home either. He had a couple of beers with them, but eventually needed to pull the cord.

When he got home, Kate was there waiting for him. She wasn't impressed by his state but was glad to see him.

"All I wanted to do was go to bed. I was already starting to feel hungover and I'd had an absolute skinful."

Kate being Kate, she apparently wanted action. Nigel went to the toilet and when he returned to the bedroom, there was Kate with a full set of lingerie on. He told me how fit she looked. Full on suspender belt, stockings, heels, lacy bra and thong. He said no one had ever dressed up for him like that before in his life. In fact, he didn't know anyone that even owned underwear like that. She was like something straight out of Agent Provocateur. He paused.

"Go on," I moaned. "don't stop now you twat! Did you get involved?"

Nigel confessed to feeling guilty, given he knew he was going to do the off, but said at the same time she looked phenomenal. He then detailed how he took off his shirt and approached her. I was hanging off his every word, picturing how she must have looked. Kate was a good-looking girl and I wanted details.

"I planned to kiss the side of her tummy, and then take her bra off. She looked incredible. I didn't want to rush the moment. This was going to be installed in the wank bank for all time! The thing is, as I knelt down in front of her, I came over a bit faint. Almost as if I lost my balance."

I suddenly stopped thinking about Kate naked. "Go on…"

"Well, I thought it would pass, but I felt a bit dizzy, so I tried to style it out and placed my hands either side of her hips. Only she didn't realise I was steadying myself. She thought she was going to get a peck on the moomoo."

I couldn't wait to hear what was about to happen next.

"The problem was; I suddenly felt bubbling in my stomach. By the time I thought I'd better excuse myself, it was already too late. I threw up all over her."

I couldn't believe my ears. "You did what!?"

"I projectile vomited all over her. It must have been the kebab followed by the beers. I couldn't help it. I was devastated."

"You were! What about Kate? What did she do?" I had to hear this next part.

"Well, she started to wretch too. I mean, having your waist and legs washed down with bits of doner and chilli sauce doesn't bode too well for anyone's stomach."

I looked at Nigel. I couldn't fathom what he was telling me. "Wait, did she puke?" I asked.

"I think a little, but am not entirely sure as I was still heaving. She skipped over me to run to the bathroom!"

Nigel rolled his eyes and took a deep breath. He knew this story was shameful, but he also knew it was going to be one he would be telling until the end of time.

"She had a shower and then threw me a mop and bucket. She was furious."

I wasn't surprised.

"She then went to sleep on the sofa, leaving me to clear up all the chunder. By the time I got into bed this morning it was 7am. She was gone when I woke up."

Poor Kate. I did feel for her. I mean, no one deserves that. I also thought it was the sort of experience that might scar a person mentally and permanently. Can you imagine what would go through her mind in the future? Every time she tries on some nice lingerie, every time she's getting intimate with someone, and that person decides to take a trip down south, she's going to be thinking about Nigel and his kebab.

Once the incredulity subsided I started to laugh. Within a few moments, Nigel started too. I told him to look on the bright side: at least he wouldn't have to say anything to her about splitting up, as it was now certain he was being clocked out for that.

"And if she doesn't give you your P45 then you need to propose," I said, "because no other girl in the world is going to put up with that!"

He felt too rough to think about it, but my prediction proved correct. At lunchtime he received a visit from her. She effectively told him it was over. Said they were on different trajectories, wanted to stay friends and so on. She made light of what had happened the night before but then skipped out quickly. By the time he got back to his room to change for the evening, she'd already been through it and had removed all of her belongings. He felt bad for how it went down, but was relieved she'd pulled the plug.

It just so happened that all this coincided with Cara leaving. She was flying out the next day to be with her family. She wouldn't be coming back out to Ibiza this year, as there wouldn't really be much of a season by the time she returned from Oz.

We planned to meet up after work. I'd bought her a little going away gift. It was only something silly. It was a small, handmade Ibiza picture frame. I'd managed to grab a copy of a professional photo that had been taken of us one night when we were out. I popped it into the frame and had it wrapped in paper with a small ribbon. It was only a small thing but she loved it. We shared an evening together and, before she left, we exchanged contact details for when we were both back in the UK.

CHAPTER 21
SHAVEN RAVENS

Another good group of lads who came out to San An' in the summer of '99 were from Brighton.

I remember them well. They were slightly older than the rest of the guests and all were working in the trades. They had a bit more cash to spend, and had a bit more life experience than their peers. They were hilarious, and if they weren't pulling pranks on each other, they were pranking the reps or even other guests. They gladly paid for the trips and made the most of every single opportunity that was put in their direction, whether that was free alcohol or the chance to grab a girl.

There were six of them and they had one goal in mind. To party and get laid as much as possible. They were only out there for a week, but they tried to fit a fortnight's worth of fun into it. They were boisterous, loud but charming. Despite them being a little rough around the edges, they were popular with the other guests.

I could tell these guys were going to be good fun when I first learnt about their self-imposed rules and games. They would play spin the bottle every single morning. Those who were yet to get laid, they had to participate. Those who'd got their nuts in, they were out. Whoever the bottle landed on had their head totally shaved. That person was then effectively out of the game, meaning as the week went on, the number playing got less, and the chance of getting a skinhead increased.

In order to keep your locks, you just had to shag. Not only that, there needed to be confirmation. Either the girl owned up, or there was a witness, etc. This made it more complex. It was well thought out though. They were there for seven days which was essentially six nights, so if none of them managed to pull, they would all essentially be going home looking like an extended Right Said Fred tribute act.

They'd flown in late Saturday night/early Sunday. Rather than hit the hay, they'd immediately gone out for a few drinks. By the time they actually got to any bars though, they were well past the peak and so had returned relatively empty handed. We woke them up a few hours later for the welcome meeting.

They enjoyed it. They agreed to come on the trips and handed over the cash without hesitation and I thought that was that. Along with the other reps that had come to my hotel to introduce themselves, I began to make tracks to move on to the next hotel to present at the next welcome meeting.

Suddenly I was stopped. One of the Brighton lads asked me for an extension lead. Though I was a little surprised, I managed to find one behind the bar. When I asked what it was for, he'd told me it was for spin the bottle. Intrigued, I followed him out to the pool side where the other five were sitting around giggling but anxious.

They all spread out in a circle and asked one of the girls if she would crouch in the middle of it and spin a glass bottle of mineral water. They had their arms around each other's shoulders like a sports team in a huddle. They fell silent as she released the bottle.

As the bottle started to slow, the guys began to make noise. A few short seconds later, it pointed in the direction of one of them.

"Oh, for fuck's sake. I knew it," he complained.

The rest of the group let out a sigh of relief and then began to laugh at the Chosen One. The rest of the pool area, and some of the reps, were bemused to say the least. I asked them what was going on and that was when they told me about their pact.

The Chosen One tried to offer resistance, claiming that last night wasn't a full night and that he should be shown some leniency. The rest just cut him down and dragged a chair over. The ring leader asked the girl if she would do one more thing for them. When she learnt she would be shaving his head, she became reticent. They insisted, and eventually even the chosen one told her it was okay, it had to be done.

She reluctantly agreed, and within a minute half of his hair was gone. The rest of the pool looked on in amusement while the Brighton boys were pissing themselves. Well, all except the chosen one who was feeling nothing but anguish.

Another minute passed and the deed was done. His head looked like it had never seen the sun. It was as pale as Gollum's ass. I immediately advised him to slap some factor 50 on and find a hat, but it fell on deaf ears. The only thing going through the Chosen One's mind was how he was going to get laid with his new, shiny, aerodynamic look and feel.

The ringleader took the girl's hand and kissed it gently. He hammed it up, but it was enough to get a smile out of her. He escorted her back to her sunbed and a couple of the other lads followed.

I could tell they weren't messing about. The other half of the group tidied up the mess and tried to console the newly bald eagle! I didn't have time to hang around as we had another welcome meeting to do, but was really glad they were in my hotel. I was expecting big things from them for the week ahead.

By the time I made it back to my hotel it was the middle of the afternoon. I was tired and hungry. I walked through the reception out to the pool area, put my bag down on a chair and ordered pizza. I wasn't really in the mood for any rep stuff, in fact, I wasn't even in the mood to smash. I just wanted some down time to myself.

As I dropped all my stuff down on the table and emptied my pockets, I was suddenly met with an opportunity. A couple of the Brighton boys were standing close to the pool edge, alongside another couple of lads. They looked like they were talking to some girls across the pool and generally being loud. There were four of them, but they were so close to the edge. It looked like they were going to head out as they had t-shirts on. I tried to ignore it, but I couldn't resist the urge to get them in.

Quietly, I kicked off my trainers and socks, and took off my t-shirt. I made sure I had nothing in my pocket and slowly crept away from the table towards the back of the group. Some of the guests could see what was about to go down, including some of the Brighton boys. I put a finger to my lip to stay silent and they all did as they were told. In fact, one of the Brighton boys asked a question to the group to distract them. As they looked towards him to answer I decided to pounce.

They didn't see me coming. Five or six big strides later and I was upon them. As I took off, I tried to turn myself horizontal, thinking that if my arms would miss the one on the end, my legs wouldn't. By the time I made contact with them, it was at their shoulder height. They all flew in, much to the amusement of the rest of the pool. I of course followed them in, but that was only to be expected.

By the time they'd realised what had hit them, I had already surfaced and was laughing with the rest of the group. They began to laugh too. One of the boys had declared to the group that I'd just opened "an account." Meaning, I would be a target from now on. This made me chuckle as the banter flowed.

We all went to the bar to grab a drink. The lads from Brighton, plus the other two new arrivals whom I had managed to soak, started to fill me in on their plans.

The other two lads were from Guilford and had turned up with the Brighton boys on the same Gatwick flight. Somehow they'd got talking to each other in the airport and had started to get on the piss with them. It looked like the group of six had become eight, although the other two weren't quite ready to commit to spin the bottle, despite being continually encouraged. It didn't stop them from putting the beers away though.

By the time we went out in the evening, the Brighton boys knew everyone in the hotel and had already started to pick up some female attention. The problem was that everybody in the hotel knew if they got laid, they'd get a pass on spin the bottle, and so I think one or two of the girls were holding out on them intentionally.

They had a great first night out. We took them to one of the bigger clubs. They were drinking and dancing and most of them pulled, although no one managed to actually seal the deal. Or at least, wasn't able to prove it.

The following morning the pool was already antici-pating the next round of spin the bottle before the guys had even appeared. I'd already got the extension lead ready, together with the dustpan and brush. Within half an hour, they started to appear. They grabbed another girl from the pool and asked her to do the honours.

As the bottle began to spin, the rest of the pool started to make a wooing noise. The kind of noise you make when the opposition is about to hit a penalty. As the bottle fell on the next member of the group, the pool cheered. Two minutes on and his head was as smooth as a baby's bum. This was really funny to watch. Even Nigel began to pop over to witness this morning ritual.

Some of the reps from nearby hotels had also learnt about the pact and had begun to tell their guests. They said if any of the girls fancied the boys from Brighton, not to sleep with them until the end of the holiday, thinking it would be funny to see them all with shaved heads.

Though if anything, this just earned them notoriety. I'd have girls from other hotels asking me to point out who they were. Whenever this happened, I would literally grab the girls by the hand and lead them directly to the group and force an introduction. As time went on, it would become a big game.

The next evening was basically a carbon copy of the one before. Lots of drinking, dancing, kissing, alas no cigars. The morning after, the third member of the group lost his hair. One half were now bald, the other half yet to succumb to the clippers.

Two of the ring leaders still had full heads of hair. I'll never forget when one of the lads decided it was time to up the ante. He thought some of the girls were holding out, on purpose, just to see them get shaved and it was annoying him. He was a good-looking lad, mixed race, and had a massive personality. What I didn't know was that he also had the equivalent of a third foot! That's right, he was hung like a horse.

On the third day, after his mate had his head shaved, he

proudly announced to the group that he wasn't messing about any more. He asked me to get some scissors and then went off to his room to fetch something. The rest of the boys were laughing. He emerged a few minutes later with a new pair of white swimming shorts in his hands. I handed him some scissors and he proceeded to cut out the inner lining of the shorts.

You see, the inner lining does two things in a pair of trunks. Firstly, it's supposed to make them more comfortable. Some shorts are made of an abrasive material which could chafe. Secondly, they're supposed to keep your junk in one place so you don't suddenly find yourself hanging out the side of them on the sunbed. In a pair of white short swimming trunks, the lining would basically stop his old boy from being seen, both in terms of outline/shape and actual transparency.

Now we have this hero cutting it out. The lads were sniggering as he snipped. Within a minute or so, the guts had been removed from the trunks. All signs of support, cover and comfort had been removed. He handed me back the scissors and headed off to the toilets for a costume swap.

On his return, you wouldn't really notice anything different at first glance. I mean, his shorts were brand new so they were clean and white. You couldn't really see anything. It was when they were wet it would be game over. He suggested a swim, as it was hot, and a couple of the lads agreed. Before he took the plunge, he told us all to look at the girls' faces opposite the pool steps. We all got comfortable, and started to smirk.

We watched the lads as they barrelled into the pool. They swam around for a few minutes, then started to look over. One of the lads started to speak to the girls opposite the steps. This meant they were directly in the line of fire, and at which point Horse decided he'd had enough. He put himself in between the girls and his lads and ascended the steps slowly, smiling at them the whole time.

The girls naturally smiled back, but then one of them noticed the Brighton rock that was being dragged ashore and her eyes couldn't help but stand out on stalks. She even nudged her mate, giving her the heads up that they could both be in danger.

At this point he'd already turned away to play it cool. The rest of the lads, us included, burst out laughing. He walked the whole length of the pool back towards us. Some noticed, others didn't, but if they hadn't seen it, it wouldn't be long before they did.

By the time he was half way towards us I could see what she'd seen. It was ridiculous. The outer white fabric of his shorts was effectively semi-transparent. Not only could you see his length with about 75% clarity, but the fabric was effectively clinging to it. The 25% you couldn't see had effectively been outlined and traced instead. He sat down and started to giggle, still trying to play it cool.

"You better be careful you don't get arrested with that thing," I joked.

"What for? Being nude?" he answered.

"No, carrying with intent," I said. All the lads in the group started to laugh.

"We'll see how long they can hold out for now," he quipped. With that, he ordered a round of beers and went back in the pool to join the others.

My pizza had arrived, so I left them to it. I was looking forward to telling Nigel this one.

I inhaled my pizza within seconds. I didn't have long to wait before we had a sales meeting, so I was going over my paperwork, making sure everything was in order.

The horse came over to me a few times. Initially I

stopped what I was doing to ask what he wanted. He just smiled and told me he was checking that I was okay. Pretty soon it became apparent that he was simply using me as an excuse to get out of the pool again and complete a circuit. It did make me laugh. On the third time, I didn't even bother looking up from my folder.

Just before I had to leave for my meeting, I called him over. I shouted across the pool that I needed him for a moment. He got out of the pool — slowly — and wandered to the table.

As he approached, I said, "I'm off, enjoy your swim!"

He laughed, we bumped fists and then he took his sea snake back to the pool.

At the sales meeting I told Nigel about the white shorts. He found it highly amusing and said that we should reward such ingenuity. I took that to mean that he was basically going to spread the word in his hotel that I had a human python in mine and thus start the campaign to get Horse laid.

We also had something more pressing to discuss. Jack had been fielding requests from some of his guests to try and arrange an inter-hotel football tournament.

Truth be told, I had no interest in doing this, nor had Nigel. Nigel was against any form of physical exertion unless it was shagging, and whenever I wasn't doing the repping bit, I was shagging myself, so to waste an afternoon chasing people up and trying to sort out a football tournament was an unnecessary ball ache.

Thing is, Tony and Frank jumped on the bandwagon immediately. Tony was desperate to do anything to try and help coax a sale out of his guests, and giving them a football match might help soften them up. Frank fancied himself as a bit of a sportsman, and figured if he showed people he could play, it might help his popularity with the guests. Prick.

The girls also said that they would ask their guests, so Nigel and I didn't really have much choice. The girls also thought it would be a nice idea to try and arrange something for those that didn't want to play football, and settled on a boat trip to Formentera. I'd have much preferred to flirt with the guests in the crystal blue waters of Formentera than watch Frank trying to win the ball simply to prove he's not a cunt.

At this point in the season, I had more girls than guys in my hotel, but before I could suggest I would be better suited for Formentera with my guests, Damien weighed in and agreed to the girls' suggestion. Nigel asked if he could go to Formentera and got cut down immediately. I decided to save my bullets and kept quiet.

CHAPTER 22
A WINNING STREAK

I n the bar that evening, we reluctantly started to ask the guests if they fancied a football tournament and, for those who didn't, if they preferred a day out in Formentera instead. Everyone understood it wasn't part of the package, so we'd need to collect some funds on the day for either a contribution to the stadium hire or boat tickets.

Most of my guests opted for Formentera, but the Brighton lads and the rest of the boys who'd attached themselves to Club Anaconda were up for the footy. The reps would be putting forward a list of names and rooms to the other reps responsible for organising the events that evening. Jack was on the footy, Emma was sorting the boat trip. Nigel was split fairly evenly, so he would have more guests to entertain at the football than I would.

The following day, Laura arrived around 9:30 and began to collect all the guests going to Formentera. She had around 30 of her lot in tow already and took a further 30 from mine. I think a few of the lads saw the light when they started to see just how many girls would be there and quickly swapped from football to Formentera. Something Nigel and I really wanted to do too.

After a few last-second wake ups they were gone. The hotel felt instantly empty. Most of the lads were out on the piss the night before and were still asleep. Even the Brighton boys hadn't surfaced yet for their daily bottle spin. The football was due to kick off at 11:30 and was only a 15 minute walk, so everyone still had plenty of time.

I was in reception swapping posters and flight schedules when a rather petite but attractive girl hurried past me. I didn't recognise her and assumed it was the walk of shame. Undeterred, I proceeded to ask her how she was and if she'd had a good night. She couldn't even look me in the eye.

I found the whole thing funny. But it was only when the Brighton Boa followed out and said he'd catch up with her later did the penny drop. She'd been on the receiving end of it. Poor girl. As soon as she was out of earshot, I asked him, "don't tell me she took the Brighton rock?"

He put his hand on my shoulder, looked me in the eye and said, "Luke, she loved it. I was magnificent."

I started to laugh.

"You coming?" he asked.

"Coming? Coming where?"

"To shave someone's head of course!"

I'd completely forgotten.

The length was sitting relaxed as he'd got laid, and because the lads had all heard it he had received the full certification. One of the other lads got close but no cigar. Three of them had already been sheared, and with the rattlesnake already earning a pass, it meant that spinning the bottle was now between just two of them. The Guild-ford lads who had attached themselves to the group were still refusing to join in, believing their chances of smashing were higher with hair than without.

There weren't many people left to witness this, so they got on with it without any pomp or ceremony. I spun the bottle, and Horse wielded the clippers. Two minutes later and the fourth member of the group was doing his best Moby impression.

Once all the tittering had subsided, they retired to some sun loungers and chilled for an hour before it was time to leave for football.

We left the hotel as a team of about 13-14 strong. Nigel's hotel was en route, so as agreed prior, we went to Nigel where we met him and his guests.

Nige was vocal in wishing he could have gone to Formentera instead. While I shared the sentiment, I kept that to myself. He had about twice as many lads as I did, and they all seemed keen to have a kick about.

As soon as we were all together, the lads started to chat to each other and the banter followed. Nigel made a beeline for the Brighton boys and confessed to Horse he was impressed with his resourcefulness. Horse wasn't quite sure how to take it initially, but soon warmed to Nigel and they were laughing like a pair of school girls within minutes.

As we walked to the stadium, the sun was belting down. It was hot as hell. Most of the guests were hungover so we thought it would be a good idea to organise a quick whip round. Once we'd collected some cash, Nigel and I went into a mini supermarket and came out with as many drinks as we could carry. Mainly a mix of bottled water and electrolyte filled drinks, Lucozade, etc.

We kept some of the cash back as we were going to get beers for the guys after, but didn't want to get them right then otherwise they'd be warm within half an hour.

By the time we got to the stadium, you could see the rest of the guests were already huddled under some shade. The stadium had a full-sized pitch, but was tired. The surface was closer to hay than grass, but it would do.

You could see the guests watching ours refresh themselves with cold drinks. When they asked where we got them, one of my lot said Luke and Nigel got them for us. This made me chuckle. It's not like we actually paid for them, but it was enough for them to look less fondly at their own reps for not thinking ahead.

Frank was dressed in a Rangers top and shorts. I think he only supported them as they'd won the league the season before. He was stretching and looked like a bell end. Nigel started to wolf whistle at him and, with some of his guests immediately joining in, Frank looked less than impressed, choosing to focus on touching his toes instead.

A short while later, Jack arrived with between 30 and 40 of his guests. It was a good turn out, to be fair, but all this meant was that we had a lot of customers to accommodate.

Jack stepped up and started to organise teams. It was loosely arranged by hotel, but as some hotels had more than others, pretty soon people just formed their own.

There were three subs per team, and each match would be two halves of ten minutes. One team would play in t-shirts, the other in skins (i.e. topless).

We must have had about 12 teams in total. What it meant in reality was that, in an hour, there could be only three matches, so six teams would play, the others left sweating their nuts off and scavenging for shade.

Right from the off, Nigel and I decided we would take absolutely no part in playing football at all. We chose to shout abuse from the sidelines and to get to know the guests. Despite it being hot, the atmosphere was chilled and a lot of the guests were happy to relax and get to know each other too. Everyone was swapping stories and general banter with each other.

As the first teams started to play, it became apparent that people were going to need liquids. I arranged another whip round and grabbed a handful of guests to come with me to help carry back drinks.

We walked back to the mini supermarket where I promptly bought them out of all mineral water, Lucozade, and anything that looked even remotely hydrating.

I also told them to stock the fridges with cold beer and that we'd be back shortly. I wasn't sure the supervisor believed me, but I waved my reps tag and told him we had 150 brits playing football. He agreed and ordered his underlings to fill the refrigerators.

By the time we left, we had just about enough to give everyone a drink. We returned to the stadium only to have the bags emptied within seconds.

As the teams continued to play, more and more people were struggling with the heat. I think Nigel, Tony and Jack did a drinks dash. The only one not to do it was Frank.

Frank was more interested in playing football or refereeing. Nigel and I seized on the opportunity to do some stirring.

"Why's your rep not getting you lot drinks?" Nigel asked the group from his hotel. "He did get you some beers on the way over here though, right?"

Horse piped up, "Yeah, we all had a few cold ones just before we got here. Luke had told us it would be hot. Nigel even brought us some snacks."

Good lad. He could tell Frank was a tool and we were stirring, so was happy to get in on the act.

One of Frank's lads said, "He didn't give us shit. He's a tight bastard."

My eyes widened intentionally. "You're kidding me? He probably hasn't organised the burgers and beers for half time either, has he?"

His other guests started to all pay attention. "What beers? No one said 'owt about burgers?"

Nigel chimed in again. "All the reps were supposed to look after their guests and arrange for drinks and a bite to eat. We took some small contributions from everyone, but we've laid on beers and burgers at half time for our hotels. We're getting the beers, it's our way of saying thank you to the guests. I guess Frank must have another plan in his mind."

Our guests knew we were on the wind up, but Frank's didn't. One by one, you could see the group start to get rattled, as if they were missing out, or they'd been somehow cheated by Frank. Some even started to abuse him from the side-lines.

"Where's my beer, ya tight bastard?"

"You better have sorted burgers, you lazy fucker."

"What's for lunch, Frank?"

Nigel and I started to giggle. Frank was irritated at being distracted.

Rather than pause for a moment, he just shouted back, "Nothing's arranged, it's up to you to sort yourselves."

With that, he kept playing.

Another of the Brighton boys stepped up, "That's poor form. What a wanker!"

He too knew we were pulling their legs, and found it amusing to play along. "Don't worry, our reps will look after you."

It was funny. Yeah, it was a bit cruel to set Frank up

like that, but after hearing him boast about this and that every single meeting, we didn't feel too bad about doing it.

Sensing some of the guests were beginning to get restless, Nigel and I decided it was time to get the beers in. We took a whip round again from everyone, and I grabbed another bunch of guests to help me carry.

I went back to the supermarket as promised and saw the supervisor. He couldn't have been more helpful. We promptly bought every single beer he had in the fridges, and he found some boxes for us to carry them in. I think he was pleased. He asked if I would be back tomorrow, and I felt bad telling him that this was a one off but, if we do football again, I'd give him advanced notice.

We were greeted like heroes on our return. Everyone dived into the bags again. This time we managed to get enough for everybody, and even held enough back for those that were playing on the fields.

Nigel had thought ahead and had brought a couple of bottles of schnapps with him. He got those out and started to play various games with the guests, dishing out shots whenever someone made an error. That was good fun, but pretty soon we were out of booze again.

Undeterred, we took yet another collection and this time a couple of groups split the cash and went on the scavenge. Within half an hour we had bought two more small shops out of beer. We couldn't physically get enough beer to buy, meaning we had money left over. Rather than redistribute it, Nigel came up with a good idea.

"Why don't we organise a little competition?" he said. "Let's do a race around the pitch naked. The first one to get back wins the pot?"

Everyone started to laugh.

"Does that sound like a plan? Or do you all want your small bit of change back?"

No one wanted to get the equivalent of a pound back, or whatever it was, but people weren't exactly volunteering either.

"Come on, someone must fancy the pot?"

Nigel looked down. There must have been £120 in pesetas there.

I immediately looked to Horse and the Brighton bunch. "Let's be having you, Brighton!"

The lads backed out immediately. Even Horse wasn't up for it. I couldn't understand it. He'd been so intent on hanging it out all day, every day, all around the pool, but here he could actually get paid for it, and had inexplicably gone shy. I continued to tease them.

"What's up, you worried someone else is bigger?"

Four freshly shaved heads started to bob up and down with laughter.

"Come on lads don't let me down! What about Frank's boys? Any of you fancy a go?"

Everyone just looked down at their feet. Nigel and I started to rib the groups.

"Frank, you up for a naked race?" Nigel hollered over.

Frank had just come off the pitch, looking red as a beetroot and was about as enthusiastic as a death row inmate. "Get ta fuck," was his reply.

Nigel was about to bait him when someone in the crowd challenged us to do it.

"You guys race, if you're not chicken."

This comment was immediately followed by an encore of agreement. It was like a lazy parliament session.

"OK. We will, if you guys are too shy."

Nigel looked over at me. I was already undoing the knot on my shorts. I counted the money out and handed it to Jack for safe keeping.

We decided on the start and finish line directly next to

where the crowd were standing. Nigel and I pulled our shorts down like it was the most natural thing in the world.

Nigel was wearing a kind of sports sandal. If you can imagine Nike sponsoring Jesus, this would have been the sort of footwear you could expect. I had trainers on, so immediately I had the upper hand.

We were both standing there, stark bollock naked, surrounded by 100-150 lads.

"Anyone else fancy trying for the pot?"

The lads stayed silent.

"Reps? Fancy winning the cash for your guests?"

They declined. I turned to my lot and said, "If I win, beers are on me!"

They all started to smile back. Shortly after, they started to encourage me. Horse was leading the charge. He shouted out, "Smash him, Luke."

We both looked at each other and glanced back at him. "Umm, not in that way," he quickly added. Everyone started to laugh, ourselves included.

Jack stepped up to count us down.

On your marks… get set… go.

We were off. We went as quickly as we could. It must have been ridiculous to watch. Two hairy arses bobbing in the sun and a couple of pricks bouncing with every stride. I can't tell you how free and easy it felt being totally naked aside from footwear. Streaking was a revelation!

It was neck and neck—pun not intended—for the first two turns, but then Nigel started to tire. At this point, his hotel started to scream at him to go faster. This gave him a boost. Truth is, I had plenty left in the tank and was merely toying with him. I wanted it to look more of a race.

As we got to the last turn, I was ahead by a few metres. Both our hotels started to cheer us on. Even the other lads were whistling and hollering at us. I swiftly powered away, leaving Nigel eating my dust. Moments later I crossed the line and the race was over.

We were both panting like animals. It was hot as hell. One of the lads handed us a beer to share, and Jack wandered over to hand me the cash. I gave the cash immediately to Horse and asked him to get as many beers as he could find. He and the group left to go grab some.

We both put our shorts back on and slumped down, ribbing each other about the race. Nigel said I cheated. I was teasing him. I was trying not to make him look bad.

The rest of the group continued playing football. Half an hour later the boys returned with more beers. They had only managed to find about 50.

I distributed them to my hotel guests and gave the rest to Nigel. He then dished them out to his lot. We had another 12 or so left, and it was decided to give them to the winners of the football. The remaining funds were returned to me. It was about 30-40 quid.

I tried to distribute it to my guests, but they kept declining, telling me it was fair that I should keep it as I'd won. Eventually we settled on a compromise. I told them I would put it behind the bar for them later.

The rest of the hotel guests looked on as our guests drank San Miguel. You could tell they wanted in. I think Frank's guests even started to wind him up about not running the race and winning beers for them. This made Nigel and I smile. We sat back and continued to cool down in the shade.

Inevitably, as time went on, the boys started to fade. Some had played two or three games and were flaking under the remorseless Mediterranean sun. Others were sheltering in the shade, but they too were beginning to tire. My guys had already decided they couldn't be bothered to play football anymore and were more intent on chasing skirt or drinking.

Suited me fine. I caught Nigel's attention and told him of the upcoming mutiny I was about to start. Before I could even ask if he was in too, he called his lot over. I wanted to do this on the quiet and just slip away so as not to provoke the wrath of the other reps. I thought we could do it in a nicer way.

Nigel had different ideas. "Right, you lot, what do you want to do? Stay here, sweat your bollocks off to watch or play football with a bunch of hot sweaty men, or do you want to come with us on the piss and find some girls?"

As you can imagine, the word "girls" was repeated back to him about 25 times in quick succession.

"That decides it. Let's go."

We didn't even bother to tell the other reps, we just started to head out towards the exit. When asked where we were going by some of the other guests, one from Nigel's hotel said, "Beers and a minge hunt."

"Sounds like a plan."

He and his mate immediately walked across to join us.

Next thing you know, about 20 more were following and others were considering it.

This now represented something of a problem. We wanted to hit the beach bars, but initially there were 30-35 of us, so we'd pick the quietest one and just take it over. Now we were closer to 60. We needed to re-evaluate.

In the end we decided to press on and stick with the original plan. We figured Café del mar or Mambo's could take us and, if there was overspill, we could all sit on the rocks in front of them.

We started to move off, much to the protests of the others. We just said the guests were tired and wanted to chill. We told them where we were going and left.

We travelled along the narrow streets as one big group. We were expecting the Guardia Civil to appear, but thankfully it was daylight and, much like the rest of Ibiza, they don't work when the sun is up.

We moved through the West End like locusts. Any shop selling beer would have its shelves stripped. Nigel hurried ahead to try and organise something in terms of seating and an area for everyone.

It turned out that Savannahs was the best choice. Nigel also knew the guys there as they often worked with us. Savannahs wasn't particularly busy and there were only a few couples having a bite to eat, and they looked like they would be finished soon. By the time I arrived with the group, the tables had been cleaned and 20-30 beers had been placed out on the tables. The staff were hurrying to pull more out.

We were having a great time as we drank our way through Savannah's inventory. Everyone was mixing and bonding. Every time an attractive girl walked past... scratch that. Any time any girl walked past, she would be clapped. Most laughed, some blushed and hurried on, some actually sat down with us.

By the time the rest of the group caught up with us, everyone was pretty pissed and waiting to watch the sunset as was customary in the bars along this strip. Frank, Jack and Tony turned up with some of their guests, but there was hardly any room left. They ended up sitting in front, on the rocks.

The other issue was that, because we'd effectively monopolised the restaurant, the wait for anyone else to get drinks was long. We'd effectively told the waiters and waitresses to just keep them coming and that we would drink whatever they brought out. We would divide the tab along the tables. The other guests and the reps were getting irritated at not getting served. Pretty soon they left to go else-where while we enjoyed a boozy sunset.

Once the sun had gone down, everyone paid up and we left for our hotels in order to get ready. Everyone was pretty pissed, including Nigel and myself.

While we'd all been together as a group, Nigel and I had begun to discuss war stories about the UK weekender. We were laughing and joking about it, and naturally people started to ask what was it about.

Before you knew it, Nigel and I had pitched to pretty much the whole group. They loved the idea of it. We told them it was just a deposit they were risking and that they could decide in October whether they could afford it and still wanted to go. Guests were realising that it was effec-tively a free option, to which we agreed.

Once we got to the hotels, pretty much everyone dived in for a swim. I was thrown in, any guy or girl in the surrounding area was thrown in, and the party continued.

One group of lads asked me if they could book on the weekender. This was music to my ears. I got out of the pool and started to draw up the paperwork. Three signed up there and then.

While I had the paperwork out, I shouted across to Horse if he and the lads were coming, as these guys had just signed up.

"Count us in," came the response.

"Guildford, you in too?"

Horse replied for them, although they were quick to agree. Within the space of about five minutes I had eleven people done and dusted.

There was only one pair left who hadn't signed. I approached them in a calm manner. "Hey guys, just checking while I still have all the paperwork out, you guys coming back for the weekender? You're the only two that haven't done the deposit, that is of course if you're interested."

"Is that the weekend you and Nigel were talking about where you basically drink and get laid?"

"Yep. Not sure I can really sell the idea any more than that."

"Yeah, we're on."

Bingo. Full house. Every lad that I had out with me paid up and signed on the line.

By the time I got to the meeting with Damien, I was tipsy. Nigel was in a similar state. Damien looked less than impressed, but before he had a chance to cane us, Frank decided he wanted to give a run down to Damien about the football.

He said how many guests he and Jack had managed to take along, and how Nigel and I basically mutinied half way through. I sat silent allowing this little shit more rope to hang himself with. Nigel followed my lead. With every pop he took at us, he effectively put another coil around his own neck.

When he'd finished whining like a bitch, Damien looked at us and asked, was this true?

I placed completed weekender booking forms on the desk in front of him. "I took 13 people to the football, that's 13 people signed right there i.e. 100%. Nigel?"

"Me? I took 22 to the football, and there's 16 on the forms. The rest said they'll sort it tonight in the bar."

I think Nigel had surprised himself. Damien changed tact. "How many reunions did you sell today, Frank?"

Frank tried to back pedal with some story, but Damien wasn't having any of it.

"How many?"

"None, but I have…"

Damien interrupted him. "Maybe you should focus more on your own performance first."

Frank didn't say anything. If I was a better man, I would have kept quiet and took the moral high ground. Thing is, I wasn't. I wanted to teach this dick a lesson.

"Frank, Nigel and I were talking with your lads. The two lads from Manchester want to go on it, and also the five from Huddersfield. They're keen too." I stopped there, thinking that was enough.

Nigel, ever my wingman, decided he wasn't just going to fuck Frank, he was going to tuck his back wheels in too. "Yeah, they seemed dead keen. Also, your two from Devon. They were asking us how to sign up. They went on it last year and were surprised no one had mentioned it to them."

That was as subtle as a skeleton wanking in a biscuit tin. Damien was almost beside himself.

"Frank, what the fuck are you doing over there?"

Nigel sat there with a big innocent look on his forehead. What you couldn't see was him fist bumping me under the table. Frank was trying to defend himself, but it was falling on deaf ears.

Damien had heard enough. Out came the usual threat. "If you don't get these guys booked on the reunion, I'll be sending Luke and Nigel in. If they close any that you couldn't, I'll bang you like a broken drum! Are we clear?"

Frank cut his losses and just nodded. Damien moved on to the others. Their numbers weren't particularly stellar either, but because they hadn't been trying to snitch on us, he let them off.

By the time the meeting was finished, Nigel and I were practically untouchable. Frank left in a huff without saying a word.

We went back to our respective hotels to get ready for the night ahead. By all accounts, the guests who'd been to

Formentera had had a really nice, relaxing day, and so were refreshed and ready to party. Most of the guys who had spent the day with us hadn't stopped partying, so there were bound to be fireworks ahead.

What made it extra special was that out of the Brighton six, four had shaved their heads already. Horse had his pass, leaving only one guy left. If he didn't get laid tonight, he was getting clippered.

Despite them having another night left, there was no one else he could play against when spinning the bottle. The whole hotel knew it. The girls in the hotel were already teasing him about it. He decided to play it differently.

Rather than wait for the inevitable shearing and risk being teased again, he decided to do it himself. He surprised everyone by waltzing into the room like something out of the marine corp. He got a full round of applause and we all toasted him.

You could sense the pressure was off the group now. A couple of the boys had already begun to pair off with a few girls in the hotel, so romance was beginning to blossom.

If anything, the pressure fell back on Horse. Given he was the only one without a shaved head, the others started to lean on him to join them. He wasn't having any of it though. Well, at least not initially.

I started asking girls if he'd be more attractive with a shaved head or not in front of him. The girls naturally said yes, even if they didn't believe it. After about the tenth girl said he'd look sexier with a shaved head, it got to him.

We had already moved out of the hotel bar towards the strip when he suddenly made his excuses and doubled back. He emerged 20 minutes later a shaven raven. He'd joined the gang. Regardless of whether he actually preferred it or not, the process and the reception he received from his mates gave him such a boost.

That night the whole group did very well! They were pulling left, right and centre. A couple of the lads even nipped off early for cuddles. I saw Horse kiss a couple of different girls before we'd even made it into the club.

Once in Eden, I saw him lock on to one cute girl he'd had his eye on. Before you knew it, he was making a quiet exit out of the side also. I guess she developed a thing for Brighton rock, because she ended up spending most of the next day with him, including their last night!

CHAPTER 23

ZOO LIFE

One of the best days out we would lay on for the guests was an all-day dance event in the hills of Benimussa, in an old abandoned zoo. We would invite the larger named DJs to the event and it always pulled in a big crowd. Every fortnight we would have the likes of Brandon Block, Alex P, Tall Paul, Roy the Roach, Sash — I think we even had Carl Cox and Judge Jules there once, but don't quote me on that.

Anyway, this day was decent and sold itself. Our sister company also sold tickets to this event, so by the time the big day actually arrived, we would have thousands in attendance. It was also one of the most glamorous events we did. All the guests would show up, and we would bus them in, done up and looking their best.

Initially it was always a bit of a struggle. We would leave just after lunch, but most people wouldn't have eaten properly as they were getting ready. They would be hungry, maybe even a little tired. It would always be roasting hot too. So to begin with, people weren't up for dancing, choosing instead to find shade where they could and generally chilling out.

The reps were no different. The last thing I wanted was to be called to an empty dance floor at 2pm in the afternoon and told to dance, or at least encourage the guests to. I learnt early on to wear black. It might have been less heat reflective but it stopped me from looking like a sweat-drenched pervert at the same time. I would always mention this to the guests I liked, and conveniently forget to tell those who were getting on my tits.

All the reps would scatter like mice and hide to avoid dance duty. Given the location was an old zoo, it meant there were lots of areas and paths you could get lost in. It was the perfect place to hide from management, and it was the perfect hunting ground too. You could normally shark amongst the girls without fear of getting caught or management hoisting you out.

And though a fantastic day out, it was also a long day out. A lot of the reps would need pick me ups at various points throughout the event. This normally took the form of a vodka-Red Bull which was the poison of choice at the time, but sometimes it would be something more chemical.

I always stayed away from drugs. Not because of some inherent fear I would suddenly drop dead if I took a pill or snorted a line of coke. It was because I was an absolute weapon on alcohol, and lord only knows how bad I would be if I became chemically assisted as well! I may have been a permanent skirt hound on booze, but I was also careful.

Careful not to upset anyone. Careful in terms of bagging up. Careful to always be kind and respectful. Who's to say I would retain those qualities after a gram or two, or whether I'd be the first one raw dogging anything remotely resembling a female, bare back? In an abandoned animal park?

Before you know it, I could have nostrils like a pair of

afterburners and spots on my cock making it look like an angry Mr Blobby. I couldn't risk it. Plus, it was hard enough to wake up day after day during peak season. If you throw a comedown into the mix, I could just see it all turning to shit. I had a good thing going on here and the last thing I needed was to fuck this up by getting on the powder. In fact, to this day, I've never tried any of it. The closest I've come to a chemical rush was a packet of Haribo Tangfastics followed by a lemon bonbon!

Not everyone applied the same logic and some of the reps would partake. You could always tell which ones did, as they would stick together at Sundance and try to disappear somewhere together. To be honest, I never knew who exactly was serving them up, but just occasionally you'd spot someone with a frosty lip or an overactive jaw.

Some of the guests were definitely on it. Within an hour of touching down at the venue, you'd begin to see them on the dance floor, gnawing at something invisible like a confused rat while swinging their arms in circles. If they'd been at the Colombian, they'd be striding around with their chests out, or just standing there, bold as brass, feet pointing out at 45 degrees giving sermons to randoms as they walked past.

I wasn't one to judge—after all, this was their holiday and their day. If they chose to get on the skittles or partake in the talc', who was I to stop them? The only thing I did object to was them not knowing their limits or forgetting to pace themselves. I guess with drugs it's always harder to tell how strong something is. That said, you'd think it would be prudent to take it easy i.e. topping yourself up, bit by bit, on your journey to Valhalla. I mean, you wouldn't expect Tony Montana to grab a fistful of cocaine in the opening credits, right?

Predictably, time flew and by the time the sun began to

set, most of the guests had been on it since lunchtime. There were always going to be casualties of war but sometimes the guests got involved in a big way. I'm talking about groups munching bags of pills before they'd even gotten off the coach. It was ridiculous. What this meant was that when the guests inevitably started to overheat after only half an hour, you'd be called up to sit with them and nurse them back to normality.

There was a main area, where there were medical facilities and a bar where you could get them sprite or water, but it was nowhere near where the party was. If you were unlucky enough to have the cookie monster in your hotel, it usually meant you were missing out on a fair bit of the party!

It wasn't just the drugs either. Many of the guests would simply overdo it on the sauce and would dehydrate themselves. Normally they just needed to sleep it off, so you'd give them a few pints of water, maybe a coffee, then find a tree to park them under. Sometimes they'd be throwing up and you'd need to take them to the medical area. You would encourage them to chunder as much as possible, give them some water, and then find a place they could recover.

Sometimes the guests would require proper medical assistance. This nearly always meant you'd need to go in the little ambulance with them to the hospital. You would have to attend to the guest initially, wait while the orderlies arrive and then together you'd all head back into the local clinic or hospital. Thankfully, throughout all my time there, there weren't any serious casualties at this event. Those that overdid it, usually just ended up getting a stomach pump or a couple of bags of saline pumped into them. Even the slightest piece of medical assistance though, meant you would be chewing through reams of paperwork once you got there. We would wait for him/her to be treated, then either take them back to the hotel or leave them there to rest/recuperate further.

Most of the time, if one of the guests was going for medical treatment, a friend would go with them, but not always. A couple of times I had it where the friend didn't want to go because they were having too much of a good time. Though I understood the motive, it did mean more work for us because we would have to normally stay longer there. This was sometimes grating, because despite the warnings we would give, our festivals would be effectively cancelled because someone thought they'd try and make a name for themselves on the party circuit.

On the whole, the ambulances didn't like taking anyone other than the patient and the rep. They'd occasionally allow a second guest, but that was it and it depended on the driver. Anyone else and they needed to take a taxi. I guess it was for insurance reasons or simply that the less people in the back, the less that could go wrong.

On occasion, if the patient was on their own, I would grab my cuddle interest and, if she was happy to leave, would pretend she was the girlfriend of the guy who needed the hangover drip. She'd put on some emotion, they'd reluctantly agree, and she'd file into the ambulance alongside me. We'd all be whisked back into San Antonio to the main clinic.

On arrival, she would stay with the guest while I would plough through the paperwork. Once the guest was treated, he would be either released or put to rest. Once the patient was in the clinic, they were given treatment immediately, so within 15-20 minutes they would normally be sleeping it off already, or would be throwing up into a bowl being held by a nonchalant nurse. This meant we would then be free to enjoy each other for the rest of the afternoon and early evening. Everyone else would be none the wiser. The hotels were like ghost towns on Sundance day as everyone was at the venue, so there were hardly any witnesses.

I remember one Sundance in particular. It was peak season. Nigel and I were on fire. We'd had a fantastic cabaret the night before, and both of us had a good bunch of guests and plenty of options for adult entertainment.

I remember getting to the venue and immediately getting collared by Damien for dance duty. I was less than impressed. I intended to do some damage that afternoon, and the last thing I wanted to be was dripping wet with sweat after 15 minutes. Thankfully I wasn't the only one, and it wasn't long before Damien was called away for some reason or another.

I immediately clocked him disappear. I stopped dancing and went to talk to Nigel instead. While talking to Nigel, he introduced me to some girls who were staying at his hotel. They were both cute and were being playful with the pair of us. We were all flirting outrageously and having a good time.

Suddenly, I felt something move in my back pocket. As I put my hand into the rear of my jeans, it became apparent that someone had put a room key in my pocket. I didn't want to interrupt the flow of banter between the four of us, so I left it there. I didn't break contact or look around at all. I didn't know who had done it, but figured they'd let me know soon enough.

Eventually, the two girls left us and I was conversing with Nigel when another girl came up to us to say hello.

"I don't suppose anyone's handed in any keys, have they?" she asked with a mischievous smile, looking directly at me.

I'd noticed her at various events that week but she wasn't in my hotel. Her name was Phillipa, or Pippa for short. We'd shared a couple of light conversations, but nothing to warrant a key drop. Or so I thought. Nigel didn't even bother to look at her face and just continued to stare at her body. He kept quiet, waiting for me to respond.

"You don't mean these, do you?" I said, pulling them from my rear pocket.

"Oh yeah, they're mine, where did you find them?" she asked.

Saving her blushes, I just told her I'd found them near the dance floor. She played coy and muttered some corny line like, "However will I repay you?"

I mean, okay, so the script was straight out of Pornhub, but it was highly effective. I was enthused. She had mousey blonde hair, almost amber in parts, and a nice smile with an absolutely cracking figure. I wanted to play it cool, even though I was aroused merely at my thoughts. I just told her that we'd work it out and smiled. She gave me a peck on the cheek and with that was off.

"Luke, you're going to be up to your nuts in guts this evening!" I nearly spat out my drink. This was classic Nigel.

I just replied, "That's affirmative, Big Daddy."

We then turned our attention to a couple of blondes who were by the dance floor. Every time we looked over they started to giggle between them. We had been on their case all week. I'd already been with the shorter of the two. Her name was Carly and she was fit. She had a small frame but was busty and had sporty but toned legs. I'm talking dance instructor level fit, not shot put!

Nigel had previously attempted to roll on to her mate, but for one reason or another didn't seal the deal. I liked my one, she was quirky with a good sense of humour. We decided to roll with it and approached them to see how they were doing. Pretty soon, we were heading off away from the dance floor towards a quieter area of the zoo.

Towards the back there was a raised swimming pool surrounded by some kind of amphitheatre seating. In its previous life it would have been used for various animal or reptile shows, but those days had long passed.

Nigel and I split the girls up. He started to walk past the pool while I took a seat with Carly and surveyed the area, looking for other guests or reps. We were all on our own. Carly and I started to make out almost immediately and I didn't even stop to see what Nigel was doing.

Pretty soon things started to intensify. We stopped at one point, looking to see if anyone was around us as things went a bit further, but thankfully we remained on our own. Nigel and the friend were at this point making their way towards a small patch of woodland. There was a copse of sloping olive trees and some foliage which could afford you some privacy if you were happy for a roll in the bushes.

Thankfully, as we were already by the pool, I knew a place where we could get some privacy of our own. Underneath the raised concrete, out of sight from the seating area, there was an old wooden slatted door that was kept shut not by a lock but rotting hinges. It was effectively wedged shut. I'd been told about this place in my first year by one of the seniors but kept it to myself.

I pulled on the handle with a sharp tug. The door sprang free, scraping along the concrete floor as it moved. We both went inside, and again the door scraped behind us as I pushed it shut.

The room was dimly lit and crammed full of maintenance parts and pipework. On one side there was the boiler and filtration system. It was covered in a thick layer of dust and looked like it hadn't been touched in years. On the opposite side there were stacks of wooden chairs and a rickety old table leaning up against a wall. It, too, looked like it hadn't seen human interaction for ages.

I quickly surveyed the table, but there was no way it would support our weight. The concrete floor was covered with dust so neither of us would have wanted a tumble there. I could already feel second thoughts were beginning to creep in, so quickly grabbed her again and continued to make out. I didn't want to lose the moment.

At this point, we were both horny. I broke away, grabbed one of the wooden chairs off the top of the stack, and put it in the centre of the room. I sat down on the chair and she instinctively followed. Another minute or so of kissing and wandering hands and we were on. She stood up and removed her thong. I instinctively undid my belt and jeans and raised my ass off this makeshift wooden throne just long enough to pull them down. With adequate protection applied, she lowered herself back down on top of me.

I won't lie, it was uncomfortable as hell. This rickety old wooden chair was unforgiving on my back and backside. She was half squatting, half standing around it. It didn't matter. Comfort takes a back seat when you're on fire.

At one point she suddenly froze. I asked her, what was wrong? She said she thought she'd heard someone. I leant sideways around her and scanned the room. The door was firmly jammed shut. I told her it was in her head. I wanted to continue. There could have been a brass band marching past the door playing Abide With Me and I would have sworn blind the entire place was deserted.

She stopped moving completely and held me still as she surveyed the risk. Satisfied that no one was in the room with us, inside or outside, she slowly started to continue again. We then began to build up a steady rhythm.

Things were proceeding nicely when, all of a sudden, she stopped dead again. Much to my annoyance she was once again convinced she'd heard something.

I started to doubt the whole thing. I didn't know what

was going on in her head. She seemed to be enjoying it, and had been a willing participant, but I think she was paranoid about getting caught in the act. Frankly I didn't give a shit about getting caught. We weren't making any noise, and besides, hardly anyone knew about this place and the vast majority of the guests were over by the main dance floor where the DJs were.

I convinced her again that we were alone and again we continued to get back into it. She'd actually moved position slightly and was kneeling on top of the chair seat, either side of my thighs. It definitely suited her better, and as we began to get a pace on, once more she began to relax into it.

Another couple of minutes and we were hammering away. Not only had she forgotten about the random noises, but she too gave up on any concerns about being heard or being caught. She began to moan and ride harder. Sensing she'd picked up the pace, I too began to relax in anticipation of the finish line. It was at that moment, when we both least expected it, that it happened.

One minute she was on top of me grinding against my chopper with total teenage abandon, and the next there was a huge cracking noise as our wooden love lounger finally gave up the ghost. The chair just fell to pieces, like something out of a cartoon.

All four legs gave way under our weight at the same time, choosing to splay outwards in opposite directions. She was still sitting on my lap, but I was now sitting on the floor with my legs outstretched. I'd fallen back on my elbows so, if anything, she was even more comfortable than before.

I was thankful that we'd collapsed as we had. She had been on a down stroke, but had she been on the up, or if one of the legs had stayed or we'd fallen to the side, she could have landed on me awkwardly and broken my cock. It makes me shudder to think about it even now. I just laughed, desperately wanting to continue, but she was totally spooked and got off me immediately.

I quickly surveyed downstairs to check everything was in order. I was still standing to attention, and there was no blood, which I figured would not have been the case if there was any tissue damage.

As she straightened herself up and stood up, she noticed she'd picked up a war wound herself. On the inside of her right thigh she had this huge splinter. It must have been about four or five centimetres long. The top centimetre or so was sticking out, but you could clearly see the remainder laying underneath the skin. She began to focus on it, wincing.

I remained seated on the floor and pulled her towards me, asking to have a look at the splinter. There was a small amount of blood but I think it was the thought that was more painful than the splinter itself.

She started to freak out. I asked her to remain still while I had a closer inspection. She started to panic that I was going to make it worse. I told her, relax, I was just going to look at it. I slowly and gently pinched and tugged at the exposed end of the wooden shard. I looked up at her and asked if it hurt.

She opened her mouth to respond, but before she had a chance to make a sound, I yanked the splinter out in one quick motion. She let out a small involuntary yelp before inspecting the skin to make sure it was all gone. It was. She rubbed her hand over the region several times and there was no pain at all, just a small mark where it had broken the skin earlier.

At this point, I tried to continue with what we'd been doing previously but was met with an instant cock block. I rose to my feet, my undies still down by my knees, and despite protests was told it was over. Our dalliance would need to be concluded some other time.

As if to make matters worse, we heard a voice in the distance which really put the panic on. She pulled her knickers up, adjusted her dress, and simply bolted. She didn't even wait for me to get dressed and lose the mini windsock. I wasn't offended by it, but was frustrated as hell.

On emerging from the pool house, I looked for Nigel but he'd already cleared off somewhere. There wasn't a soul in sight. If I was horny before, I was absolutely gagging now, but knew there was no chance of luring Carly back.

I moped off to the main area where all the guests were. I was sulking. I looked around for Nigel to tell him what had happened when someone caught my eye. It was Pippa. She was smiling at me from across the dance floor and beckoned me over to join her. I made my way through the crowd and got to where her and her friends were dancing. The DJ had decided to play a more garage style set, opting to keep the trancey, hands-in-the-air style Ibiza bangers for later that evening. The stars had aligned!

As Pippa twisted and teased in front of me, I started to get the demons. I danced right up behind her, allowing her to tease me, and she kept looking back at me, laughing. I seized the initiative and pushed right up behind her, effectively parking my lunch box in her rear. She could clearly feel that I was hot to trot, the question was, was she?

I leant in and with about the same creativity as she'd shown me earlier with corny lines, I asked her if she fancied a cuddle. She stopped dancing and turned to face me. The reaction was a familiar one.

"A cuddle?" she quizzed.

I leant in again and whispered, "Yeah, an adult cuddle."

She started to smile. With that, I said "follow me" and left the dance floor.

I didn't look back once. I headed to the pool house again, taking the long way round to avoid bumping into Carly or her mates. It was only when I got near to the pool did it occur to look behind me and, sure enough, there was Pippa. She just grinned. I dragged open the pool house door again and went inside. Seconds later she followed me. I closed the door behind us.

This time it was different. There were no niceties. No encouragement or persuasion needed. Pippa and I launched at one another as soon as I let go of the door handle. When we weren't kissing, she was talking dirty to me. There was a complete, incautious urgency this time around.

I kicked the chair and broken legs out of the way and made my way towards the rest of the stacked chairs. I needn't have bothered. I had turned my back on Pippa for a moment to lift another wooden death trap off the stack before she'd loosened her clothing and hitched up her dress. Without saying a word, she turned around and leant against the boiler. I couldn't believe my luck. All thoughts of running the chair gauntlet were immediately abandoned.

By the time we got back to the masses, both of us looked dishevelled. She went one way, I went the other to avoid suspicion. As soon as she got back to her mates, they all started giggling. I ordered myself the largest vodka Red Bull the barman could make without blushing, and started to refuel myself.

It was while I was at the bar talking to some of the guests that Nigel suddenly appeared. He looked especially pleased with himself. He told me that he'd managed to grab a cuddle with Carly's mate, despite her having a boyfriend at home. I'd assumed Carly had a boyfriend at home too. I didn't directly ask, and she didn't directly mention it, but you could just tell.

Apparently, Nigel had used us as an example of how her mate should let her hair down on holiday. He'd even used that gem of a line, "What happens on tour, stays on tour!" Whatever he'd said to her, it must have worked. I told Nigel what had happened to me and he couldn't believe it. I was all shagged out. I finished the first drink before quickly ordering a second. The pressure was off. It was time to drink and be merry with the rest of the guests.

It was a little bit awkward that night, as I was bouncing between the pair of them. Carly, despite abandoning me, still wanted to conclude what we started. I was playing hard to get. Initially I was wary of getting too close, in case Pippa saw, but eventually alcohol got the better of me and I was flirting and grinding with anyone and anything in the blast radius. Pippa would see it, but she'd just smile and continue having fun with her own friends and other guests from the hotel.

As the night went on, the drinking intensified. By the time Nigel and I left the club, we were ruined. Somehow, I managed to make it back to Carly's where we continued what we had previously started. That's not to say that I then left Pippa high and dry. She and I continued to make more memories over the next week or so of her holiday.

CHAPTER 24
FRANK THE PRANK

As I mentioned in Ibiza '98, pranking was commonplace throughout the hotels in Ibiza. People would be smurfed (i.e. coloured in), shaved, tied up, stripped and whipped. You name it, it happened. But it wasn't always the guests who were in play. Many of the reps also partook. Sometimes with the guests, other times without. There were several examples of reps getting pranked big time. Escapades ranged from soft but annoying to harsh and devastating. You had to keep your wits around you. You could fall victim at any time.

I already documented in my first book, and in great detail, how a group of girls had loaded Rice Krispies into my Gary Glitter while I was asleep. Well, I wasn't the only one to have my ass played with while out for the count.

At one point in the season, some of the female reps decided to try and throw a bit of a wine party back at their apartment. For one reason or another, everyone was finishing slightly early that day and, rather than hit the West End on the piss, they decided they wanted a break and to open a few bottles of wine instead. As soon as it was mentioned, nearly every female rep in San Antonio wanted to attend. If there were female reps there, then soon enough the males would follow.

Not all of us though. Frankly speaking, spending a night surrounded by reps in one apartment guzzling Rioja wasn't my idea of fun. When reps got together, it often became too competitive. Someone would relive an experience or tell a story, but then everyone else would clamber over each other to show that they had an even more outrageous story, or who got drunk the most, or who had the worst experience and so on. It wasn't exactly relaxing. Besides, there was also a fair amount of jealousy within the various teams. As time went on, people would become more cliquey. Some would fall out of favour and get bullied. Unfortunately, in this time of extreme highs and lows, emotional responses were magnified.

Nigel and I intended to go to the apartment, just later on. We were happy to shark amongst the guests for a bit and to have fun with them. Jack and Tony were happy to join us and we stayed out on the piss. The reps meeting was done and dusted by 12:30, and most headed off to the apartments, fetching cheap bottles of plonk along the way. Our merry band of horn dogs went back into the club.

By the time the clock hit 2am we were pissed. Someone had orchestrated a kissing competition and between us I think we'd managed to get nearly every guest in the bar to French kiss everyone else. It was a true feat. At one point, even Nigel managed to stick one on the barmaid who was watching with great intrigue.

By the time we left, just before 3am, we were crabbing. One step forward, two steps to the left, two steps to the right. Rinse and repeat. We got to the apartment and, somewhat predictable, the reps had been deep in conversation, boasting and arguing. Most of them resembled The Joker, with red wine stains on the edges of their lips, others looked like extras from a KISS concert, with dark, wine-stained tongues. Some were asleep in chairs, some were on the terrace trying to calm down or be comforted after what I can only imagine would have been some kind of verbal onslaught.

The fact that we'd arrived loaded and happy was in stark contrast to the rest of the group. We were as welcome as lions in a deer enclosure. To make matters worse, we hadn't brought any alcohol with us. Thankfully, I don't like wine, so my boozing stopped there. Nigel looked like he was about to pass out, so he wasn't interested in continuing either, but Jack and Tony managed to find some red and practically poured themselves half a pint each, much to the girls' disgust. The atmosphere felt pretty toxic. I didn't know what had gone down, but it was a far cry from the snog-a-thon we'd engineered in Koppas an hour previously.

The conversations continued, and both Nigel and I sat in the corner and started to discuss what the plan of action was for the coming weeks. Nigel still had his mates from the UK due out, and he was telling me about some of their heroics from back home. Tony and Jack continued to guzzle anything they could find in a bottle. I think at one point, Tony even started to minesweep, i.e. any glass left unattended was fair game and he'd finish that off too.

After about half an hour, the reps were beginning to turn in. As more and more of them started to leave, a space opened up on the sofa. Tony immediately filled the void and promptly passed out. I looked across at Jack who was asleep in a chair, snoring like a wounded camel. The pair of them were well and truly sozzled. Frank, whom we had done our best to avoid, suddenly decided he was going to prank the pair of them.

Both Tony and Jack were practically comatose. Both

were snoring heavily. Frank, with the help of the girls, gently undid Jack's belt and somehow managed to pull down his jeans to his ankles, while leaving his boxers somehow covered. They left him like that. The girls were tittering as they did it.

Next it was time for Tony. Tony was laying face down. One of the girls reached under him and undid his jeans. She moved with such speed and efficiency you'd have thought she was a cat burglar in her previous vocation. Frank ever so slightly tugged down Tony's jeans and boxers, leaving his little peach looking up at everyone in the room. He then proceeded to pull out a condom and unroll it, asking for a pencil, chopstick or something thin, together with some milk. Much to the girl's horror, he tipped a little bit of milk into the johnny and with a straw carefully poked the latex sock just in between Tony's cheeks. He then tipped a few splashes of milk on the back of his jeans.

Once done, he cleared everyone out. People were laughing as they left. The idea was that Tony and Jack would wake up and think that they'd had a go on each other, without remembering it. As they were the only guys in the apartment, and the hosts were all female, there was no one else it could really be. This was an incredibly cruel joke. Too much for Nigel and I to carry out, but neither of us wanted to go against the flow.

Within minutes, Nigel and I were kicked out. As neither of us lived by the apartments this season, we decided it would be easier to play Knock-a-door smash in my hotel than walk back across the strip. As we walked across we both agreed that the joke was indeed a stretch too far, but we remained somewhat optimistic about the chance of Frank getting a smack in the mouth for it from either Tony or Jack. By the time we got to my hotel it was touching 4:30am. We were both rat-arsed and tired. We quickly found a pair of girls who took pity on us and promptly passed out on their couch. The only thing we got horizontal with was each other, top to tail on their sofa.

We overslept and woke up some 40 minutes later than we should have. We were already used to cutting it fine, because every possible minute of sleep counted out there, but it left no margin for error. Nigel was already in Damien's bad books due to sales figures, and I'd already overslept a couple of times in the last few weeks and didn't want Damien tearing me a new one.

We shot out of the hotel like something out of a cartoon. I had an emergency pair of shorts in reception, but as my apartment was closer than Nigel's, I chucked them to him and I grabbed a pair from my balcony. We were five minutes late by the time we got to the meeting.

Apparently, I still had the folds of the pillow across my face. Laura and Emma were already there, nursing red wine hangovers. Frank arrived a minute or so after us, with Damien arriving a minute or so after him. Tony and Jack were nowhere to be seen. Damien asked, had anyone seen them this morning? Frank quipped that the last time he saw them, they were together. He promptly started to giggle to himself, leaving Damien somewhat confused. Neither of the girls made any reaction, and I think they were more focused on the throbbing headaches they were both experiencing. Damien started the meeting anyway, detailing the itinerary for the following few days as well as hotel targets and figures.

By the time Jack and Tony turned up, the meeting was nearly finished. They both looked like shit. Damien decided to lay into the pair of them, but it didn't even register. They both looked at the floor in silence. Sensing something might have happened, Damien changed tack.

"Are you girls ok? Something happened?"

Neither of them said anything. Frank was sniggering, and even the girls seemed to be smirking. Sensing something was clearly amiss, Damien left it there and finished the meeting. He hung around for a few minutes, making himself available in case anyone wanted to chat.

Neither of them wanted to. Frank asked if they were okay after telling them they both looked like shit. Emma offered them both a sachet of aspirin which they both gratefully accepted and immediately poured into their bottles of water. After listening to the girls complain about their hangovers for another minute or so, we all left to go back to our respective units. On the way out, Nigel and I were debating on what had gone down that morning, when either one of them had woken up, and whether they'd discussed it or pretended like nothing had happened.

Tony and Jack had both got on well and bonded over the season. They also had gotten on pretty well with Frank, what with them all starting out at the same time. I wondered if this would damage their friendship but Nigel started to laugh. I asked him what was funny. He told me that if he was going to get done in the bum, he would be honoured if it was by me. I started to chuckle, replying that if I did shag him, he couldn't add it to his "list" and would be a notch for me.

I left him at the corner. He went home for a shower, I went to the pool instead. It was quicker and more efficient. I was always rugby tackled into the pool within a few seconds of me arriving anyway, but I was always able to order my breakfast just beforehand!

As the day wore on, everyone had forgotten about the prank. Everyone except Jack and Tony, that is.

The next time everyone was together again was on the bar crawl. We'd all assembled towards the back of the bar. Nearly everyone was looking human again after their red wine indulgence. Tony and Jack still weren't really saying anything. Frank asked the pair of them why they were looking so down. They both shrugged. Neither of them wanted to volunteer anything. Frank, of course, didn't let up.

"Tony, what's the matter mate, you look like you've been fucked in the ass without any lube? You're in Ibiza, lighten up."

Tony immediately changed his stature. "What the fuck is that supposed to mean, Frank?" Frank had clearly pushed the right button. Tony now stood tall, his posture instantly changing. Frank tried to back pedal.

"I'm just saying, look where we are, why are you looking so miserable?"

Jack intervened. "Cut it out, Frank!"

Frank started to laugh, which irritated Tony all the more. Frank quipped, "No need to be so touchy, you pair of fairies."

Jack told him to fuck off. Tony started squaring up towards Frank, his emotions started to show through. It was at this point that Laura stepped in.

"Calm down, guys. It was just a joke. Frank, tell them!"

Frank was too busy laughing to hear her properly. Laura insisted once more. Tony looked like he was about to either blow a valve or throw a punch, possibly both.

Frank came clean. He was pissing himself with laughter. He didn't even come close to apologising. He was revelling in it. You could see and feel the relief roll over the pair of them. Jack looked like someone had lifted a 50kg weight from his shoulders. Grateful to find out that he didn't smash his mate's back doors in. He looked across at Tony.

It took Tony a few seconds to register that he hadn't actually been ploughed by his teammate. He looked across at Emma and Laura, who both looked back with a look of regret that they'd allowed it to get this far. Next thing you know, Tony lashed out and smacked Frank straight in the side of the jaw.

You could hear the noise of fist connecting with face above the music. Frank recoiled immediately, nearly falling into the guests behind him. Tony immediately walked out, with Jack following closely behind him. Frank didn't see that coming.

Nigel and I just tapped our beers together. We'd been leaning against the bar watching the whole episode unfold. Laura checked Frank was okay, but no one had any real sympathy for him. The girls stood around awkwardly, clearly remorseful for not stopping things sooner.

Some of the guests who'd witnessed the punch started to come forward and check everyone was well. Some were looking to defend Frank. Others were coming down on the side of Tony. Obviously, none of the guests were in the loop about what happened, and we weren't about to tell anyone. Nigel and I moved off the bar to diffuse everything and put it all down to a big disagreement. We got the guests some shots and herded them back on to the dance floor.

Frank spent pretty much the rest of the evening explaining to people what had happened, and how he didn't mean for it to get out of hand. Jack and Tony decided they were effectively off duty. If Damien wanted to pull them up on it, so be it. They figured Frank would come off worse if it all came out, meaning Damien would be forced to reprimand him, possibly even formally.

Nigel and I continued to work and look after the guests. I felt a bit guilty that I didn't do anything either to stop the prank initially, or at least to try and end it earlier in the day, but there were going to be more people in the firing line ahead of us, so I didn't feel too bad. Besides, seeing Frank get smacked and become the pariah was immensely satisfying.

Jack and Tony didn't reappear until just before 2am for the debriefing outside the club. Damien appeared none the wiser of the altercation that had happened previously. No one said anything, and no one was going to say anything. It was a short meeting, and we were done for the night.

Frank tried to make amends with the pair but Jack and Tony didn't want to know. They just walked off. Nigel and I went back into the club. It took several days before Jack and Tony would end up acknowledging Frank and allowing him to attempt to bury the hatchet. They smoothed things over, but it was never quite the same.

CHAPTER 25
SPEARMINT RINGO

Another popular prank was messing with people's hair in one way or another. Pranks with clippers would be played out on both guest and rep alike.

One night, Nigel and I had been with our guests in Es Paradis, the pair of us fuelled to the brim with Vodka and Red Bull, not to mention tequila chasers (someone previously had introduced us to the TVR—Tequila, Vodka, Red Bull—not that we needed a kicker, but it tasted good and got you sideways nicely).

Anyway, we were back at Nigel's hotel in one of the guests' rooms at silly o'clock in the morning. The initial idea was to climb on to a pair of angels from London whom we'd been outrageously flirting with for a couple of days, but as we were having so much fun with everyone, our little menage-a-quatre became a floor party, with groups from up and down the corridor all hanging out and drinking with us.

Determined not to lose out on the chance of laying one of the angels, Nigel decided to get extra flirty and laid across her on the sofa. Not only did he immediately begin to receive a nice massage and gentle shoulder rub, but he was also marking his territory so the rest of the lads knew what was up, because up until now, it had been a bit of a free for all, with everyone and his dog trying to fire into the Londoners. Not to be outdone, I then sat next to the other one and we cosied up on the opposing sofa style chairs.

At this point I had switched on to tea, as had the Londoners, while the rest of the group continued to drink heavily. One by one they all started to fall by the wayside and the rest of the guests began to drift out of the room and back to their own apartments to crash out.

Nigel, however, had committed a cardinal sin. He'd fallen asleep. He'd overdone it on the booze, and had allowed himself to relax too much under the soft hands of his would-be assailant. I don't know how we got on to the topic, but with him snoring softly to himself, the rest of the room began to talk about hair styles.

Nigel had a bit of a quiff and someone remarked that it needed trimming. There was a pair of scissors on the coffee table and a needle and thread from a previous last minute dress alteration. I wasn't really paying too much attention, as I was trying to get inside the other one, but I remember looking across and seeing Nigel's angel take a sudden snip at his hair. The next moment, I see part of his little coiffure laying on the sofa looking back at me. She was laughing. Her mate was laughing, and the last remaining guests who hadn't quite taken the hint were also laughing. I said he was going to kill her when he woke up, but she simply rebuffed me telling me it's his own fault for falling asleep and neglecting his duties. My one giggled at that, which I took to be a good sign that I was getting laid, as long as I didn't fall asleep too.

We continued to chat for a bit until the other guests finally took the hint and left us all to it. Nigel was still sound asleep and I was drinking tea to make sure I didn't fall asleep too. After giggling again that he looked better for the trim she'd given him, I might just have made the remark that he looked like a gorilla below the waistline, and maybe she should spend some time attending to that. Both the girls started to laugh and, next thing I know, she's managed to pull his denim shorts down enough to expose the cheeks of his ass.

Nigel had a little tuft of hair poking out of the back of his boxers, and I watched in surprise to see her go to town on it. With a few, short, sharp snips, he was suddenly tuftless.

"That's better," she said.

I couldn't believe it. This girl was game for anything, and it's not like it took much encouragement either. Just the hint of a suggestion and she would immediately obey and carry out the idea. Whenever I would explain that he was going to kill her, she would laugh and say he shouldn't have fallen asleep on her, or that she was going to make it up to him in the morning. My one would continue to giggle.

Truth be told, Nigel was my mate and I didn't want to see him get stitched up like this, but at the same time, I was fascinated seeing this girl go to work on him. She was unflinching, very pretty, but icy cold underneath. She was happy to use sexual gratification as reward or apology, and wasn't afraid to show it.

I could see this had legs. I thought, let's test her resolve. I casually mentioned that I'd fallen asleep on a girl the year before, and had woken up with a full make up job, feather boa wrapped round my sausage, and breakfast cereal stuffed up my starfish. The girls found it hilarious.

Next thing you know, the lipstick came out, and Nigel resembled the joker. Next, some eye shadow, and he looked like an extra from a David Bowie video. It wasn't enough though. This was rookie level stuff. Unprompted, Nigel's angel of the South removed the piece of chewing gum she'd been gnawing on for the last hour, and pushed it lightly into the crack of his ass. What did I just see? My face must have been a picture. This beautiful, voluptuous specimen of a woman, from arguably one of the most cultural capitals of the world, has just inserted a spent piece of Wrigleys into the crack of my comrade's ass.

She looked up at us. We looked at her, before she simply muttered "oops!" and the pair of them started to piss themselves. I too found it funny, but also a little unnerving. I mean, was I just witnessing the birth of a stalker or serial killer here? Is this how it starts? One minute you're falling asleep on her and the lipstick is applied, the next she's interfering with your nether regions? I mean, where do we go from here? Wasabi smeared on his helmet? Mustard brushed over his sphincter? Before you know it, your child's rabbit has been boiled alive and it's looking at you on the family stove!

As funny as it was, I felt the need to try and rein things in a little here. Not through fear of what might happen to Nigel's genitalia, but in case my one got ideas from Glenn Close. I jokingly remarked that she was going to be blowing Nigel for a month to make up for that, and she would have to cut the gum out of his ass because I wasn't doing it. She just looked me straight in the eye and told me, "Don't worry about it. I'll take care of him. By the time I've finished with him, he'll be drinking milk for a month!"

Wow, just wow. I felt a sudden pang of jealousy. Nigel had unwittingly and unknowingly hooked up with the human sperm extractor, and even if it cost him a restyled shitter, he would be milking the sympathy blowy every day for the next week or so. Right there and then, I wished it was me who'd been violated with Orbit around my orifice.

Not to be too downhearted, I looked at my one and

decided to take things up a notch. "I hope you're as good as this one," I joked. It was already late, and I was hoping a little bit of friendly provocation might bring things closer to a conclusion.

"Follow me and you'll find out."

She stepped up and made her way over to the bedroom. Bingo. I bid Vidal Ass-soon a good night and quietly shut the door behind me.

The following morning, we both woke to the sound of Nigel whining like a child. She wrapped herself in the top sheet and I slid back into my boxers to open the door and see what all the fuss was about. It was a sight I will take with me to the grave.

Nigel was naked, on all fours, doubled over on the sofa. Glenn Close was standing behind him brandishing scissors. Nigel was spreading his cheeks, showing his pencil sharpener to the rest of the room, while she was pulling at the now-hardened chewing gum. Every time she got a hold on it, she had to pull it further away from his fold to try and cut the hair that was anchoring it to him like a limpet.

"For fuck sake," I muttered as I watched the back of Nigel's undercarriage sway back and forth. "No one needs to see this in the morning."

My one just tittered. I started to laugh.

Nigel was massively over dramatising. "Luke, this is so painful. Is there any blood?"

I couldn't help but roar. "Of course not, you silly sod. Cinderella's only put gum in your beard, not stolen your rectum."

"But she said you did it!"

"You can stop that shit right there. That deviant with the scissors played with your back doors, you can leave me out of it."

Edward Scissorhands threw me a glare.

I pressed on. "Don't look at me like that Darling. You were the one boasting about how you were going to milk Nigel dry every single day for the rest of your holiday to apologise."

My one also came to the rescue. "Yeah, you did say that as you put the gum into his butt crack."

Nigel stopped wriggling. "Princess, are you really going to milk me dry?"

I laughed again. The comment alone was comical but the fact that it was coming from the head end of what looked like a 75kg bent over turkey, tickled me all the more.

Before she had a chance to answer, he continued. "See, I knew you liked me really. Although, this is an unusual way of showing it."

She just laughed. "I suppose I could help you out, once or twice."

"You said every day!" I replied.

She tried to make another cut, but it was no good. She couldn't get the kitchen scissors close enough. Eventually, she came to the conclusion I wanted to both hear and watch.

"Nigel, I think we're going to have to just rip this out." As Nigel gulped, I watched his bean bag lift slightly, which made the situation even funnier. "On the count of three, okay sweetheart?"

She took a grip on the small ball of matted butt hair and chewing gum and started the countdown.

"One, two…"

I interrupted her on purpose. "Do you think it will hurt?"

She just glared at me and said, "No, it will be quick and painless." She continued the countdown. "One, two…"

I interrupted again. "Are you sure it won't hurt? I'm

worried you might tear the skin. It already looks weak." I was grinning from ear to ear.

"Nigel will be fine. I know what I'm doing." She began the countdown again, only for Nigel to interrupt her. Ignoring him completely, she went ahead and ripped on two, forcing an involuntary yelping noise to come out of Nigel's mouth. He flinched massively and suddenly found himself sitting on the sofa, wincing. She walked over to the bathroom and said goodbye to the gummy critter she'd just freed from his chute.

The fun didn't stop there. As if the dingleberry removal procedure wasn't enough for my poor friend, I signalled to him, pointing at his hair. He walked over naked as the day he was born to the mirror.

"For fuck sake. Where's my quiff? Who did that? And can someone tell me, why am I wearing makeup?"

It was too much. I took a seat in my boxers and started to laugh. I don't think Nigel was that bothered but he definitely wanted his money's worth out of this encounter. He walked over to the curvy Londoner as she dried her hands."

Are you responsible for this, too?"

She just smiled and threw back her hair.

"But why, princess? Why? I really liked you, I thought we shared a connection. I was hoping for a cuddle, instead I got physically assaulted. I don't understand!?"

This was typical Nigel. he'd gone into sympathy/helpless mode. Any moment now, she would feel some guilt, grab him by the hand and lead him into the bedroom. I anticipated this, so I went to get my clothes out of it.

Sure enough, no sooner had I emerged from the bedroom with my jeans and t-shirt, they went into it and closed the door behind them. I made my girl a cup of tea and got dressed. I gave her a polite peck on the cheek and set off for my hotel.

Nigel only had to walk downstairs, I still had to get changed. I skipped out of his reception feeling somewhat chirpy. I'd got laid, Nigel had made me laugh—despite having seen his giblets that morning—and I wasn't feeling hungover at all. Even Nigel's hotelier, the crazy catholic, couldn't dent my mood as he spat his venom at me on passing. Today was going to be a good day!

CHAPTER 26
ROOKIE MISTAKE

Not everyone reacted so well to falling victim to some impromptu styling. One of the reps, an Essex boy called Adrian, had also succumbed to some unwarranted trimming. He was a peak season rep like myself and Nigel and a good lad. Always cheerful, always up for a drink. He got on well with the guests and could always be found leading them on an after hours bar crawl, or arranging a dance off somewhere. If you wanted to party onwards, he was always someone you could rely on to be out with you. Nigel would often marvel at his stamina, but whenever you asked Adrian, he said he would sleep when he was dead.

Adrian was in his final year at university and had finished his third-year exams before flying out to Ibiza. He was already in his second season, much like us, and he knew the score.

Towards the end of the season, Adrian needed to fly back to the UK for his graduation ceremony. Despite not wanting to bail out midway through and lose his momentum, the company had agreed to fly him home for three nights and then immediately back out. It would give him enough time to attend his graduation ceremony but not enough time for him to fall out of sync with the rest of us and for the sleep deprivation to take hold of his soul.

I don't actually think he wanted to go back to the UK as he was loving his time in Ibiza, but he understood it wasn't just about him. His mum and dad wanted to see him accept his scroll, etc. and, given they'd been funding him up until now, it was the least he could do. The girls would have to wait. Besides, I think even Adrian was secretly looking forward to a couple of lay ins.

A lot of the reps were jealous. Not the fact he was leaving, but the fact he would be able to get a couple of days' respite from the pure chaos of peak season. Adrian got on well with most of them, though, so I don't think anyone really bore him any ill feelings. They too would simply have liked the chance to nip back to see family and friends for a few days.

Someone in his team suggested they go out for a nightcap after work, especially as it was Adrian's last night. Not that it mattered. It was an excuse for a night out. Most of his team agreed. He extended the invite to Nigel and me which was nice of him as we weren't even in the same team. A couple of others agreed we would meet by a particular bar in Eden, upstairs.

Once our respective end of day debriefings had finished, we all went back inside as agreed. Even Damien and Adrian's supervisor Jason went back in for a drink. It was a nice crowd. Not all the reps had been invited or even knew about it, but those that were there were genuinely decent and we all got along well. Even Damien seemed to relax and seemed less irritable than normal.

A couple of the guests were also present. This irked a few of the reps initially, but the guests were good as gold. They were just chatting normally. There were a few girls circling but they soon get bored. Tonight wasn't about tucking yourself in, it was about bonding with the guys.

True to form, it wasn't long before things got out of hand. Things started to get messy and we became a bit of a liability with security. Though they knew us, and were happy to have us there, it wasn't the sort of place that relied on our custom so we couldn't take the piss. Damien and Jason decided it was time to pull the cord and shepherded the rest of us to a karaoke bar on the strip.

I don't like karaoke. The only time I would go into a karaoke bar normally was when I was looking for a girl but couldn't remember which bar we had agreed to meet in. That said, I soon found myself on stage with the other reprobates roaring Tom Jones' Delilah at the top of my voice.

Everyone was bladdered. At one point, Adrian was found laying down in the toilets, only to be brought back to life by Damien and Jason for another rendition of Right Said Fred or whatever other shit they could convince the VJ to put on next.

Nigel and I were in bits. Nigel tried to chat a girl up on another table before having to pull the emergency chute. He took about four steps back and involuntarily threw up on his shoes. I found this hilarious. In fact, I laughed so hard I lost my balance and fell off the bar stool into a table of drinks. Clearly it wasn't going to be long before we were given our marching orders here, too.

After a couple more songs it was decided we should call it a night. One by one, we were losing the ability to function. Adrian had found his second wind, though, and was on fire. He'd already kissed a couple of the girls in there and didn't want to leave. Thing is, given the state of us, he was fortunate to be even standing up, let alone standing mini me up for some after-hours entertainment. The only way we could convince him to leave was to offer an alternative.

One of the other reps suggested they go back to his hotel as he knew a big group of girls that seemed like fun and would probably party on with us. This piqued everyone's interest and was the sort of proposal that Adrian found acceptable. We left the karaoke bar and staggered through the West End to the other hotel.

Sensibly, at this point, Damien and Jason left us. No one knew where they went, but it left us down to five. Adrian, Jack, Keith (who was in Adrian's team), Nigel and me. It was Keith's hotel we were going back to. Sure enough, when we got there, he knocked on the room and we went in. There were five girls inside and they were drinking and listening to music. We immediately continued to party with them for about half an hour before we started to drop like flies.

Jack was the first one to crash out. He had gone out onto the balcony to smoke with one of the girls. He'd sat down on a chair, relaxed back and promptly passed out. She just left him to it.

Next was Adrian's turn. Both Nigel and I were surprised he'd even made it this far. Considering he'd already blacked out in the karaoke bar and had found his second wind he had done well. Predictably, though, he crashed out on the sofa. Some of the girls had placed hats and glasses on him and posed for pictures. At one point I think he even had a pair of knickers on his head. There was no waking him, he was out for the count. Keith even tried to put his hand in a bowl of warm water to make him piss himself but to no avail. Even his dick was drunk.

At this point, I was still focusing on one of the girls in the room to pay too much attention to what the others were doing. One of the girls got some shaving foam and gave

Adrian a beard. Keith then moved some of the foam from his chin to his eyebrows. Completely unknown to Adrian, he was slumped there looking like a Gillette Santa Claus.

I'm not entirely sure what went down next, but someone suggested it would be funny if they could shave a little line into one of Adrian's eyebrows. You know, to make him look like someone from East 17, or that bell end from Boyzone.

One of the girls emerged with a lady shave. Keith began the arduous job of very lightly trying to carve out a little tramline in one of Adrian's brows. He was concentrating really hard, and everyone seemed to stop talking as they focused on the task in hand. Nigel, the wanker, had other plans.

Keith was patiently—and ever so gently—hacking away at the foam on the inside edge of his eyebrow when Nigel suddenly grabbed his arm and sharply pulled down and outwards. Before Keith had even a chance to react, the deed was done. Not only had the foam been removed, one of Adrian's caterpillars had gone with it. Half the room gasped, not quite knowing what to say or do. Nigel pissed himself laughing, before the rest of the room joined him.

It wasn't until Keith reminded Nigel that Adrian was going to a graduation ceremony a few days later that Nigel stopped laughing.

"Don't you dare tell him it was me," warned Nigel. "Tell him one of the girls did it. He won't remember any of them anyway!"

"Erm, excuse me," piped up one of the girls. "Don't be blaming us for something you guys did."

Keith was already in a pickle. If it emerged Adrian had lost a brow by his hand, he was in for the high jump. Adrian was a good lad but he didn't fuck about. You didn't want to be on his shit list.

Eventually, a plan was hatched out. We were going to

walk Adrian back to his hotel and leave him in reception. The following morning, he wouldn't remember how he got there, or who he partied with, and he probably wouldn't even realise what had happened to his eyebrow.

All were in agreement. We woke Jack up, who was also in a state, and managed to get everyone down the stairs. Adrian was all over the place and pretty incoherent. We managed to get him to his reception before laying him out on the sofa. No sooner had his head hit the cushion, he was out like a light bulb.

Jack had come round a bit, so we let Keith take Jack back to his hotel, while the rest of us crashed out. Thankfully, Adrian got on well with his night security guard, so he wasn't bothered to see him sleeping it off in reception. In fact, he found it comical.

By all accounts, the following morning Adrian was groggy as hell. He came round just before 9, having been woken up by his guests. He was late for his morning meeting and shot to his apartment to get changed.

Keith later recounted the story of Adrian turning up to his sales meeting. Clearly the worse for wear, he came in with a flimsy apology and slumped down in his chair, waiting to hear the music from Jason. However, when the telling off didn't occur, Adrian was puzzled. He began to look around the room, wondering why everyone was looking at him and not speaking.

Eventually, Jason said to him, "You've got your graduation in a day or so, right?" Adrian nodded. "So why the fuck have you only got one eyebrow?"

Apparently, Adrian just stared forwards for a few short moments as that statement sank in, before slowly lifting a finger to just below his forehead. It then became apparent to everyone that he, up until now, had been completely unaware of his predicament.

He initially touched the wrong side, running his finger lightly over his remaining eye brow. I'm sure a part of him must have felt a tiny sigh of relief and a small seed of optimism may even have been planted that Jason was pulling his leg. He did in fact have both brows and all was right with the world. That illusion was shattered approximately half a second later.

"Bollocks!" he sighed, as his finger rubbed across a small fresh patch of skin to the side of his temples. This new found clearing was as smooth as the egg shell finish gracing the centrefold of Playboy. "Who fucking did this to me?"

The room fell silent. No one dared to laugh, or even speak.

"This is so fucking out of order. I have my graduation in two days. What a cuntish thing to do."

He was right. This really was harsh. Even Jason fell silent. As he stood up, he went to the window to look at his reflection. He surveyed the damage. One of the girls came over and put her hand reassuringly on his shoulder.

"It's really not that bad, Adrian. You'll be able to draw one in for the actual ceremony. No one will know and it will grow back really quickly."

Adrian just stood motionless. He was seething. "Which prick did this? Was it a guest? A rep? Someone better tell me."

No one said a word. Keith stared down at the floor. At this point, Jason approached him. "Calm down dude. I'm sure we'll get to the bottom of this. Like Sarah said, you'll be able to hide it ok with eyeliner or something. It'll be alright. Now come on, let's get you seated. We need to go through your numbers before you pack and head off for the airport."

Jason coaxed Adrian back into his chair. Anger turned to despondency. If not for the graduation, I don't think he would have given a fuck at all about it. This sort of stuff was happening week in, week out. I guess he felt it had been done out of spite, intentionally, and he was thinking about how his parents would take it, which had caused the sting.

At the same time Adrian was dealing with his emotions in his meeting, Nigel approached me just before ours. "Did you see Adrian or K-man this morning?" Nigel called Keith K-man for some reason or another.

"Nope, they're probably in Jason's sales meeting. Why, you worried?" I teased.

Nigel just laughed. He certainly wouldn't want to get on Adrian's bad side, but nothing really bothered Nigel anyway. I mean, if Adrian did find out, what's he going to do? Keith will get the worst of it anyway.

"Not really, but it would be nice to know he was cool about it."

"Cool about it!? You're kidding, right? I'd be furious. He's probably sat there in the taxi thinking of ways to get back at the pair of you. That, or he's pondering whether to shave the other brow off to match and hope people don't notice he looks like an alien, or he's trying to work out which felt tip pen best matches his eyebrow colour the closest. Either way, it's going to be winding him up further. You better pray that 'K-man' doesn't grass you up, or you're really in for it."

Nigel silently pondered my response. "It'll be alright. They can do wonders with make-up nowadays."

He started to grin. I just shook my head. "Whose hotel are we hitting tonight then? Yours or mine?"

We started to discuss the rest of the week's plans on the cuddle front. Nigel was keen to get as much cuddling done as possible because his mates were out the following week, and he openly said to make the most of him as a wingman now because, when they arrive, he was going to be getting seriously smashed with them and doubted he would be useful to man, woman or beast. I laughed before starting to compare notes on who was who in our respective hotels.

Neither one of us gave another moment's thought to poor Adrian and his baby monobrow. Adrian had indeed flown back to the UK and had attended his graduation ceremony. Thankfully, his parents were cool with the whole thing and found it quite comical, by all accounts. His mum ended up drawing an eyebrow on and, according to Adrian afterwards, it actually wasn't so noticeable.

I wasn't entirely convinced on hearing this. I mean, when did gunmetal black ever blend nicely with mousey brown, but hey, who was I to judge. The good news was that the rest of his time spent with his family had gone through without a hitch, and officially Adrian now had letters after his name.

We weren't the only ones who had forgotten about Adrian and his shaven haven. Keith too had not given it a second thought. Such was the pace out there, he wouldn't have time to think about it again for the rest of the season, were it not for a sharp reminder: Adrian himself.

Keith was sitting down in his hotel reception, hanging out with a group of guests, when something must have triggered his spidey senses. For whatever reason, he glanced over his shoulder just in time to see Adrian approaching him with a pair of wireless clippers in his left hand. Keith sprung up out of the chair and started to bolt towards the closest exit.

Now, while Keith had the reactions of a cat, it was no match for his assailant who had the drop on him. Keith got about three strides towards the pool area before being roughly taken down by Adrian. The guests all knew Adrian and so they knew not to intervene, although I am sure some of them would have been quietly questioning the intensity with which Keith was thrown to the floor.

Before Keith could say anything, Adrian rolled him on to his back and managed to kneel on his chest. Adrian was significantly bigger than Keith. And as Keith struggled, Adrian took each arm, one by one, and pushed them underneath his knees, giving him free reign over Adrian's head and face. Keith knew the game was up and tried to speak, but Adrian beat him to the punch.

"You motherfucker. How could you do that before my graduation?"

Keith tried to explain, but Adrian was having none of it. He reached over to the side, careful not to let either of Keith's arms go free, and managed to pick up the clippers. Keith had longish hair in curtains. Nigel and I used to remark he belonged in a boy band. Keith played on his youthful looks and his floppy quiffs when chatting up the guests. All of that was about to end.

Despite his wiggling and protestations, Adrian held Keith's head against the floor with his left hand and, with his right, pressed the clippers hard against the side of a cheek. With one swift and rough upward motion, he dragged the clippers against the head of his opponent. Keith yelped as the blade scratched over the side of his skull. Adrian repeated this motion again and with all the grace of the first stroke. Keith cried out for a second time. Yet no one came to his rescue.

Keith would go on to later explain how Adrian's eyes seemed to glaze over, and he appeared emotionless as he continued to shear him. As Adrian cut/ripped out the curtains, you'd imagine him as a big strapping Aussie farmer shearing a sheep. No sympathy, no caress, just a job that needed to be done, regardless of the bleating.

After about the fifth stroke, and with 40% of Keith's

hair now surrounding him in clumps on the floor, Keith stopped struggling. Adrian didn't go slow enough for the blade to actually cut it all, and he certainly wasn't slowing down. The more Keith struggled, the more his hair was being dragged out as opposed to being shaved out, making things infinitely more painful. Adrian said nothing, just swapped hands and continued to do the other side with all the tactfulness and sensitivity he'd shown previously. Another four or five strokes of the clipper and K-man's curtains were no more, and he began to more closely resemble an extra in Alien 3.

Suddenly, without warning, Adrian stood up off Keith, took a step back and shook the clippers. Another tuft of hair silently dropped to the floor. Keith, sensing that it was over, also got to his feet. The guests in the reception area, who up until now had been silently watching, started to point at their rep and giggle between themselves. Adrian had shaved the front and top part of his head, but in order to get the job done properly, he would have had to flip him over.

Adrian couldn't be arsed. Once the clippers had been freed of the last remaining traces of Keith, he turned and made his way to the door. The guests made a path so he could walk through. While they'd enjoyed the spectacle, they could see that Adrian wasn't in the mood to be messed with. In fact, the only words to leave Adrian's lips were "fuck off" after Keith asked to borrow the clippers to finish the job.

Adrian left reception and headed off in the direction of the West End. Keith tried to put a brave face on, trying to laugh it all off with the guests. His face was a picture when he checked out his new look in the mirror for the first time. As he still had the hair at the back, he resembled what could only be described as a cross between Terry Nutkins and a Chernobyl ground worker.

He started asking around the hotel for a pair of clippers to finish the job but none were forthcoming. Reluctantly, he made his way down to one of the hair dressers just behind the West End to get it cleaned up. Despite this little feud, Keith apologised to Adrian later on that evening and the pair had a drink about it.

Fortunately for Nigel, he never saw any revenge. Not even the slightest slither of payback. And you know, I'm not sure that was fair or not. I mean, ultimately he had a hand in it, but then again wasn't the one actually holding the lady shave. I'm not sure if that was because Keith never grassed him up, or because Adrian felt like he'd already evened the score. Nigel was definitely involved in more pranks, but no one ever messed with Adrian again.

CHAPTER 27
THE THREE MUSKETEERS

By the time Nigel's mates from home flew out to see him, I think the whole of San Antonio had been told. Nigel was like a child at Christmas. He couldn't wait to see them, and was excited for me to meet them too. All I kept hearing, repeatedly, was how great they were, and how much I was going to love them as well. He'd even started to apologise in advance to some of the bar and venue owners for the state he/they/we were going to be in. I too was excited to meet them.

Three of them arrived on the Gatwick flight. Gary, Will and Jamie. They'd all studied together, and by all accounts shared everything from girls to drinks. They clearly knew each other really well and got on like a house on fire. They were all very different, but somehow it just worked.

Gary was from Manchester. Olive skinned, good look-ing, with a keen eye for the ladies. He was ruthless when it came to moving on to the next one. Never a hesitation nor fuss. It wasn't that he was horrible or cruel. He never led anyone on or lied. The girls always knew where they stood. I think it was that openness and their hope they could turn his head twice that allowed him to go about his business without drama. He had the ability to sink a vodka and Red Bull just by looking at it and to this day, some 24 years later, he still claims he has never ever had a hangover. Bastard.

Jamie was from Birmingham. He was about as close to olive skinned as an Icelandic Viking wearing factor 50. Jamie was hilarious. He would make people laugh right from the get go. He wasn't crude or laddish. He just saw the funny side in everything. You would have the most bizarre conversations about something as innocent as a fruit cake, but you'd be somehow pissing yourself at the same time.

While there was no doubt what was going through Gary's mind in his endless pursuit of the lady garden, Jamie was able to disarm and deflower in the most subtle and unlikely of ways. One minute the girl would be laughing about some childhood TV series, like Blue Peter or the Teletubbies, and the next she'd be getting scuttled. Out of the blue, without warning. He was similar to Nigel in that he would play the sympathy/helpless card. In fact, I believe the pair of them found great success at university by focusing on a niche of girls that were looking for someone to mother!

Last but not least we have Will. Will was a Brit pop poster icon. Originally from the South, he was as Oasis as Manchester. Equally as funny as Jamie and Gary, in his own way, but chic with it. He was trendy without even trying. He also played it much cooler than everyone else. If the girls were even remotely into fashion or music, they were attracted to him. He was so laid back you'd think he didn't care if he hooked up with a girl or not, yet I think this contributed heavily to him getting laid. He too had a good sense of humour and didn't appear to be fazed by anything.

Nigel had met them off the plane the night before. I hadn't been to the airport, so the first time I got to see them was when we conducted a welcome meeting at Nigel's hotel. I'd quickly been introduced to them as soon as I'd arrived and we spoke for a minute or two before the meeting commenced.

Nigel had managed to secure them passes for everything anyway, so while they sat in on the meeting, no one tried to sell them anything. I sat with a pair of lads who were basically out to misbehave, so I quickly closed the sale within a few minutes of the meeting concluding. Nigel, as always, was struggling to close his deal, so it meant the three of them were on their own. I approached and sat with them for 15-20 minutes while we watched Nigel in the distance attempt to sell the trips.

"What do you think then? You think they'll bite?" I asked the group.

Without hesitation Gary replied, "Fuck no. He couldn't close a door let alone a sale."

Jamie added, "Put it this way, I've got more chances of selling the package to that pair, and I don't even know what's in it!"

Everyone tittered before Will asked, "Why do you even allow him to talk to the guests? He's a liability."

That was it, I started to laugh. They clearly had the measure of Nigel.

As we spoke further, I began to hear more about how they all knew each other, and heard more stories of their antics at uni. They were super friendly and I don't think I stopped laughing once while sitting with them. They were mercilessly laughing at Nigel, as well as each other, which really resonated with me. They were asking me about Ibiza and if I was enjoying the repping. To my surprise, they knew a fair bit about me from Nigel, and Gary added he was looking forward to winging with me. At this point, Nigel returned to us.

"How did you get on?" I asked.

"Nil Points!" he replied, in a bad French accent. "You?"

I just shot him a look as if that was the most stupid question on earth. Nigel shook his head. He faced the group and accused me of taking all the easy ones. They shut him down immediately, and we all laughed again.

Before we could get into anything else, Damien appeared. "What are you two still doing here? Go to the next meeting unless you've got paperwork to fill out."

Before Nigel could say a thing, Damien said, "I know you haven't got anything to book in, you twat." The group laughed again. Nigel and I made our excuses and headed onwards.

I didn't see the other three until later on that evening. A feeling of expectation hung in the air. Nigel had already introduced them to pretty much everyone in the bar and was doing his best to loop them in with the female guests. Not that he really needed to do that, given they were already embedding themselves nicely with the fairer sex. Gary looked like he was on a promise already, and Will had exchanged contact details with one of the girls before they'd left the hotel. Even Jamie looked like he was making strides as he held court with a group of girls from Birmingham.

I asked Nigel what was the plan for the evening. He said the plan was to get smashed and go from there. He told me to stay close, because after work they were going out for a big one. It's a shame he could never sell the trip packages with the same intensity as he sold a piss-up. He would have cleaned up.

As the night went on, the guests began to get more and more raucous, and Nigel's friends were no exception. After a stint on the dance floor with my lot, I went off to find them.

By the time I caught up, everyone was completely battered. Jamie had his belt out and was hosting a limbo competition for some of the other guests, Will was at the bar knocking back aftershocks with an attractive looking blonde, and Gary was making out with this tall bird. She was pretty but big. Not just physically big, she also had a large forehead. Will remarked that it looked pregnant and Jamie laughed that she looked like Vigo out of Ghostbusters 2. Every time they looked like they were going to come up for air, Gary would just bury his tongue deep into her mouth again.

I approached Will to say hello and ask where Nigel was. Will tried to buy me a shot but I stopped him. Instead, I nodded to the barman who sent me three more, on the house. "One of the perks," I smiled.

Along with Will and his blonde bombshell drinking partner, we proceeded to down them. As we put the empty glasses back on to the bar, Nigel suddenly appeared out of the crowd. He looked worse for wear. He was clutching the hands of two attractive girls from his hotel. One of them looked like she'd applied lipstick with a spray gun. Strangely enough, it matched the shade that Nigel seemed to be wearing all over his face. I just laughed.

"State of him!" exclaimed Will. I chuckled.

"Where's Gary and Jamie?" Nigel asked. Before I had a chance to answer, Will chirped up.

"Jamie is over there, trying to promote Brummy limbo, and Gary is trying to kiss that neanderthal back into the painting." This little Ghostbusters quip made me laugh but soared straight over Nigel's head.

"Get the lads over here now, Will, we got a challenge on our hands."

Will did what he was told and wandered over to Jamie who at this point had already fallen onto the floor after being totally crap at limbo. I turned to face Will's suitor, who looked a bit out of place without her beau and I made small talk while we waited for the troops to return.

Jamie came over to Nigel and was immediately introduced to the two girls Nigel had with him. Will then approached Gary, who at this point was grinding up against this giraffe of a woman. Without any tact, hesitation or niceties, Will stuck his fingers into Gary's mouth, immediately ending their kiss.

As Gary started to protest, Will came out with an immortal one liner. "Kick Vigo into touch, Nigel's got you an upgrade."

Sensing something was better around the corner, Gary took one look at the girls next to Nigel, apologised to his belle, then put his arm around Will and bundled him over to where we were standing. I broke off conversation with the girl Will had been speaking to, thinking he would want to pick up where he left off, but he didn't even acknowledge her. He was more focused on what Nigel had in store for them. Within a few moments, she left, irritated, leaving just the five of us and the two girls that were listening intently to Nigel.

I don't know exactly what was going through Nigel's head when he had proposed this to the girls initially, but he'd basically challenged the pair to a snog-a-thon. He claimed that, despite the girls being attractive, he and his mates could snog more girls than they could guys. Both the girls were fit and knew that they'd have no problems picking up guys in the club. It was more a question of forfeit for the losers.

Nigel had conceded that, as the girls were attractive, and guys are guys, they had it easy, so to make it more sporting he wanted to have more players. On hearing this, I immediately disqualified myself from taking part. I figured Damien was lurking around and, in any case, I'd been active within the hotel that week. The last thing I wanted was a public showdown on the dance floor with one of the female guests spying on me as I poked my tongue into other people's throats.

Despite Nigel's protestations, I was out and happy to watch the carnage unfold. Besides, someone needed to keep count. The girls were happier with me out, as it meant the pair of them, against 4 not 5.

I hadn't seen Nigel this pissed for a long time. Everyone was listening to him try and explain the rules. He was describing the order of play in an animated manner. I didn't realise there was a technical or strategic way to play snog-a-thon, but I guess I was mistaken. I ordered a round of tequilas for everyone involved, while my immoral friend fleshed out the finer points of what consisted of a snog and what was actually a peck.

The girls were going to go first, and had a minute and a half to frenchy as many people as possible. They couldn't go for the same person, and they couldn't go back to one. Nigel and the three musketeers would keep count, and then it was the guys' turn to have 90 seconds to get off with as many as possible, under the watchful eye of the two girls. The kiss had to be witnessed for it to count, so no one could stray too far from the current position.

The girls were already giggling between themselves before Nigel started to count them down. I was surprised they'd be playing this, to be honest. These two were nice looking and not the usual sorts to resort to such antics. I watched on with curiosity.

As Nigel started the countdown from 10, others joined in. I helped too. Some of the surrounding guests were also counting down, although judging by the puzzled look on their faces, I'm not quite sure they knew why. The girls started to get into the crouching start a sprinter before the gun goes off. They were smiling and giggling until we got down to the last few digits.

3... 2...1... Go!

Immediately they bolted forwards. The blondest of the two leapt on the guy closest to her. He nearly dropped his drink as she jammed her mouth over his and pushed her tongue in. Instinctively, he tried to reciprocate. No sooner had he put his hand on her hip, she was off.

She practically threw herself straight onto his comrade a few steps away. She pulled him with the same subtlety she had shown a few moments before. The guys were laughing. I cast a glance over to her mate who pretty much had done the same thing to a couple of lads who were closest to her. 15 seconds in, and the girls were four for four. The guys had their work cut out.

After about 30 seconds, you could sense that some of the lads in the nearer areas had twigged what was going on and began to move closer to the epicentre. It didn't take long for their bravery to be rewarded with an oral assault lasting a few seconds. It also didn't take long for the girls to reach some guys that weren't up for it, and you could tell the shock of being knocked back put them off their stride. Aware that the clock was ticking, they weren't sure whether to try and over turn the guy's objection or move on to the next one.

Having exhausted everything in the immediate vicinity, the girls seemed to run out of options. Either the guy was shy, not interested, or maybe he was part of a couple. The pace of kissing quickly deteriorated. When it reached their last 10 seconds, Nigel started to count them down loudly and was soon joined by everyone else. There was a last moment dash for one unsuspecting lad but they couldn't get to him in time. I think the poor guy thought he was going to get murdered the way they ran at him.

The girls returned to the bar, flustered but giggling. They felt confident. Between the pair of them they'd manage to kiss 17. This was good going. In a sense, Nigel and the guys had got lucky because no one had cottoned on to what was happening. Had people realised there was a chance to get a free snog with one of these two angels, that number could easily have doubled or tripled.

Everyone took another drink as the banter started to flow. The girls, supremely confident in their results, started to bait Nigel and the boys. It was funny to watch. We'd managed to draw a crowd which played in the favour of the guys. People could sense what was coming next, and a fair few girls had closed in to see what the commotion had been about previously.

Not wanting to lose momentum (or the crowd), Nigel instructed me to count us down. I managed to make a little area in the centre of the bar, then started to count down loudly from 10. Along with the two girls, some of the other guests started to join in. Nigel coordinated the group, giving directions as to who was going where.

Gary looked totally poised. You could see he already had his kissing chain lined up. Will was focusing on the countdown, trying to prepare himself for the love to come. Jamie, on the other hand, was like a deer in the headlights. He was trying to confirm with Nigel what direction he was supposed to head in, and by the time the count finished, and the other guys had gone, he was still standing there like a lemon, much to everyone's amusement. I just shoved him in the direction the others weren't.

From the off, Nigel wasted no time. He sprung like a surprised cat onto two of his guests. Much like the girls had done, he'd kissed them both within seconds and pounced off to the next. Gary and Will had both managed to get points on the board early on. All three had been well received.

So would Jamie have been, had just leapt before looking. Instead, he was asking permission, which came across as awkward. I think by the time the other guys had been on two or three each, Jamie was still negotiating. This was hilarious to watch. Eventually, one of the girls in the crowd interrupted him and plunged her tongue into his mouth before he had a chance to go elsewhere. Everyone cheered, and this seemed to give him the kickstart he needed, as he then grabbed this bold maiden's friend and proceeded to smooch with her too.

Nigel didn't let up once. He was a machine. In fact, I think the majority of the girls in his hotel were practically lining up behind each other. That's not to pour scorn on Gary and Will. The olive-skinned lothario and britpop icon respectively were putting in the tongue work. I must confess to losing count, and wasn't sure the other team had been accurately recording the oral interactions either, but I knew things were close as the last 10 seconds started to get counted down.

Nigel must have been on about 7, with Gary and Will on 3 or 4 each. Jamie had managed just the 2. The others had pretty much exhausted all options around them, leaving Jamie in the final seconds to close in on one of the few princesses who hadn't been kissed by a frog. Everyone gestured to him wildly to get it done. She looked like Bambi in the spotlights of a locomotive, and Jamie seemed to freeze in his tracks.

You know what didn't freeze? The countdown. Everyone was roaring as the countdown got to 5…

"Go on Jamie, kiss her," hollered Nigel.

"Get it done, Jay," roared Gary.

At this point, the girl started to grin, ever so slightly. Well, I say grin, it was more a twitch in the corner of her mouth. Jamie, pressured by what seemed like the rest of the bar, needed no second chance. He moved in, and the girl instinctively began to turn her head to the side.

3… .2… 1… shouted the girls.

It was no use. No matter how loud, or how fast they counted, they couldn't stop the young crummy from this kiss. Their tongues were chasing each other like a washing machine. I'd had bouts of food poisoning that were more romantic, but everyone accepted it was enough to see the guys ahead.

As Jamie retreated from his newly discovered friend, the others returned to the bar, congratulated by guests. Nigel immediately began to wind up the losing team. Whenever anyone asked what the forfeit was, he just replied it was a secret.

As others began to join us, we all stood around laughing about what had just transpired. I think a lot of the guests were bummed they had only been bit part players in this event, and hadn't been invited to participate from the start. Every time I heard, why didn't you invite us to play, I referred them to Nigel as it was his gig. As people would try to speak to Nigel, he would be ignoring them as he was busy whispering in the ears of the two girls, presumably trying to carve out some sort of prize for the boys.

You would have thought that, seeing these lads swap spit with a good percentage of the bar, some of their potential suitors might be discouraged. I can assure you, they were not. As I surveyed the scene, I could see the pretty girl that Will had been ignoring shuffling her way towards him. Some of the girls that Nigel had kissed were standing in the wings, and even Vigo, who'd been unceremoniously left by the wayside, was casting a watchful eye on Gary. It was like being monitored by the eye of Sauron. Some of the males that had managed to get a kiss in were hanging around too, but they had no chance. Nigel stayed loyal to the cause, and these girls weren't going anywhere.

After a few minutes of sniggering and negotiations, it appeared that Nigel and the girls had struck a consensus. Nigel had clearly laid claim to one of them, which meant that the other had free rein over the rest of the guys. And as Nigel began to retreat from the others, girl in hand, the friend—the blonder of the pair—grabbed Will by the hand and led him away too. With that, his fate was sealed.

Everyone else continued to drink and have fun. Jamie even resurrected the limbo game again, only to see him fall flat on his arse for a second time, much to the concern of the girls he was playing with. They immediately picked him up off the floor and dusted him down. Gary decided to pick up where he left off, and once again began to climb the beanstalk. Her patience was rewarded; it wasn't long before they too were heading towards the exit.

This left Jamie and me. I didn't really have anything on the go, so decided to have a chat with the girl who was with Will. She was fit but I didn't really get anywhere with her. I think she was too fashionable for me. She was into Will, and I think her ego had already taken a bit of a beating.

After another hour of hanging about with the guests, I decided to call it a night. Jamie was on the same wavelength and we walked back together from the bar. We were both heavily intoxicated. He said he was starving, so as we walked through the West End, we stopped for him to get some grub. He opted for a kebab with all the trimmings. Despite it looking like a culinary masterpiece, I was too tired to eat.

When we reached the cross roads, I pointed him in the

direction of his hotel and we parted ways. By the time my head hit the pillow, it must have been close to 5am.

I managed to oversleep the following day. Thankfully, Laura had given me a knock after an hour so it wasn't terminal. Apparently, one of her guests had seen us walking home in a crab-like fashion and told her we were ruined, so she decided to check up on me. I'm glad she did. I opened the door to be greeted with a cheese toastie and a cup of coffee. I could have kissed her. She had saved my ass, big time. Without her, this could easily have been a mid-afternoon lay in. Luckily there was nothing to do in the hotel and so I didn't miss anything. I got to the sales meeting just in time.

"Jesus Christ, you look like dog shit!" hollered Damien as I walked in.

I just ignored him. I wasn't in the mood for any of his lip. I wanted to find Nigel and get filled in on the night's events. He was nowhere to be seen, so I quietly sat in my chair and tried to hide behind my bottle of sprite.

Eventually, Nigel staggered in. Damien couldn't help himself. "Fuck me, you look worse than this dick," gesturing at me. Nigel also ignored him and slumped down in the chair next to me.

"How are you feeling?" I moaned to him.

"Absolutely terrible. You?"

"Same, I'm knackered" I replied. I got the run down before Damien really got into it.

Nigel had managed to negotiate cuddles with the two girls for him and a friend. Obviously, that was him and Will. When I asked about the others, he just replied, "Luke, I can only lead a horse to water." Nigel and Will had then gone back to theirs and completed their assignment. They both bolted this morning and nipped back to the apartment to find Gary in bed with a girl.

"I don't know how to describe her," he said, before I chimed in.

"Massive?"

Nigel smirked, "Oh, you know the one I'm talking about?"

"Yeah, the giraffe." I replied. Nigel started to laugh. I asked how Jamie was.

Nigel said he saw him on the sofa this morning, but he was asleep, so he didn't wake him. I told him how I'd taken him for food and crashed out. Nigel was already planning the night's escapade and so I told him I was down for whatever but didn't want to talk about it now as I was feeling rough. We were interrupted by Damien who then proceeded to carry out the sales meeting.

"You two ladies finished? Good. Let's crack on."

CHAPTER 28
EVICTION NOTICE

I don't think I even started to come round until the afternoon. I was struggling. I think the lack of sleep, over indulgence and general behaviour of the past few weeks had really begun to catch up with me.

Thankfully, one of my playmates was staying in the hotel. She too had over indulged and was feeling under the weather. Her friends had gone to the beach but she wasn't in the mood. I bumped into her as she was returning from the West End. She'd gone to buy some paracetamol and some water from the shop.

When I learned that her friends had gone to Cala Bassa, I quietly asked if she fancied a duvet day? I made sure I was out of earshot of the other guests. She started to smirk and then asked me to clarify exactly what that entailed. I told her it involved a massage and then a kip. I said I was down as long as she didn't snore! She just laughed and began to walk away, leaving me standing there. Without looking back, she asked me, "Are you coming then?"

I didn't need telling twice. She made us both a cup of tea to wash down the paracetamol she'd just taken. Once the intro was out of the way, we got down to pleasantries. Both of us felt rough, but that short time was a moment of respite from the hangovers. But, as you know, the minute that's all finished, the hangover comes back with a vengeance!

Within a few minutes we were both fast asleep. I don't recall being that tired in '98 and it was certainly the first time I'd needed a full afternoon off this season. I only stirred when her friends returned from the beach just before 6. It was somewhat awkward, but they were cool about everything.

When I looked at my watch, I'd managed to get a good additional five hours of sleep. I'd gone straight through lunch. I couldn't believe it. This was more sleep than I had managed in any one night in months. I felt human again.

I apologised to the girls for needing to cut and run, but I needed to be back at the hotel in an hour, changed and ready to work. They understood. As I closed the door behind me, I heard an eruption of giggling and exclamations. This made me smile.

I went to the hotel bar and managed to squeeze a quick meal in. I was famished and keen to avoid a repeat of the hangover, so asked the barman to get me some pasta. I demolished the plate within minutes and was off, back to the apartment to get ready for the evening. I hadn't spoken to Nigel, so had no idea what he had planned, but figured it would be something along the lines of get drunk, get horny, get lucky or get pissed.

By the time we all met up in the first bar, everyone was already relaxed and looking to party. Something was off though. Gary, Will and of course Nigel were there, but Jamie was missing.

"Where's Jamie?" I asked.

Nigel filled me in. Apparently, Jamie had eaten something bad and, from the moment he'd got out of bed this afternoon, he was turning himself inside out. He had experienced a complete biomedical breakdown. Gary described it like bleeding a radiator. This expression had me howling with laughter. I knew it must have been that kebab.

I wanted to check on him to see if he was alright or needed anything, but the others just laughed. Gary said it served him right for eating shite. Will seemed to be slightly more empathic, adding that they'd already got him some Sprite, boiled rice and some brown bread from the supermarket, so he should be well on his way to getting plugged. Nigel didn't seem bothered in the slightest. He was more intent on scouting for a suitable group of girls he could latch his band of brothers to. With that, no one mentioned it again and everyone promptly proceeded to get pissed and go on the pull.

It didn't take long for Sauron to walk in and start to flank Gary. It was like standing next to the Eiffel Tower. Everywhere you stood, you were in her shadow. Rather than try and be pleasant, Gary simply grabbed the nearest girl who would even look in his direction and started to dirty dance with her. It didn't take long for his long-legged friend to get the message, retire and seek refuge elsewhere.

Will was doing ok. The girl from the previous night was showing renewed interest. He played it cool, tempting her in with the odd glance or flick of the hair. I remember Nigel was being baited by some Welsh lads in his hotel. They kept challenging him to a drink. Every time he tried to refuse, they mercilessly caned him. Once we joined in, he folded like a deckchair and would chug whatever the Cardiff contingent would issue. This theme would continue throughout the night, and by the time we rocked up to Summum, everyone was staggering.

Summum was a small, alternative club located on the

outskirts of San Antonio, in the bay area. It was cheesy as hell. It was done out in a Greco-Roman style, with imitation marble columns and statues everywhere (think cherubs on the ceiling and so on). We would still host famous DJs there, but the nights would be a lot smaller than those going on in some of the super clubs. We would need to take a coach to take guests there, and frankly speaking, there wasn't much around there, so even if the guests got bored and left, they would usually come back in once they realised there wasn't much else without taking a taxi back to the West End.

What this meant was that the club stayed busy throughout the evening. Most guests couldn't be arsed to find a taxi, and would sooner wait until our coaches took them back to the West End in the early hours. The club was affectionately labelled as 'the sweatbox' by the reps. Even if you were sitting under the air conditioning and not moving a muscle, you would still be boiling.

Theme nights were all held at Summum, and whether it was 70s, 80s or fancy-dress nights, we'd all be there and in full costume. Nigel and I both knew that, having gone to clubs like Es Paradis or Eden (not to mention the super clubs like Amnesia or Privilege), being herded into Summum was always going to disappoint. The venue wasn't great, the location was even worse, and the DJs, while decent, were strictly B- or C-list at that point. We needed to make sure the guests had a good time.

Laura was on board with this, so we made sure that, on nights we were heading to Summum, we did the best we could to keep the guests engaged. We would do our utmost to entertain everyone. This meant deploying the full suite of entertainment measures. We would play blindfolded kissing games, dirty dance offs, drinking competitions, team and solo games. You name it, we did it.

It didn't stop when we got to Summum either. We would continue the effort inside. By the time the party was in full swing the guests would be on fire. They wouldn't have cared if they were dancing in an open air amphitheatre or Joseph Fritzl's basement.

This particular evening was particularly hard core. The guys from Cardiff had effectively broken Nigel. That's not to say that he hadn't done himself proud, I mean, the wheels had fallen off of the Cardiff carriage too, but Nigel was in a pretty bad way. Even his mates from home were laughing at him.

"Look at the fucking state of that dipstick," muttered Will, as we watched Nigel try to crowd surf but fail miserably.

"Luke, looks like you're our wingman tonight," added Gary. "At this moment in time, Nigel is the equivalent of an anchor."

We all started to chuckle. Two of the Welsh boys had already been put to sleep in the corner of the club on sofas. Some of the girls from their hotel were babysitting them to make sure security didn't throw them out. The remainder were giving each other rugby lifts and downing beers while hoisted far above everyone else.

We spent the remainder of the evening marvelling at Nigel's antics, and chatting to anything even remotely female looking. Will had finally managed to push up on the fashionista who had been on his case since the first night, and Gary had managed to immerse himself in a love triangle. He had spent an hour or so dancing and flirting with two girls from different hotels, all while under the watchful eye of Sauron, whom I believe had plans to swoop in and extract him with the panache of an Eastern European snatch gang.

As for me, well, I was no bueno. I was tired as hell. It

was an effort just to keep my eyelids off my cheeks. I was determined to stick it out though, so each time I felt my head beginning to nod, I grabbed a vodka and orange. The calories and the sugar injection would manage to ward off the desire to snooze for another 30 minutes.

By the time Gary had made his choice, Will had gone in for the kiss and Nigel had fallen over. I was relieved. It was just before 2am. We just had to see the sales meeting through and we were done. I was going straight to bed. I could hardly keep my head up, let alone anything else.

Damien went through the meeting quickly. I was practically propping Nigel up. Every time Damien turned away, Nigel stroked my face and I started to laugh. Every time Damien looked at us, we would freeze. This carried on for a few minutes before we were dismissed.

By this time, Gary and Will had emerged with their girls, and we piled on to one of the coaches heading back to the West End. Just being outside of the club in the fresh air made everyone feel instantly better. We all began to receive a second wind.

The banter on the coach was raucous. We were dropped off opposite the bars by the promenade and made our way up the hill towards the square at the top of the West End. Gary and Will flipped a coin. Gary won, and chose their room, so he and his belle were heading there. Will went back with the fashionista to hers.

Nigel and I were heading back ourselves when I heard a familiar clamour. The Welsh lads were also in the West End and, on seeing us both, immediately started to bait the pair of us into drinking with them. This was the last thing I needed but I didn't want to be rude. I looked round to ask Nigel what he wanted to do, but he'd already begun to head over.

We walked into the bar expecting to find it half empty

as most of the punters would have turned out towards the clubs. To my surprise, the bar was packed, mainly with our guests. A commotion was made as we entered and Nigel was immediately given a cocktail to neck.

If I could describe it, I would have to say—in terms of consistency and colour—if you put a parrot in a blender, you'd arrive at something similar. I didn't even want to think about what was in it. Thankfully, when one was handed to me, my dignity remained larger than my ego and I refused it.

"No chance am I putting that in my mouth."

Pressure was immediately applied on me to change my mind. I refuse, politely. "No fucking chance I am drinking that shit." Again, I was met with resistance.

Fortunately, I didn't get a chance to refuse again. My hand was grabbed and I was pulled backwards away from those that meant to do my liver harm. As I turned around to see who my mystery assailant was, I was pleasantly surprised to see it was Leanne, my afternoon cuddle buddy.

"Hello trouble, thanks for that! How are you?" I asked.

"Seems like you needed saving there," she replied. "I'm fine, thanks. We had a great time. You had a good night? He looks like he has!" She gestured at Nigel, who was on the cusp of downing his second liquidised cockatoo.

"Yeah, we've had a good night, but can I let you into a secret? Just don't tell anyone else." I leant towards her, and she instinctively leant back in towards me. "I am absolutely shattered," I whispered in her ear.

She laughed. "Not again!"

"Yep, I am getting old. I think I'd be better suited to repping the blue rinse brigade in Eastbourne."

She laughed louder. "Fancy going back for another kip?"

"You took the words right out of my mouth," I replied.

She wandered over to her friends and, a couple of moments later, we disappeared towards the rear of the bar and left quietly through the side entrance. I didn't spare a second thought for my face stroking accomplice.

We headed back towards mine. I figured it would allow me another 30 minutes of sleep if I didn't have to leave hers to go to mine to get changed in the morning. It did mean that she would have to do the walk of shame in the morning, but why should she get all the luck!

As we walked back towards my apartment, I joked that she was getting a sleeping partner and not a cuddle buddy. It didn't bother her, she said she was tired herself, and was sleeping badly at the hotel anyway because her roommate snored like a horse. At 2:45am we were back at my apartment. At 2:47am I was asleep.

By all accounts she was only a few minutes behind me. Thankfully, I didn't need to be at work particularly early and the sales meeting had been postponed an hour because Damien was needed in the office. This meant we could afford ourselves a somewhat lazy morning.

The flip side was that the later she left, the more obvious it was she'd stayed out. It's one thing walking back to your apartment at 8am in the clothes you wore the night before. I mean, you could easily be coming back from a club. It's another thing wandering back at 11am!

I promised to walk back with her to give her some moral support, though I am not sure if this did her any favours. Clearly, she felt better having someone with her while passing scores of holiday makers tucking into their breakfasts, but it also marked her out as someone who potentially got drilled by the rep next to her! I took a slight detour so we didn't have to pass along the main strip, dropped her off at the hotel, rather awkwardly, and checked in with Pepe to make sure all was well.

Having done my inspections and changed the notice board over, I decided to check in with Nigel and the lads to see how they got on. As I turned to the door, I was surprised to see them walking in.

"Oi oi, was just on my way over to see you!" I hollered. "How did you get on?"

Nigel looked damaged. Will and Gary started to laugh. Something had clearly happened. I looked at Nigel again, he looked different somehow. It took me a moment to realise what it was. He was rocking a mono brow. Yep, my partner in crime had lost one of his caterpillars.

I started to laugh, which kicked off Gary and Will again. "Who did that?" I asked.

We took a seat in reception. "Luke, I might need a favour from you," said Nigel.

Now I was intrigued. "I'm not giving you any money, you bell end."

"I don't need cash. I need a place to live!"

Will and Gary pissed themselves.

"What are you on about?" I said. I was bemused.

Nigel began to recount the tale of how he lost his brow. Apparently, after I'd left with Leanne, he had stayed around for a few more drinks with the Cardiff contingent at his hotel. They'd all got in a terrible state, returning to the hotel after 6am. Nigel confessed he needed to be assisted to get home. In fact, they all did.

Thankfully there were some girls from the hotel who were out with them, who helped steady them and walk them all back. Rather than go to bed as he should have done, he ended up in one of their rooms to continue the party. They drank for another hour or so. Nigel said there was lots of rugby banter but then things became boisterous. When I asked what this meant, he said they all started play-fighting and wrestling.

Now, Nigel being all ribs and dick meant he didn't stand a chance against anyone, so he started to play dirty. He ripped the shorts down of one of the guys in front of the room, exposing him to the girls. On the face of it, everyone just laughed, but it marked Nigel's card.

One of the lads crashed out on the sofa. Nigel had floated the idea of giving his eyebrows a little trim. The lads were in agreement, but as the razor and the foam came out to play, the guy suddenly came round. He saw what was about to go down and managed to squirm away. He then got the group to turn their attention to Nigel and, within half a minute, Nigel was an eyebrow lighter.

This made me laugh. Served him right for even suggesting it. I guess this was his comeuppance for what had happened to Adrian earlier on in the season.

Nigel said things didn't stop there. They continued to drink and laugh it off, but matey boy who nearly lost a caterpillar wasn't done. Unbeknown to Nigel, he'd run a cold bath and chucked in a couple of bags of ice they'd bought earlier in the day. I think everyone was too pissed to even register why someone was running an ice bath. They continued to drink until Nigel excused himself to use the loo.

As an unsuspecting Nigel entered the bathroom, he was suddenly pounced upon by the group. After the shortest struggle in combat history, Nigel was stripped naked and thrown in the bath. Despite his protestations, he was laughing and trying to wriggle out. They continued to hold him down in freezing cold water. After a minute or so they deemed the inevitable shrinkage had taken place, so dragged him out of the bath and carried him out of their hotel room along the corridor.

They each had an appendage and made plenty of noise as they carried him along like a stretcher, stopping only to wait for the lift. Nigel continued to protest about his treatment, but they—and everyone else who'd come out into the corridor to see what was transpiring—simply laughed. The lift doors opened, and the four carrying Nigel, squeezed into it. Those that couldn't fit into the lift made a dash down the stairs towards the front desk, anxious to witness the reception that was going to be received.

Nigel apparently didn't stop whining about how the hotel manager was going to go mad, something which served only to bolster their enthusiasm. Despite all his warnings and pleadings, the plan was going ahead.

The lift pinged as it reached the ground floor. As soon as the doors opened, Nigel was jettisoned onto the tiled floor, directly opposite the front desk. His naked torso landed in a heap of wrinkles. He stood up quickly, using his hands to cover his brooch and earrings.

If the owner of the hotel didn't like Nigel before, he was absolutely incensed now. Why the hotelier was up and about so early in the morning, we will never know. Everyone stood there laughing at Nigel. Well, everyone with the exception of the night security guard, who was about to clock off, and the owner.

The security guard shook his head but didn't say anything. The hotel manager, on the other hand, was some-what more animated. He started to shout at Nigel in Span-ish, and began to shake his fist. Rather than get out of there quickly to shield everyone's embarrassment and get some clothes back on, Nigel decided to try and fight his case, there and then.

I think this only wound the hotelier up further. There was no way he could take Nigel seriously while he was standing there, holding his plums, trying to protest that it wasn't his fault. Not only that, I don't think the hotelier could hear what Nigel was saying over the constant barrage of insults he himself was shouting.

This stand-off lasted for about 45 seconds before the hotelier flipped. He came from around the counter, grabbed Nigel around his neck, and frog marched him through reception and out the main entrance. He shoved him into the street and told him not to come back.

Nigel stood there on the pavement, dick in hand, asking for forgiveness, or at the very least his clothes. These requests fell on deaf ears. The hotelier simply turned around and walked back to his office, leaving the security guard, who by now had withdrawn his baton, covering the entrance to make sure he didn't come back through it.

It was at this point that the guests quickly dissipated. The lads from Lisvane quickly shot into the lift and back up to their room. I can only imagine how they began to wonder if they'd gone too far. They quickly went on to the balcony and could see Nigel, bemused, sitting naked on a bench. They called down to him to wait there. One of them quickly grabbed his clothes from their bathroom and nipped down to give them to him.

It must have been a sorry sight to see him dressing himself like a homeless lothario. I was laughing as Nigel told me all this. When asked what he did next, he said he went to a café to grab some breakfast. He ordered a breakfast bocadillo and promptly fell asleep at the table. He said he woke up an hour later, finished his sandwich, then sat back on the bench waiting for the others to emerge.

It was at this point that Gary and Will started to chime in and fill in the missing pieces. What was apparent to me, though, was that Jamie was still missing.

"Where's Jamie?" I inquired.

"He's still on the shitter," replied Gary, nonchalantly.

"You're kidding?" I said.

"Nope, he's wringing himself inside out still. He's not been off the throne for more than an hour in two days," claimed Will.

"Does he need to see the Doc? Maybe he needs treatment?" Gary shot me down immediately. "No, he's ok, just needs to drink water and rest. He's eating Imodium like skittles! Soft cock. That'll teach him to eat shite."

Clearly there wasn't much sympathy for their missing wingman.

"Never mind Jamie's ring-piece, what about my situation? I'm homeless!"

I started to laugh again, instantly forgetting about Jamie's stint as a human squid. "What did the hotelier say? Have you spoken to Damien or the office?"

I wanted to make sure Nigel had covered all the bases before offering out my love pad as a place to crash. Last thing I wanted was a roommate, but I was obviously going to help him. I suggested he tell Damien what had happened so he could fight his corner, in case anything got escalated. He asked if he could crash at mine if he needed to. I said he could, but only if he put me in touch with some of the girls in his hotel. He laughed and then claimed he couldn't believe I was blackmailing him. Gary quickly chimed in that it was only fair. Of course, I was joking but I wanted him to work for it!

In the end, Nigel told Damien what had happened. He did it in front of some guests who backed up Nigel's story that he was essentially kidnapped, stripped and shoved into reception. As much as Damien figured Nigel had done something to deserve it, he couldn't really go against the story. He went to take it up with the hotelier.

Trying to get him to back down was apparently like pulling teeth, but eventually, Damien wore him down. I think it was the threat of us taking the hotel guests to another bar every evening if Nigel was not allowed back that did it. I mean, if Nigel wasn't allowed to use the hotel, he would have to 'supervise' the guests elsewhere.

That being said, the hotelier reluctantly agreed he could come back, but only at the weekend, which meant I had him for the next 2 evenings. Damien agreed. Laura was told to swap with Nigel until then, so she was looking after his guests and he was looking after hers.

Gary, Will and Jamie stayed with us for the rest of the week. The evenings were pretty much a carbon copy of their first night. Everyone continued to get wasted, someone would bring up a particular game or challenge, we'd all play it, and the other guests would get involved. At the end of the night, different combinations would end up with girls while those without would end up hammered.

I don't think I saw Jamie until maybe a day or so later. He never really made it back out fully. His stomach had properly turned on him. He would venture out for an hour or so, but even the mere mention of the word beer had his sphincter twitching like a rabbit's nose. I think he returned to Blighty paler than he was before he arrived, not to mention a good 5kg lighter.

It was a shame to see them go. They were a great bunch, and am proud to say that I'm still friends with all of them to this day.

CHAPTER 29
THE FORMENTERA FLOATER

As we were nearing the end of peak season, we were all beginning to tire. Nigel would frequently confess that he routinely ended up falling asleep in the sack rather than performing. I wasn't immune to the effects of sleep deprivation either. Rather than the lady's lion, it was more often a case of the lazy leopard.

We weren't the only ones. Most of the team were knackered by this point. The sales meetings became a point of friction. Someone was always pissed with someone else. People were oversleeping, getting more drunk on duty, or just not doing what they were told, causing Damien to come down harder as he tried to maintain discipline. Damien himself was getting tired, meaning his mood swings were becoming all the more unpredictable, adding to the stress.

On nights out, the girls would often sneak off for a sleep in the toilet cubicles, meaning that we would end up having to cover their part of the entertainment as no one could find them. This left the guys feeling salty.

Even my sales figures began to dip, causing Damien to ask me if everything was ok. I told him I was shattered. He suggested I try and get some sleep rather than trying to pile through the guests. I just smiled and told him I wasn't that sleepy. We both shared a grin. He appreciated I was clearly enjoying myself out there and that to try and stop me from any extracurriculars wasn't really an option.

Thankfully, I'd stayed away from drugs, so despite being tired, I was still pretty much firing on all cylinders. The same couldn't be said for some of the other reps. Some ended up getting into the habit of a booster. Whether that was a line of coke here or there, or a couple of pills, they were in a worse situation than me, physically and mentally. Although nothing was ever said publicly, it was obvious who had been using them. The paranoia and fear of being caught out only added to their mood swings.

It wasn't just mental issues that people were carrying. Many of us were struggling with physical issues, too. Even at the grand age of 18-20, hitting the parties as hard as we were began to take its toll. People were struggling with everything from continual throat infections to gastric problems. Some would get the shakes, presumably from the alcohol. Others would be in a perpetual state of having thrush or cystitis. Some would be carrying war wounds from nights out: broken wrists, ankles, even the odd broken nose were common injuries amongst the reps.

Nigel had a cough that lasted what seemed like months. I myself struggled with gastritis and, from time to time, gastroenteritis. It basically meant that I was continually having various stomach ailments. I'd often suffer heartburn and general tummy aches. I think this helped to see me through though, as it meant I'd be forced to slow up on the booze and drink more water than normal.

The gastroenteritis was a different story though. One minute you were out with the guests, or chilling by the pool, and the next minute, the countdown was on. That small tingling that started off as a few bubbles in the bottom of my belly would, within no time at all, turn into an arm-wrestling match between my colon and my intestines. I knew then that I had between 30 seconds and a minute to find a throne before the contents of my stomach and, seem-ingly, part of my spine would be ejected from my tea towel holder without any thought for my respect or dignity.

This would come and go but, in general, I was being careful—if not downright lucky—to make sure I always had a turn out before I went out, or took the relevant medication with me if I was showing any symptoms. Luck, though, like anything intangible, doesn't last forever.

It must have been midway through August when Jack and Frank brought up the idea of doing another football / beach day combo. They claimed they had guests that had wanted to play against other hotels in a football tourna-ment, and were being pestered daily about it, but this was of course bollocks. Very few guys aged 18-19 want to spend the day taking part in a football tournament rather than chasing beers and bikinis in Ibiza.

On hearing their plea in front of Damien, Nigel rolled his eyes. I was somewhat more vocal. Seeing that their idea looked to be gaining some traction, I felt the need to chirp up.

"No interest in taking my lot to play football. They'd prefer to relax by the beach," I said.

Frank, sensing I was trying to torpedo his efforts, went on the attack. "You just don't want to play. How do you know they don't want to play a tournament? Did you ask them?"

I wasn't in the mood to play nice, so snapped back. "I've booked almost everyone on the weekender, and have higher sales figures than you've had all season. Don't be telling me what my guests do or don't want."

Damien sat back for a moment, while I let Frank mari-
nate on the saveloy I'd just laid across his plate. He didn't
say anything, forcing Damien to mediate.

"Okay, okay. Luke, would you prefer to go to the
beach?"

"Yeah, on this occasion, I really would."

With that, Damien started to divide up the group. He
didn't bother asking one of the girls to swap with me and
go to the football, given he knew what the outcome
would be.

It was at this point that Nigel chirped up. He got as far
as "Damien…" before he was swiftly denied.

"No chance. You're playing football."

Nigel took it on the chin and just sat there imitating
heartbreak.

They mapped out the event for the day after next. Tony
had already phoned through to check the stadium was free,
so it all came together rather quickly.

I put a couple of posters up in reception detailing football or the beach and told all the guests about it. I put in the
bare minimum effort into selling the day. Predictably, those
who were interested went for the beach.

When the big day came, all of my guests, bar one or
two, were up for the beach. I'd woken up feeling relatively
okay. I had managed to get a relatively good night's sleep,
and as a result felt pretty normal.

I led everyone down to the pier and we boarded a boat
destined for Cala Comte. I was the only male rep on the
boat, with an overwhelming majority of female guests relative to males. In fact, I think there were only a handful of
lads present outside of my hotel guests, so the numbers
were heavily skewed in our favour.

This went down well with my guys. I'd already briefed
them when we assembled earlier that, as far as ratios went,

this was as good as it was going to get in Ibiza, so told them to capitalise on it!

We boarded the boat. The weather was perfect and everyone was smiling. A number of female reps made a few light hearted attempts to poke fun at me in front of their predominantly female guests. After 10 minutes, I think the whole boat cottoned on early and soon realised that a) I didn't have five kids b) wasn't married c) wasn't gay, and d) wasn't riddled with crabs.

I smiled graciously and just took it all in. I then went to the front of the boat and made a little bed for myself on the deck. Within a couple of minutes I was in the foetal position and off into the land of nod.

One of the guests was kind enough to give me a nudge as we pulled in. Apparently, I looked very sweet as I slept. The guests couldn't believe how quickly I —and some of the female reps too—had dozed off, and how I managed to stay perfectly asleep on the floor of a boat laden with 100 guests and loud music. What little they knew! I think I may have inadvertently been posing for pictures with various groups of guests. Not that I cared. The sleep was worth it.

We reached the disembarkation point and made our way off the boat onto the beautiful sandy shores of Cala Comte. If you've never been here before, the water is crystal clear and the current is extremely light. There are a few rocks and some small islands jutting out of the calm, turquoise sea. You had a handful of restaurants and bars, but these were extremely basic, more like shacks on the beach.

It was all very Bohemian. It added to the character, particularly as there wasn't really much else there. There were a couple of walls and a rickety door that was supposed to resemble a toilet—and that was about it. There wasn't much shade there, so we always advised the guests to cream up.

Everyone dispersed along the beach and started to relax. It was still early so the place was relatively empty. I made sure that my guys had everything they needed and made small talk with the other guests from the girls' hotels. Despite being flirty, it was all very chilled. My plan was to do the bare minimum, then find a spot for some more sleep. I smiled to myself, thinking of Nigel being shouted at by Frank for not playing football hard enough.

I wasn't smiling for long. I was holding court with about six or seven girls. Everyone was being very smiley and friendly. They were asking me about what it was like to be a rep and live in Ibiza, and I was asking them what they did at home, etc. Just the usual pleasantries.

One of the girls spoke up for me and said she didn't believe what the other girls were saying about me on the boat. I just smiled and told the group the female reps always did it to me, just to put people off me. This gathered some sympathy and I started to feel my mojo rise. Unfortunately, it wasn't the only thing I could feel rising.

Out of nowhere, I felt a stomach contraction roll through my lower regions like a slinky. It was as if some part of my pelvis felt the need to gulp. I instinctively looked over to the makeshift toilets. There was already a queue there and it looked like someone was handing out the wet wipes.

I couldn't believe it. I had been feeling fine all morning and hadn't had a bout for a few days. Surely not here. Not in one of the most pristine places in the Balearics.

I tried to ignore my inner workings. I focused intently on what the girl was saying, trying to drown out the percussion that was gathering both pace and power somewhere behind my belly button. It was no use. The game was up.

Another wave came and thankfully passed. I briefly pondered to myself if this was how women felt after their waters broke, or how Kane felt, in Alien, just before the little guy started to burst through his guts. I didn't give too much time to either thought as I was aware that, in about 30-40 seconds, my own waters were going to break.

I looked again at the makeshift shacks. Still a queue—as if that was going to have changed since I initially looked at them. I quickly surveyed the area again. There were no bushes, no rock formations, no cover. I even looked to see if there was a boat I could squat behind. No bueno. Fuck it.

I felt a few beads of sweat form on either temple. Another contraction hit me. This time it managed to make its way further along my digestive system. I abruptly, but very politely, broke off the conversation with the girls and began to walk away. I didn't know where I was going, but the last thing I was going to do was shit myself in front of seven ladies who had been expressing sympathy towards me not a minute earlier.

I looked towards the female reps but they were preoccupied with putting sun cream on each other and making themselves their own little beds for some much-needed winks. There was no saviour there. Bollocks.

As I started to drift along the beach looking for inspiration, or at the least praying for intervention, my stomach threw another motion towards my ankles. The way I saw it, I had two choices. Sea or sand. It really was that simple. There were a few people paddling but nothing I couldn't swim through. The issue was that the sea was absolutely, conspicuously, crystal clear. It would be the equivalent of emptying a catering jar of Branston into a white porcelain bath and hoping no one notices.

I was convinced it would only be a matter of time before someone would spot it. People would flee the waters like an

Amity Island shark attack. To make matters worse, there was no current at all. It could lurk there all day, just offshore, waiting to attack. Just below the surface. Silent and deadly, like a German U-boat.

I tried to stay calm. I casually took off my t-shirt, flip flops and discarded my bag onto the sand. As I approached the water, I felt another intestinal hula hoop roll through my abdomen. This felt more urgent. I felt my starfish let out an involuntary hiccup. This was it, no time to lose. Didn't care how much of a tool I looked, I needed to get out to sea and quickly.

With great purpose I strode forward into the azure waters. I immediately stepped onto a sharp rock or shell. Despite me wincing, I carried on. I heard someone calling out to me. I figured it was someone from my hotel, but there was no chance I was stopping to talk to them. We were going to be knee deep in Bovril any moment now.

They called again. I ignored them again. To save my blushes, I dived forwards into the water and began to swim. Not a casual 'I am in crystal waters with a bunch of chicks' swim, but a 'Michael Phelps Olympic domination' type swim. I properly powered ahead.

Normally, when doing front crawl, you would lift your head to breathe every two or three strokes. I was lifting every eight. Breathing would come later. I was more preoccupied with not leaving a gravy trail, and didn't stop until I was at least 50 metres behind the last person. Problem was, the sea was still shallow.

I decided to go out more diagonally now, albeit at a slower pace. I feared I could still be seen from the shoreline. Remember, I still had to pull my shorts down. Further out I went. Another 25m, 30m, 40m. I was now a good 100m from the shore. I could tread water without touching the bottom or being seen. No time to lose.

Trunks off, placed in front of me. I couldn't bear the risk of having a nugget anchor itself to my shorts, effectively betraying me when I made land. I could hear the nicknames now: Shitter, Pooper Scoop, Bertie Squirty, Two Bob, I could go on. Predictably, it wasn't long before my stomach turned again. This time I was ready for it.

Within a few short seconds, I had essentially adopted a squid like pose and had committed my turd to a sea burial. The minute I emptied myself, I stopped treading and started to swim away. I couldn't look back. I think the feeling of shame must have washed over me. How could I defile such a beautiful place? I looked below me and, despite the water being a good 8-10 feet deep, I could clearly make out ripples in the sand. With such clarity, the fear of seeing my little kinder egg returning to me like a boomerang began to return.

Convinced within minutes that people would be detailing what I had for breakfast, I pulled my shorts back on and decided to swim parallel with the shore as though I was exercising. I figured the longer I was out for, and the harder I swam, people would think I was a swimmer as opposed to a serial crapper.

Now, while I had always swam, two seasons in Ibiza had taken its toll. I swam up and down repeatedly until my arms were practically hanging off. Thankfully I was still relatively slim so I could pass it off as exercise, but by the time I got back to the shore, I was exhausted. I was careful to exit the water a fair way off from where I entered the water to further break up the chain of evidence.

One of the guests remarked that I was like a fish. I just smiled and told them it was rare that I got to exercise and the water was so nice, I couldn't resist. Of course, that was utter nonsense, but I felt more confident issuing that white lie than admitting I was effectively incontinent. I picked up my bag and clothes, found a little area close to where the girls were, and promptly crashed out. True to form, within minutes I was asleep.

By the time I came to, the place was much busier. A procession of boats had emptied their passengers along the shoreline and people were happy chilling and swimming about. I figured that, because I hadn't been woken by any screams or commotion, I must have been in the clear. Besides, you'd be hard pushed to blame that on me. I instantly began to feel better.

"Hello sleepyhead," a voice rang out. I turned around to see it was one of the girls I'd been talking to earlier. She'd brought me a water. "I thought you might be thirsty."

"Thank you very much, you didn't have to do that," I told her.

"I know I didn't, but I wanted to," she replied, handing me the bottle. She took a seat next to me. Her name was Lauren. She was cool, a year or so older than me, just graduated from University and doing some clerical work in London. She had long, dark hair and pretty brown eyes. We basically continued our conversation from before.

I apologised for bailing so abruptly earlier, telling her I was hung over and I suddenly got the sweats. I told her I needed to cool off in the sea. She didn't seem fazed by it. We continued to chat, and it didn't take long for the conversation to take a familiar turn.

"So, I guess you get lots of girls out here then?" she asked.

Here we go. "What makes you say that?"

"Well, because you're a rep, and everyone looks up to you lot," came the reply.

"Well, I'd like to think if someone was interested in me, it would be because I was attractive to them, or at the very least a nice person."

Checkmate. She was flustered. "Oh, I didn't mean it like that, I mean, erm, well…"

I cut short her pain. "Relax, I'm teasing you. Yeah, some girls want you only because you're a rep. I guess it's a trophy thing for them. Others want to sleep with us mainly because we look good naked." I paused to smile at her. I could see the cogs turning as she digested what I'd just said, before we both started to smile.

She playfully flicked sand at me, which I thought was a good sign. We talked further for another 10 or 15 minutes, before she suggested we go for a swim.

With all thoughts of my emergency turn out erased from my memory, I went back into the cool clear waters. We stood around in the shallow area talking to other guests and reps for a while before we started to venture out further into the deeper blue. By now a few boats had arrived and had moored up to the side of the main area. We began to swim and float about near them. There were a few guests around us also paddling.

Slowly but surely, as time went on, the others would swim back to shore, leaving us more and more isolated. As we began to move towards the shoreline, we found ourselves behind one of the boats. Neither of us could reach the bottom and stand, so to save energy we ended up balancing on one of the lines the boat had tied itself to. We continued to chat about this and that for a while before it suddenly became apparent we were both alone, flirting, and very close to each other.

I wish I could say I took the initiative and grabbed her by the waist, but the truth be told, it was her. She pulled me into her and we shared a cheeky snog. Initially I was some-what startled but within a few moments we were making out like a couple of teenagers.

It felt weird. Normally, most of the interactions out

there were in the evening. Mostly under the influence of alcohol or during some random meeting in the early hours of the morning. Here I was, in the middle of the day, sober as a judge, having my tongue tickled by an older educated girl in the middle of the sea. It was much more stimulating.

Things continued for a few minutes before we reached a point where we were either stopping here, or we were going for it. As dolphin style wasn't on the menu, we both pulled back, deciding to head back to the beach.

Unfortunately for me, it wasn't the first time that day I had been forced to swim up and down away from everyone else. This time it wasn't because I was fleeing human waste, but because I'd developed a keel and needed to swim it off before exiting. She found this hilarious, and by the time I'd lost my stabiliser and exited the sea, she was already gossiping with her mates.

I went over to see the female reps. Laura had clocked me emerging from behind the boats. "You better not be messing around with my guests," she hollered at me.

I just feigned shock, smiled and sat down with them. We hung out and chilled for another hour or so before we had to make tracks. We put everyone back on the boat for the ride back to San Antonio.

As the boat was pulling back from the makeshift jetty, we heard a shriek followed by some raucous commotion and laughter that made most of the guests turn around in their seats. I couldn't make out what all the fuss was about, but some guests from a neighbouring boat were also laughing and chattering like monkeys. Was it just an adventurous crab, or had my faecal float returned to base?

I guess we'll never know. I quickly constructed my temporary quarters and, as regular as clockwork, was asleep within minutes.

CHAPTER 30
LOOKIE-LOOKIE

After the beach we returned to our hotels. At mine, everyone had a quick dip and a beer as the sun began to set. It was probably the most chilled I'd seen the hotel all season. With everyone sitting together, I did the rounds and closed the last few remaining guests on the weekender.

I was pleased with this. This not only brought me back up to 100% for the hotel, but more importantly, it would allow me to tea bag Frank in front of Damien. Frank had fuck all chance of getting numbers anywhere near as good as these, and I figured it would allow me some autonomy going forwards choosing between football or the beach.

Once the sun set, people began to turn in. I returned home to get changed for the night ahead. I was in a relaxed but thoughtful state and even managed to make my dinner last longer than a minute. I tucked into some chicken and plain rice as I contemplated what had occurred during the day. I thought about my beach emergency (hence the rice), and I thought about Lauren and our marine encounter. I was especially keen to see her again and go from there.

I caught up with Nigel and Laura in the bar. I threw

Nigel a fist bump and planted a big wet kiss on Laura's cheek. She recoiled in terror, much to my amusement.

"Laura was just telling me how you fucked one of her guests in the sea." Laura shot Nigel a sharp look. You'd think he'd just spilled her innermost secrets. I simply laughed.

"Nothing happened in the sea."

"Sure, sure," teased Laura.

I quickly changed tack. "Why, what did this guest say?" This threw her off balance.

"Um, nothing was mentioned," she responded meekly.

"Bullshit. She said something, didn't she?"

Nigel also came to my aid. "Laura, does your guest want to bonk Luke?" She was cornered with nowhere to go. I felt my ego swell with every second passing. "Out with it, Missy!"

With that, Laura capitulated. "Well, she might have said you were fit and you might have shared a kiss and cuddle by the boats." I could tell that admitting this was an irritation for Laura.

"Luke, I think you're staying over at Laura's hotel tonight," he said, high fiving me while smiling defiantly at Laura as he did so.

"You had better not. Take her to yours. I don't even want to think about you spreading your filthy behaviour throughout my palace of sophistication."

I just smiled. Nigel couldn't help himself. "Laura, do you know how many times I've smashed in your hotel? Your hotel is notorious for going over. Luke and I stopped going there because it became boring, it was too easy."

Laura kicked Nigel in the shins. I kept quiet. With that, we all started to chuckle again. Of course, Nigel was exaggerating and trying to wind Laura up. The truth was that while we were frequent visitors to her place of business, that didn't mean we had to be public about it. Thankfully, some of our guests came over to ask a question and the topic was immediately changed.

I only briefly saw Lauren and her friends at the end of the first bar. We exchanged pleasantries and I introduced Nigel to her group. Get your end in, get your friend in became our mantra.

Pretty soon he had cemented himself within the group. We started to round up the guests as we were moving onwards to the next bar: Koppas.

Koppas was one of my favourite bars on the strip. It always had a great atmosphere and you rarely lost guests. It was at the bottom of the hill and directly beneath it was a small, cheesy club. No matter how wasted you were, this place would always let you in. If you were going to Eden or Es Paradis, Koppas was on your way.

It was always a nice place to meet before moving onwards. The only downside about Koppas was that it was close to the restaurant area, opposite the promenade. If you hung around for too long you'd run into hordes of ticket touts. They would not only try to poach the guests into other bars or restaurants, they would also bombard the guests with offers to buy all manner of goods.

The first group of touts were easy to deal with. Our company was large enough that, if a complaint was made to the owner of the bar or restaurant the tout was working for, it could cause them issues. With a turnover of 3-4,000 clients a week, we were a tour operator you wanted to stay on-side with.

The second group of touts proved significantly more cumbersome. Most of them had travelled to the Balearics from Africa. Initially they would try and offer the guests things like sunglasses, silly hats, and other plastic neon infused shite. They often would holler, "Lookie-lookie" as a way to embed themselves with the guests. The guests would often take the piss, banter back, laugh, etc., and then the guys would start their spiel. They were seldom alone, and more often than not, things were not as they seemed. What would start with harmless banter over a fake pair of Ray-Bans or a hookie Louis Vuitton handbag, would often quickly move on to a drug deal negotiation.

Ibiza was the party capital of Europe and, in the 90s at least, the entire world. Everyone therefore wanted a piece of its drugs business. The market was large, lucrative and well organised. Much like in any film or TV show, the business was divided up. Local dealers would handle the higher margin powdered side of things. Other Europeans would handle the dance drugs (ecstasy, speed, LSD and so on), leaving the green stuff to the aforementioned lookie-lookie men.

That's not to say things weren't exclusive, but in all my time there, I was never offered weed by anyone other than the lookie-lookie men. After two years there, going out every single night, that's saying something.

Quite often guests would get themselves in trouble. The lookie-lookie men didn't particularly hide their business well, and were targeted by the local constabulary. The guests would end up paying the guy then having to meet someone else at a particular place a few minutes later. There would often be instances where the person never showed up. Or the person would bring something completely different to what had been agreed, or sometimes others would be there to shake the guest down further still.

I'd seen and heard about this happening time and time again. That's not to say that every guy selling fake Gucci bracelets was actually trying to offload kilos of Mary Jane, nor that every visitor from Nigeria or Sudan was a drug dealer, but in '98 and '99, anyone trying to hawk neon rimmed sunglasses was basically someone you wanted the guests to avoid.

We saw them every evening and they saw us. If I heard so much as a 'lookie' I intercepted. If I heard a guest so much as mumble the words drugs, I pulled them away. If you want drugs, go buy them in the club, buy them from security, buy them from bar staff, but don't buy them from here. Every rep had this ingrained in them.

One particular evening, as we were going into Koppas, a group of guests had been collared by some of the lookie-lookies. By the time I arrived on scene, it was too late. The damage had been done and it had all kicked off. By all accounts, one of the guests had stopped to look at the wares of one such street seller. They were negotiating on the price of a fake gold chain, or something equally as crap.

The guest involved kept protesting that he didn't have enough money to meet the price of the seller. Eventually they agreed on a much smaller amount, but then the seller didn't have change. At the insistence of the lookie-lookie man, the guest showed him his wallet, opening it in front of him to display a pair of notes. They'd agreed on a price of 2,000 pesetas for this chain, which was about £8 at the time, but once the seller saw the guest had a pair of 10,000 notes, which was about £80, he snatched them out of his wallet, gave the guy two chains and began to walk away.

Strange as it may seem, this didn't go down too well with the buyer or the rest of his group. As they protested louder, the lookie-lookie man increased his pace and started to head away from the area. Not wanting to let this go, the group of three or four guests grabbed him by the arm and tried to detain him in an attempt to get their money back.

Things escalated immediately. The lookie-lookie man pulled out a small knife and began to wave it around in an attempt to ward off the group. In response, the group became seriously vocal, drawing more and more attention to the whole situation. The lookie-lookie man was immediately surrounded by the group, cutting off any exit routes. The guy who had been a victim to the snatch then picked up a bottle that had been conveniently left by the side of the curb and began to approach the thief.

Despite the lookie-lookie man not really shouting out for help or creating a scene himself, he was soon joined by three or four of his accomplices. Things were turning physical. Thankfully, his companions came and stood in between our guests and the knife that had been drawn. But as more of our guests began to hear and see the commotion, they too began to join the group and, before you know it, what had started as a small misunderstanding began to swell into something much nastier. By the time the reps were on the scene, there were 25-30 additional guests there, all baying for justice.

Word travelled quickly and several other reps left what they were doing and piled into the thick of it. We were trying to stop the guests from getting beaten, or worse. The money at this point was no more than a life lesson on dealing with filth. But the guests weren't thinking along these lines. Buoyed by their greater numbers, alcohol and a sense of justice, they weren't in the mood to let this chancer go softly into the night.

Other holiday makers, who until now had been tucking into their tapas and paellas, began to rise to see what was happening. This in turn alerted their staff and other touts to a potential flare-up. Still the guests pushed for their refund. The air was filled with cursing on both sides. English insults flew freely, as did the street sellers' indecipherable rebuttals.

Once the ratios began to climb further still, the guests started to move forwards, despite us doing our utmost to hold everyone back while at the same time trying to get the money returned from the asshole that had caused this. Realising we were losing control of the situation, I began to look around for an exit. If things were going to really kick off, and a knife and bottle were involved, this was the last place I wanted to be.

My worries were short lived though. A couple of the security guards and a barman from Koppas came rushing out and closed the gap between the bar and the crowd in a few seconds. The barman was brandishing a steel rounders bat and the security guards each had a cosh extended, ready to be used. The guests instantly parted ways for them, unsure initially as to their intentions. Once they realised they were coming to their aid, they circled around each other behind the lookie-lookie men.

Things didn't look good for the sellers at this point. The bar staff seemed to know them. Something was said and the bat was brandished in a threatening manner. The knife was put away. After some back and forth, one of the security guards took the two chains from our guest and shoved them in the hand of the thief. He initially refused to take them, but one of his friends started to argue with him. Reluctantly, he took the chains back. Watching him hand the money back to the security guard, you'd think he was being forced to hand over his family for execution.

The security guard wasn't taking any prisoners. He snatched the cash out of his hand and promptly handed it back to the guest. Sensing a break through, the reps immediately began gathering the guests back towards the West End, leaving the bar staff arguing with the lookie-lookie men. After a minute or two, they parted ways. All of the lookie-lookie men disappeared quickly into the night, leaving the rest of the tourists and random bystanders to continue on with their evenings.

As we got back inside Koppas, the guests were clearly very animated. Everyone was discussing what had just taken place. They were like chattering monkeys. The reps immediately started to dispatch shots of schnapps to try and lighten the mood.

We made a big effort that night to try and integrate the groups with the opposite sexes. After about half an hour, things were completely back to normal. No one was speaking about the incident, and everyone was too busy enjoying the music and drinks to care.

It wasn't long before it was time for us to take the guests to the next place but, before leaving, I managed to get to the staff to thank them for their intervention. They downplayed their involvement and I wasn't hearing any of it. We spoke for a few minutes. Apparently, the lookie-lookie men had been doing similar all season, and there was somewhat of a crackdown taking place. Given the nature of the underlying business, it wasn't in anyone's interest for the police to be involved, so bar owners and staff were taking matters into their own hands. They all knew each other anyway.

Just before leaving we took a shot and bumped fists. Somehow, the resort office learned of what happened, and they too were grateful to the staff for intervening. For the rest of the season, Koppas was our venue of choice.

CHAPTER 31
3,2,1... MERMAID

Having left Koppas, we made our way along the promenade to Eden. We'd crossed over so we were walking along the edge of the beach, opposite the restaurants. As we were a big group, it was easier to move along that side, undisturbed by touts.

The mood among the guests was vibrant. They were happy and keen to continue the party. With all the excitement from earlier, I'd pretty much forgotten about Lauren. I'd been so busy trying to chill everyone out and salvage the evening, any thoughts I may have had of finishing our marine encounter had completely slipped my mind.

It wasn't until I felt my bum get pinched did things return to me. I looked to see who it was, and saw Lauren and one of her mates grinning at me. If I had to guess, I'd say Lauren had been stitched up and it was her mate who had felt my peach. Despite her elbowing her mate in the ribs and protesting, I accused her all the same.

As we were moving along the road to Eden we chatted with the rest of their group. Nigel was also attaching himself to them, hopeful for some action. We were all conversing, with general conversation being interrupted with various bits of banter from time to time.

I was in a good mood and looking forward to Eden, but Nigel had other plans. We were already approaching the end of season and everyone was dog tired. Nigel decided he didn't want to go to Eden and instead we should all go somewhere else separately to bond. While I liked the sound of it, he was failing to grasp one simple fact. We were supposed to be working.

Nigel proposed we should give Eden a swerve and have our own party in one of the beach front bars. His suggestion immediately started to gain traction. A couple of his guests weren't in the mood for a club, and some of the girls liked the idea of another bar. Nigel's reasoning—that it was too early to go to the club anyway—started to appeal to a few more. Before you knew it, he'd started a revolution.

I couldn't understand what he was doing. This was completely counterintuitive to what we usually did. I took him to one side, stopping by a fountain until we were out of earshot from the girls.

"What are you up to? We can't just skip work. Damien will destroy us tomorrow. He's already touchy about reps slacking off."

Nigel put his hand round my shoulder. "Luke, you worry too much. We have a couple of weeks left. We both know I'm already going to be on airport duty for the rest of my time here anyway. What else can he do?"

He had a point. Nigel had been signed up for most of them anyway due to him not bothering to sell. It's not like he was going to get fired a few weeks before we were due to leave anyway. He leaned in to me.

"Let's just take the guests to our own little bar, far away from the masses. I'm tired, Luke, and the last thing I want to do is dance to fucking house music for the 500th time this summer." He lowered his voice to a whisper. "Wouldn't you rather cuddle up to Lauren instead of babysitting?"

I totally understood where he was coming from. The season had taken its toll on all of us, but still, the very last thing I wanted to do was get in Damien's crosshairs. It was hard enough waking up at the moment without needing additional airport punishments pushing me way over the limit.

I thought I had better reason with him. My suggestion would be to take everyone to a bar and settle them in. I would tell the others he had forgotten something in the apartment, then we could switch out at one point during the evening. That way, neither of us would go in the doghouse. I thought that would be a fairly decent compromise.

I opened my mouth to put forward this idea when I felt my body involuntarily go sideways, coming to rest at the base of the fountain, in about 18 inches of water. Mother-fucker. One of Nigel's guests had decided that I looked too dry in my evening attire and that maybe I was in need of some hydration. I dragged my ass out of the fountain, soaked from head to toe. As I turned towards the guest who had done it, he started to bleat.

"Luke, I'm sorry man, Nigel put me up to it. He said if I didn't do it, he'd give me half a pint of tequila to drink in court tomorrow. I can't drink tequila, it's awful. He said he owed you one, because you pushed him in the fountain last week."

I turned to Nigel. "You lying cock. I never put you in any fountain. You prick."

Nigel was grinning. "Yeah but you could have done it. This was a preemptive strike." He then proceeded to quote Karate Kid. "Strike first, strike hard, no mercy sir!" and started to giggle.

I couldn't believe it. This bastard has just organised me

being dunked, and here I am laughing at his corny jokes. Fucking Nigel!

"Luke, I've solved our little problem. They won't let you in dripping wet, and it was a guest who pushed you in. So then, where shall we meet?"

As much as I hated to admit it, he was right. Eden wasn't going to be keen on having one of their clientele walking around wringing wet. I would sooner have found another way to skive off work, but this was the hand I had been dealt.

Nigel had told our little group to hang back towards the end of the line. The plan was to quietly shoot off without any of the other reps or guests noticing what we were up to. I would proceed as normal to the door queue, knowing full well I wasn't getting in while this soaked. Damien would be irritated, but what could he do?

As we approached the front of the club, the guests began to line up. I walked further up to the main door. The bouncers saw me and started to laugh. In fact, the whole queue was laughing. Not that it bothered me. I was trying to find the other reps, hopeful I could pass a message to Damien without actually seeing him. That didn't work out.

"You absolute knob head. Look at the state of you!" I turned around to see the man himself looking me up and down. "You know full well they're not going to let you in like that."

"Yeah, I know. Sorry, Damien, one of the guests wiped me out into the fountain. Dickhead." His demeanour softened.

"For fuck sake. Anyone else go in? Or just you?"

"Was just me. It was a dare, apparently. I'm soaked through and I stink of chlorine, plus I look a right twat." I thought I'd try and play for some sympathy. "What do you want me to do?"

Damien let out a big sigh. "Where's your boyfriend? I haven't seen that tool all evening."

"Nigel? Haven't seen him. I think he's already in. He was leading at one point. I assumed he went straight to the bar. You know what he's like."

This was manipulation 101. Before Damien had a chance to respond, some of the guests in the queue started to take the piss. This was perfect. A group of them started to poke fun at me being wet through. It was all harmless enough, but I just smiled back at them and took it. On seeing and hearing this, Damien took me to one side.

"What are you on in the hotel?"

"100% weekender, 90% trips. I couldn't book one group as their friends are already out here and they're doing their own thing. Got them on the reunion though."

"Ok, good lad. Off you go. Get some rest."

With that, I was dismissed. Nigel's plan had worked. Of course, Nigel was going to be missed at 2am when we finished work, but as he rightly pointed out what else can Damien do? You can only go to the airport twice a week and his card was already stamped.

I made my way back along the promenade to the bar that we'd previously agreed to meet at. By the time I got there, I looked more dishevelled than someone who'd just emerged from the sea. My clothes were already beginning to dry and my t-shirt was black, so that helped me. Besides, the bar was a beach bar anyway, more boho than trendy.

I arrived to see about 15 guests downing shots. By the looks of the empty shot glasses on the table, these weren't their first. Nigel let out a cheer when he saw me, encouraging others to do the same. As I approached Nigel, he was beaming.

"I told you it would work. Am I a genius or what? Plus, you already dried out, no harm no foul." I punched him on the arm and despite him feigning injury, I simply told him, "Get me a beer, you helmet!"

I then sat down amongst the guests. Lauren asked me how I was doing and asked if I was still wet. She meant it innocently enough but it came out wrong and sounded dodgy. Suddenly she started to clam up and blush. Her mates then cottoned on and started to take the piss out of her further. She then tried to hide behind her hands. She had turned so red, she was effectively a beetroot with limbs. Rather than deliver any witty comments to further her embarrassment, I simply thanked her for asking and told her I was drying nicely.

We must have stayed in that bar for a good couple of hours. Everyone was pretty pissed by the time it came to leave. A couple of the lads and a few of the girls wanted to go to a club, but Nigel and I and some of the girls were done for. We clearly couldn't go back to Eden or risk being spotted out elsewhere. We decided to go to another bar closer to home. We figured it would help us to get laid. Nigel and one of his hotel guests had paired with two of Lauren's friends, so the numbers worked in our favour. We decided to take the long walk back, stretching right around the corner of the West End, through the port and past the ferry point and then further round towards Cafe Del Mar and the sunset strip.

As we walked along the port, Nigel stopped to take a leak off the side. This was typical Nigel, no thought for common decency or his surroundings. There was nobody around at this point, so I didn't blame him. His girl, not wanting to hold Nigel's hand as he peed, came over to talk with Lauren.

As we were chatting, I looked across to see Nigel looking out into the port, standing right on the edge. He was about 10m away. All feelings of lust were instantly replaced with revenge. I couldn't help myself.

I made a dash towards him. Nigel sensing something was up turned around mid piss to face me, but the plan was set in motion. I launched myself into a single footed drop kick, catching him on the side of his back and arm. By the time gravity had kicked in, I landed about a metre from where I took off, just short of the water's edge. Nigel landed about 3m from where he had been standing, only it wasn't terra firma. He disappeared into the blackness and was now swimming through his own urine.

I pissed myself laughing. The wall of the port was too high to climb, which meant that he had to swim over to the steps on the other side of the boats. Lauren's friend — Nigel's one — scowled at me for what I'd done, but I didn't care. In fact, if he'd inadvertently taken her in with him, it wouldn't have bothered me in the slightest. Lauren could see I was pleased with myself and laughing, so she just smiled and held my arm. The other two were too busy making out on a bench to even notice, so we just left them to it.

As Nigel got closer towards the ramp, he started crying out for help. He was playing the sympathy card, calling to his girl telling her he was tired. She took the bait immediately.

"We have to help him. He's getting into difficulty!"

I just started to laugh.

"It's not funny Luke, he could drown."

I laughed harder.

Lauren turned to me and asked if Nigel could swim. I told her he could and this was part of his plan.

"Lauren, watch this. She's going to get closer to the edge to help him get out, and he's going to pull her in."

Lauren looked onwards. "He wouldn't dare. She'll kill him."

I stayed silent, generally enjoying the show and revisiting the drop kick I'd carried out a minute earlier. Nigel continued to whinny as his beloved made her way down the ramp. The closer he got to the ramp, the more he seemed to flail about.

"Wait for it…" I mumbled, as we both looked on.

She leant down to help pull Nigel out, even though as a young man he was more than capable of climbing up a few steps. Nigel held back, forcing her to move lower and closer to the edge.

I started to count down: "3, 2, 1."

Right on cue, Nigel suddenly grabs a hold of the edge and, with a swift tug, his princess instantly became a mermaid. Lauren gasped, I started to chuckle. Nigel was roaring. She was not impressed.

Nigel helped her out on to the side of the dock before he too exited the water. He was still laughing, she was not. She was moaning. Lauren and I approached them, mindful not to stand too close to the edge ourselves.

Nigel tried to hold her hand but was given the cold shoulder. He apologised and made her laugh. Despite the initial brush off, he soon had his arm around her. We continued towards the beach. It must have been around 3am.

On arrival, we'd already started to drift apart. Nigel and the mermaid were already walking at the water's edge and we were some way back towards the road. They went skinny dipping but I wasn't in the mood for all that. I asked Lauren half heartedly if she fancied a swim, but getting wet and covered in sand in the middle of the night wasn't on her bucket list either. It was at this point Lauren asked if she could come back to mine. I asked her what was wrong with her place, but she said Laura would kill us if she found out. I started to laugh.

As we headed back towards mine for a cuddle, we left Nigel and his mermaid frolicking in the sea. By all accounts they ended up sleeping together on a sun bed, under the stars. On paper that seems passionate. Romantic. Idyllic even. In reality, it means sand in every single orifice, waking up before dawn covered in a mix of sand, dew and damp clothing that they would have used to stave off the shivers. Waking up in my own bed, dry and warm, with the sun gently creeping in through the shades, seemed a far better choice!

CHAPTER 32
THE FINAL COUNTDOWN

All good things come to an end, and a summer in Ibiza is no different. Time doesn't feel linear when you're having a good time. One minute you're at the start of your campaign, the next you've got momentum and are barrelling through peak season having the time of your life. You have months to go, then weeks, suddenly days.

Despite being absolutely knackered at this point of the season, I didn't want it to end. I was thoroughly enjoying myself. Similar to last year, a lot of the reps started to flake. Some of them were extremely irritable and short tempered. More and more of us were falling ill with a variety of ailments. On any given night out, you could guarantee that one of the team wouldn't be there. Whether they were skiving or genuinely out of action, the rest would just pull together.

We all had pretty big personalities, and we were used to operating under pretty stressful conditions—at least in terms of physical demands, lack of sleep and so on. A member of the team down meant others would have to carry additional load. This wasn't always easy and had varying degrees of difficulty. I mean, if you were a man short in a bar or club, you wouldn't really notice it, as you were mingling with the guests anyway. But if you were a man short for an airport, that's an issue. That means someone is going who previously wasn't, or someone has to do two trips to the airport in one evening. Either way, that rep is going to be pissed. If you even thought for a minute the other rep was milking it, or just couldn't be bothered, there would be fireworks.

A lot of reps had coupled up over the duration. Not every male rep had thrown up on their other halves' lingerie, and so miraculously, some were still together. But as the season was drawing to an end, this presented further issues. Was this just a holiday romance? Are the people involved returning to boyfriends/girlfriends back home? What will happen back in the UK?

Thankfully, Nigel and I had been whoring ourselves to death in the resort, so we were saddled with none of this baggage. Though that's not to say that we didn't have to endure a multitude of mood swings and catfights amongst others in the teams. Most of the time we would end up simply laughing about it, but after a while it became an additional drain.

I remember, at the beginning of my very first season, one of the senior management team advised us to write a diary and to collect photos wherever we could. They said that these were going to be some of the happiest days of our lives, and that we needed to fight to preserve the memories we were making. Of course at the grand age of 18 or 19, the last thing you had to worry about was memory loss. Here I am, a couple of decades later, wishing I'd taken that advice more seriously.

The last few weeks seemed to fly by for us. Nigel and I tried to stay around the guests as much as possible. They were happy and looking to have fun. We were keen to avoid the tensions and conflicts that were increasing with the levels of tiredness. Not only were we still keen to score, I think we were also painfully aware about how dull life was going to be back in the UK. Even university paled in comparison to the life we were leading out there. Having gone through this process once already, we were already psychologically preparing ourselves for what was to come next: a month of sleep, rehydration, antibiotics and home cooked meals, followed by another month or two of trying to fit in with the rest of the world, before eventually being assimilated.

Neither of us spoke about returning the following year. We were both too knackered to even think about it. I did start to wonder what other resorts would be like. The tour operator was all over the med: what would it be like in Greece? Turkey? Majorca? Tenerife? Having finished two tours of duty in Ibiza, would I be able to survive a third?

In what seemed like a blink of an eye, our final day was upon us. We both decided that, as per the season prior, we would leave together on the same flight. Nigel's hotel was effectively closing for the season, given the low turnout, so he had already moved to a room in one of the other units. Mine was already running on low occupancy, so Laura was going to manage what little guests we had remaining there. We needed to be back for university, and she didn't, so was happy to run the remainder of the season right down.

I remember waking up with a massive list of things to do. I'd already taken steps to start packing the previous week, so most of that was done, but I wanted to say goodbye to everyone. I needed to buy some more CDs, some t-shirts and various other souvenirs to remember the place by. I also wanted to pick up some professional photos that had been taken of us all while we were out and about.

These were probably my greatest investment in terms of memories. Each of these 12x8 inch' professional prints functions as the key to a subset of memories locked away under years of normality and corporate compliance.

The day seemed to fly by and before we knew it, the sun began to set. Nigel and I agreed to meet at Savannahs for a last beer and a quick bite to eat before saying our final goodbyes and heading to the airport. While the place was the same, we did it differently this year. Rather than get smashed, we actually paced ourselves, choosing to reflect on the season as a whole and relive some of the incidents you've been reading about.

By the time we'd said goodbye to everyone else, we were ready to leave. I won't lie, both of us shed a tear or two as we made our way to the airport. That evening would be the last evening we were together on the white island, and while I've been back several times since, I've never been back there with my partner in crime.

EPILOGUE

As I alluded to in my first book, Ibiza has changed massively. You have as much chance of finding the tomb of Nefertiti as you do of finding any remains of the terrace at Space (having been totally overhauled and buried under concrete for Hï Ibiza). I am grateful that I got to experience the place at the end of the 90s. And I am sure the people who were there 10 years before me are even happier!

That said, working there and doing the job we did, often leaves me wondering if I am yet to pay a price for all that debauchery and partying. What would I have gone on to become had I never taken the interview in '97? If my holiday rep at the time had failed to snatch that girl from me in Magaluf, how much healthier would my liver and brain cells be? Is there such a thing as Karma? Am I going to be impotent at 55 because I've worn it out? Incontinence? Dementia? Who the fuck knows? Frankly speaking, some of the reps I knew have already unfortunately clocked out, so the fact that I am still sitting here now, unsoiled and typing into a laptop, means I'm still in the game.

The second season was emotionally heavier than the first. I think it was a combination of having Jess out there as well as fatigue kicking in more aggressively than before. Whether it really was more tiring, or because you knew what to expect you would begin to notice the effects sooner, I am not sure.

I've been fortunate enough to travel extensively since University and have covered a decent part of the globe. Never have I found a place like Ibiza. Sure, I've found beach clubs and nightclubs and bar strips up and down the Med, the Black Sea, as well as the beaches of South East Asia, but they never did strike the same balance. Full-on bars, dance clubs, hippie villages, private beaches, as well as a functioning town. Ibiza has them all.

That said, some of those attractions are on the decline. Pay a visit before it's too late! It saddens me to think that the next generation of adolescents will never get to experience that bright orange fish bowl, that tequila head slammer, that drunken booze cruise or random beach cuddle after an Es Paradis foam party.

Still, at least they have fucking Instagram. #BLESSED

AFTERWORD

If you've gotten this far, and I haven't completely repulsed you, you can probably tell we had an absolute scream in the resort. The experience was completely life-changing. I managed to squeeze into two years more partying than most people do in their lifetime.

That's not to say it was all fun and games. Just because you're living a life of hedonism doesn't mean the gods won't try and balance things up a bit. In Ibiza '98, I'd already detailed some of the horrible things that I had to deal with in my first season. Unfortunately, this second season would be equally unforgiving when it came to tragedy. I didn't want to put this earlier in the book, as it kind of went against the flow, but I think it's important to shine a light on some of the work that wasn't always seen or known by others.

Regrettably, when you're dealing with between three and four thousand young holiday makers a week, statistics will end up biting you in the ass. We're talking accidents, arrests, burglaries, rapes, even deaths. We're talking fights starting with a slap or a quick dig on one extreme, to people

345

being stabbed and glassed in the street on the other. Now, this sort of behaviour and these incidents happen everywhere. They've happened before, they'll happen again, but what makes the difference is how you handle them.

It was about halfway through the season when word spread that one of the guests in Jack's hotel had been raped. I could tell something was wrong the minute we walked into the welcome meeting. Nigel and I wandered along, slightly late, and jovially. The atmosphere however was deathly silent. Rather than chew us out, Damien just asked us to take a seat. He'd told the others moments earlier. Everyone was silent. Tony had his arm draped across Jack's shoulder. Frank was staring at the floor in disbelief. Damien went on to tell us how there had been a rape in our area. Nigel and I just sat quietly. This wasn't the first time we'd been here, but it was the first one we'd had in our area this season. Laura and Emma were absent from the meeting. Given the nature of the incident, Laura—with Emma as backup—was more suitable as primary support. Nigel quietly asked what happened, but before Damien could get a word out, Jack answered.

"Fucking taxi driver! Can you believe it? Evil cunt."

Nigel and I couldn't believe it. Damien let Jack get it off his chest. The rest of the room remained silent as Jack brought us up to speed.

Apparently, a group of girls from his hotel had gone to Amnesia for the night. They were partying into the early hours and somehow got split up. Now, if you've never been to one of Ibiza's superclubs, you cannot appreciate how large they are. You could easily spend several hours walking around looking for the rest of your group, only to miss each other repeatedly. Remember, you had no mobile phone, no easily identifiable meeting points, multiple rooms, and anything up to 5,000 people (10,000 in Privilege) in darkened dance halls to walk through. In this case, after about an hour of searching, the girl who had lost the group decided to head back.

She left the venue—which in itself is a mission, let me tell you—to flag a taxi to take her back along the motorway to her hotel in San Antonio. Around four or five in the morning there is usually a small horde of taxis waiting to take weary clubbers back to their hotels and apartments, and last night was no exception. This poor girl grabbed a taxi. Not a gypsy taxi, an actual, bona fide, Ibiza taxi, with the yellow/greenish plastic indicator on the roof. He agreed to take her back.

Off they set, but then after only a few minutes of driving down the main highway, he turns off down a dirt track road, pulls over to the side, and joins her in the back. A few minutes later and this piece of shit carries on driving in the direction of San Antonio. Stopping vaguely near the back of San Antonio, Jack's guest, who until now has sat in absolute silence in the back, quietly gets out of the car without saying a word. The taxi pulls away and within seconds is out of view.

We were dumbfounded, I mean, what can you say? Her only mistake was getting separated from her friends, which is so easily done in these massive clubs. It was gut wrenching and especially hard for Jack. It was the first he'd had to deal with. Not only did he feel an emotional connection to the girl herself, as she was one of his guests, but the poor thing was still in shock and didn't want anyone near her, especially not a male. Hence, Laura and Emma got involved. The worst bit about all this, is this absolute shit of a human being was free to go about his day, his week, his summer, continuing as normal. No charges would be brought. No complaints would be filed, no investigations would ever be made. Even now, many years later, it winds me up. Who knows how many times this fucking neanderthal had done it?

It wasn't just the girls that were vulnerable on holiday. Many guys had come to experience their share of tragedy, too. In 1999, during peak season, sombre messages would be distributed to the various teams on what seemed like a weekly basis. The vast majority of incidents would be self inflicted, and it wasn't just our guests either. All tour operators were affected equally. Forgive me if I skip over the exact details — not to diminish those situations and the pain of everyone involved, more to keep the tone of the book generally lighter. That said, I wanted to show the other side of what, at face value, was the greatest job in the world.

In San Antonio Bay, in one of our larger units, we had a guest on the fifth floor climb over from one balcony to another — a common practice amongst teenagers, unfortunately — and he lost his balance in the early hours of the morning. Can you imagine being one of the first on the scene there? The reps actually lived in the unit, so they would have been there within minutes. How would you deal with his friends? How would you deal with the families that would undoubtedly fly out to arrange repatriation?

Another guy that same season had gone out big time on a bender. There was a kind of clubbing marathon that people wanted to attend. Seldom did they manage it, as most of the kids who came to us didn't have a clue they would be paying the equivalent of £40 to enter a club and up to a tenner for a bottle of water each time. The line up was something as follows (forgive my memory):

Monday night: Manumission@ Privilege

Tuesday Daytime: Space (Manumission afterparty)

Tuesday Night: El Divino

Wednesday: Clockwork Orange @ Es Paradis

Thursday: Cream / Gatecrasher @ Amnesia

Friday: Ministry @ Pacha

If you were a clubber, this was the holy grail. The biggest DJs and largest parties would be held there those evenings. Our guests would fly in on Wednesday and Sunday, meaning that if you were fully committed and supplied with enough 'supplements', some would go out Monday and not return until Thursday or Friday. I'm serious.

Some guests would disappear for the whole week. Maybe sneaking back for an hour's sleep and a change of clothes, if that. Can you imagine the state of someone who's been on it for two, three or even four nights straight? You can at least imagine them not thinking so clearly.

We had an occasion where a pair of guests had landed, dropped their bags, and gone straight out. No one had seen them for two or three whole days. They missed the welcome meeting, the follow up visits, everything. We assumed that they'd been out on it. It wasn't until one of the maids had raised the alarm that we knew differently.

One of the lads had unfortunately passed away in a pool of his own vomit. He was found in his room, slumped over the bed. Alongside his body were various disco biscuits and powders. I've often heard it said that when someone passes away, they look peaceful. Peaceful my ass. Maybe they look peaceful after a professional makeup artist has spent the afternoon applying industrial concealer, ready for the chapel of rest, or maybe when a 96 year old nods off for the last time and is checked a couple of minutes later, still warm. But when someone passes away, any pressure applied to a body part turns it blue, and quickly. Different from the heaviest bruise but no less noticeable. A body that's been lying on its side and leaking for more than a few hours does not look peaceful.

Not only were the reps summoned to the scene to assist

with the inquiries, they also had to break the news to his friend, who was nowhere to be found. It wasn't until some time the next day that he resurfaced at the hotel. And if you've ever had the misfortune to see a dead body, you'll know the images and the details surrounding them never ever leave your mind.

We had another instance where a guest came out on holiday on their own. He had a larger group of friends staying elsewhere on the island, but had managed to grab a cheap deal last minute to join them. He'd gone out for a big night to the bars and clubs on the main airport highway. I can't remember if it was Privilege or Amnesia, just that vicinity. When it was time to head home, he got separated from his group and tried to catch a car on the way back. He was knocked down and instantly killed.

Can you imagine being the one to have to pack up his personal effects and clothing to hand over to the friend or family? Having to hug and try to calm a complete stranger who's in bits? It was extremely sombre. Your stomach would be in knots before and during the meeting. Once done, you would have to bury your feelings and put your smile back on for everyone else.

At the grand age of 19, how could that not affect you? Don't shed a tear for me just yet. The job was still over-whelmingly brilliant. The highs were fantastically high, it's just the lows were just as extreme. And as you can imagine, going through such experiences at such an early age, you need to rely on and support each other. I think the bonds that I formed with my team mates there were probably as strong as any I have ever formed, aside from Frank. He's still a dick. It's why Nigel and I are still as close today as we ever were, and how we still joke about our Balearic experiences today.

ACKNOWLEDGEMENTS

It's better to be a lion for a day than a sheep all your life - Elizabeth Kenny

I am more than twice the age I was then when I first hit that white island. Am grateful to still have the friends I made there.

Glowworm, Doc, Starfish, Big Fella, Newmans, Balloon Knot, Ginger Spice and Danny. Do you think they'll let us do a reunion at 50?

Once again, I'd like to give a huge thanks to Phil for his assistance in helping me put everything together yet again. Your advice as always was precious. Big Fella, Ginge' and Glowworm, thank you for filling in the gaps.